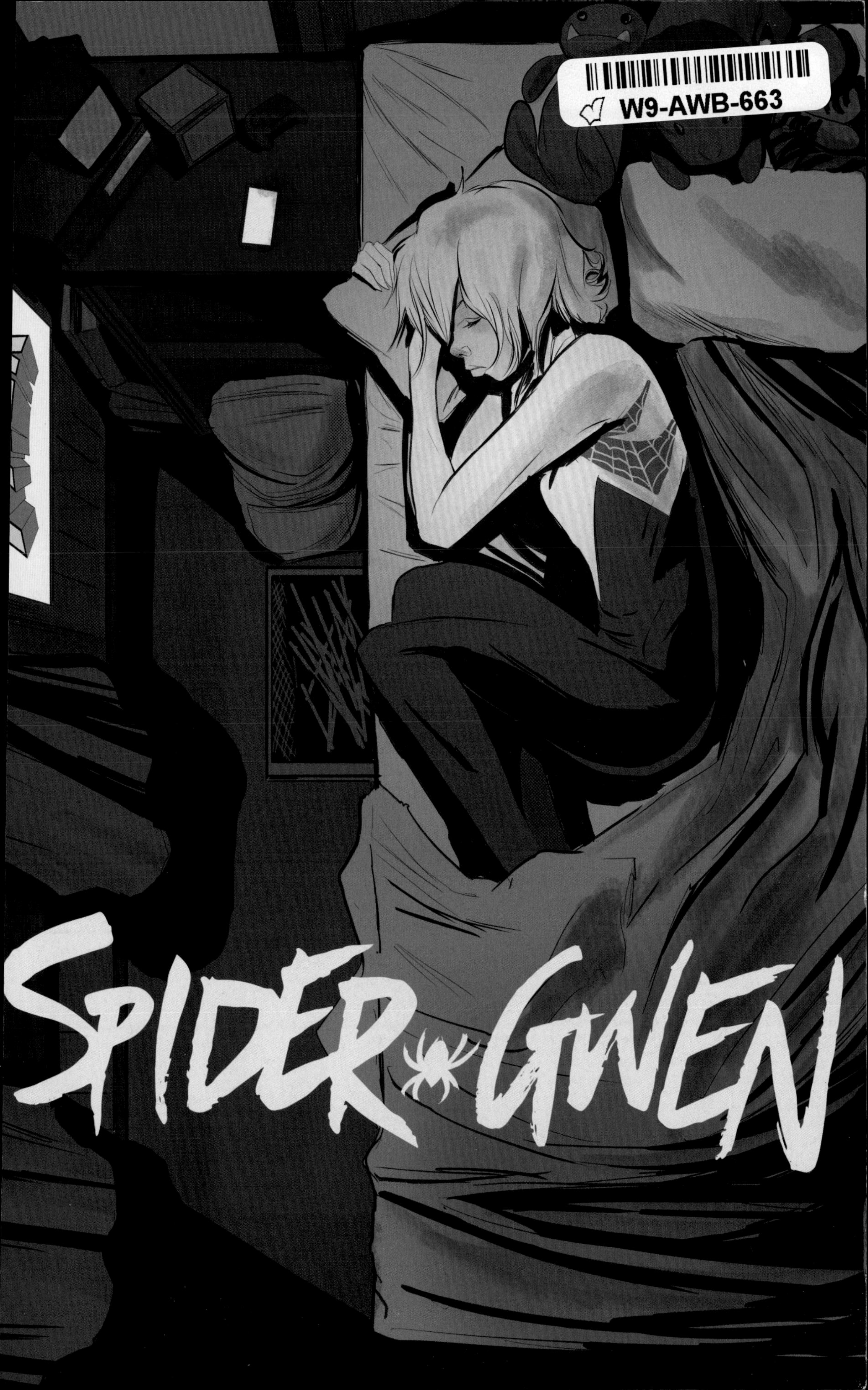
SPIDER-GWEN

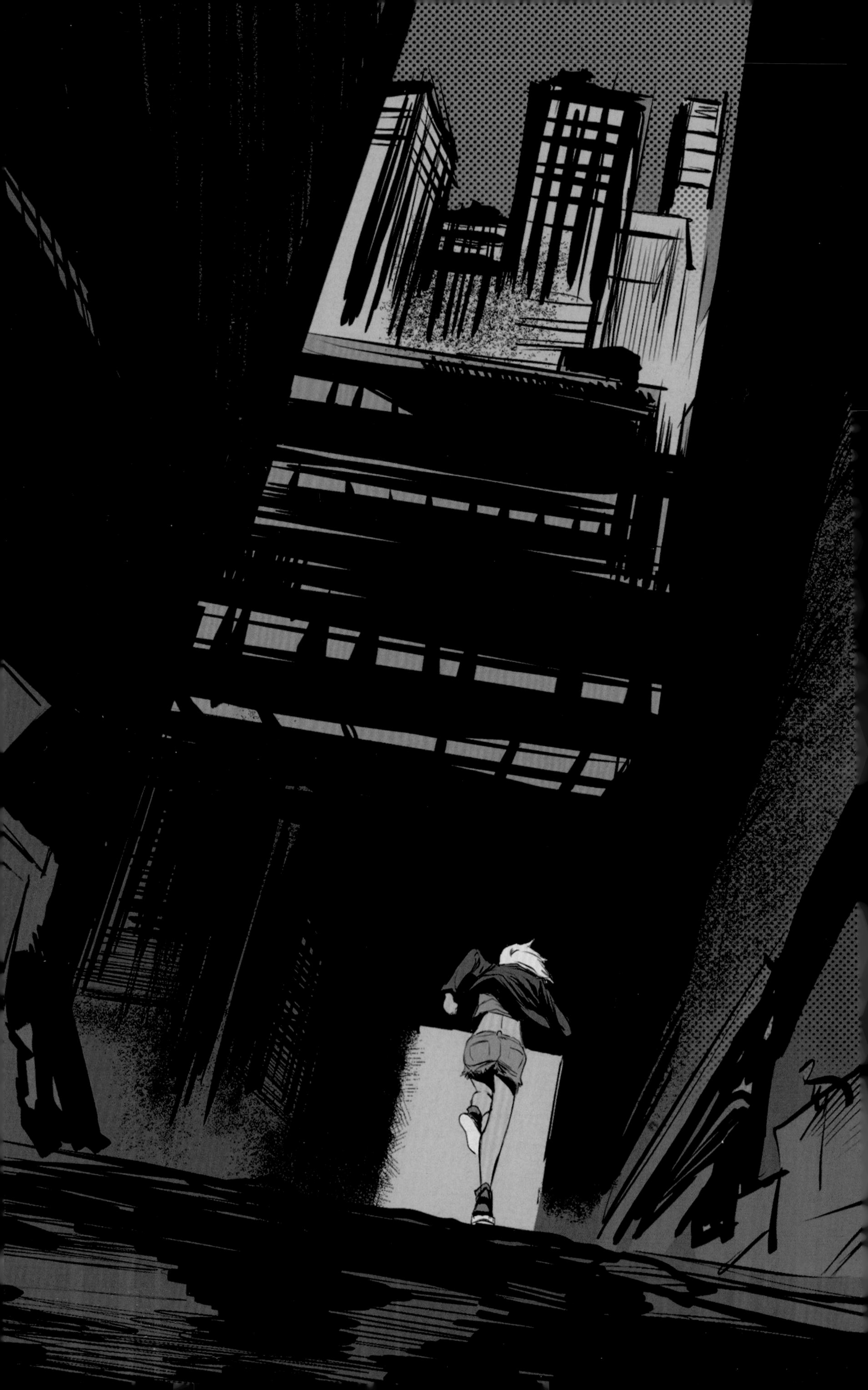

SPIDER-GWEN

WEAPON OF CHOICE

JASON LATOUR
WRITER

ROBBI RODRIGUEZ
ARTIST

RICO RENZI
WITH **LAUREN AFFE** (#10)
COLOR ARTISTS

VC'S CLAYTON COWLES
LETTERER

ROBBI RODRIGUEZ
COVER ART

DEVIN LEWIS
ASSOCIATE EDITOR

NICK LOWE
EDITOR

SPECIAL THANKS TO **CK RUSSELL**

JENNIFER GRÜNWALD
COLLECTION EDITOR

KATERI WOODY
ASSOCIATE MANAGING EDITOR

SARAH BRUNSTAD
ASSISTANT EDITOR

MARK D. BEAZLEY
EDITOR, SPECIAL PROJECTS

JEFF YOUNGQUIST
VP PRODUCTION & SPECIAL PROJECTS

DAVID GABRIEL
SVP PRINT, SALES & MARKETING

JAY BOWEN
BOOK DESIGNER

AXEL ALONSO
EDITOR IN CHIEF

JOE QUESADA
CHIEF CREATIVE OFFICER

DAN BUCKLEY
PUBLISHER

ALAN FINE
EXECUTIVE PRODUCER

SPIDER-GWEN VOL. 2: WEAPON OF CHOICE. Contains material originally published in magazine form as SPIDER-GWEN #9-13. First printing 2016. ISBN# 978-0-7851-9960-1. Published by MARVEL WORLDWIDE, INC., a subsidiary of MARVEL ENTERTAINMENT, LLC. OFFICE OF PUBLICATION: 135 West 50th Street, New York, NY 10020. **Printed in Canada.** ALAN FINE, President, Marvel Entertainment; DAN BUCKLEY, President, TV, Publishing & Brand Management; JOE QUESADA, Chief Creative Officer; TOM BREVOORT, SVP of Publishing; DAVID BOGART, SVP of Business Affairs & Operations, Publishing & Partnership; C.B. CEBULSKI, VP of Brand Management & Development, Asia; DAVID GABRIEL, SVP of Sales & Marketing, Publishing; JEFF YOUNGQUIST, VP of Production & Special Projects; DAN CARR, Executive Director of Publishing Technology; ALEX MORALES, Director of Publishing Operations; SUSAN CRESPI, Production Manager; STAN LEE, Chairman Emeritus. For information regarding advertising in Marvel Comics or on Marvel.com, please contact Vit DeBellis, Integrated Sales Manager, at vdebellis@marvel.com. For Marvel subscription inquiries, please call 888-511-5480. **Manufactured between 10/28/2016 and 12/5/2016 by SOLISCO PRINTERS, SCOTT, QC, CANADA.**

10 9 8 7 6 5 4 3 2 1

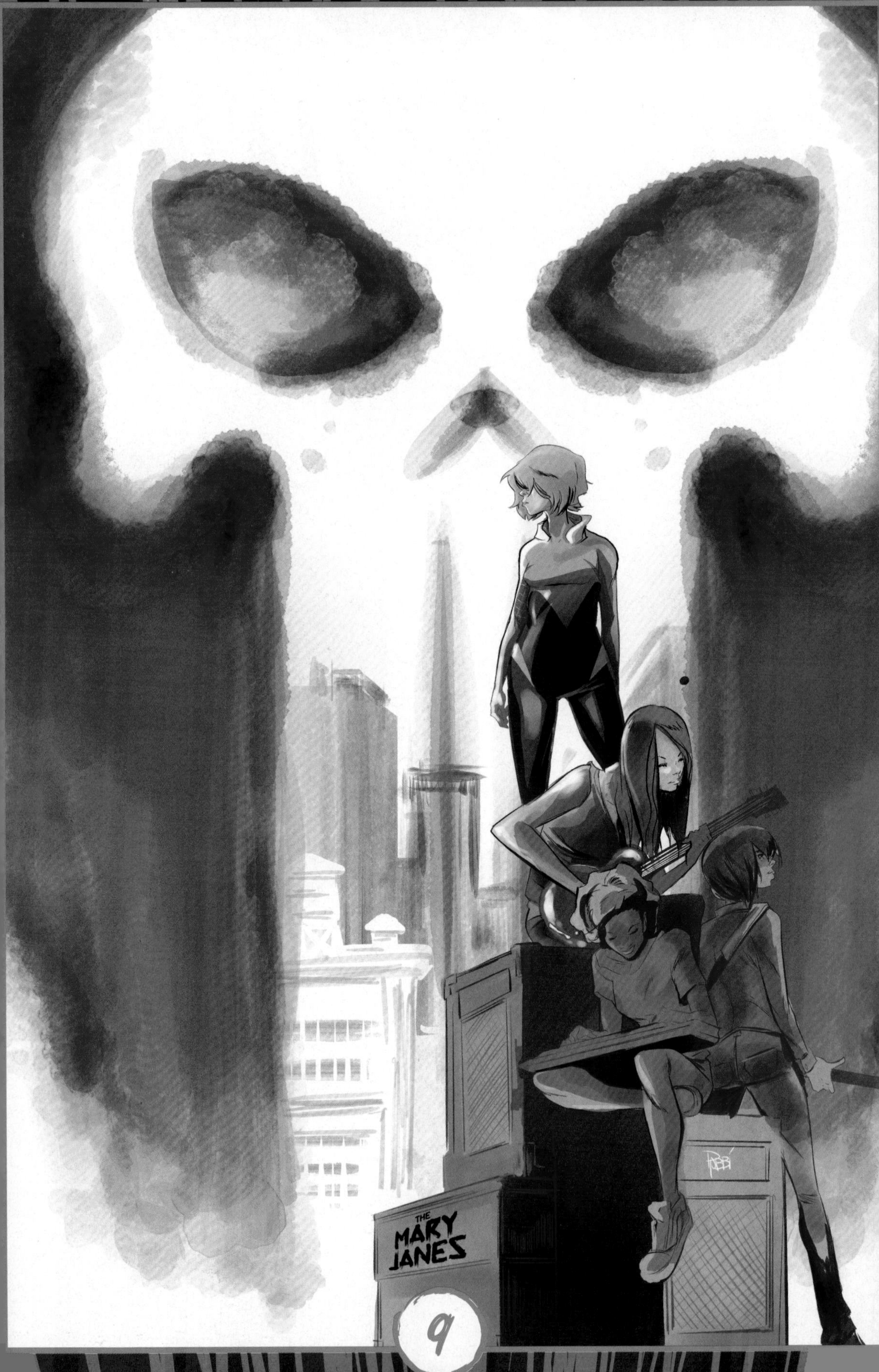
THE MARY JANES
9

AS A TEENAGER, GWEN STACY WAS BITTEN BY A MUTATED SPIDER. THE BITE TRANSFORMED HER, GRANTING HER AMAZING POWERS: A PRECOGNITIVE AWARENESS OF DANGER, ADHESIVE FINGERTIPS AND TOES, AND THE PROPORTIONAL SPEED AND STRENGTH OF A SPIDER. TO THE RESIDENTS OF NEW YORK, SHE IS THE DANGEROUS VIGILANTE CALLED SPIDER-WOMAN, BUT YOU KNOW HER AS...

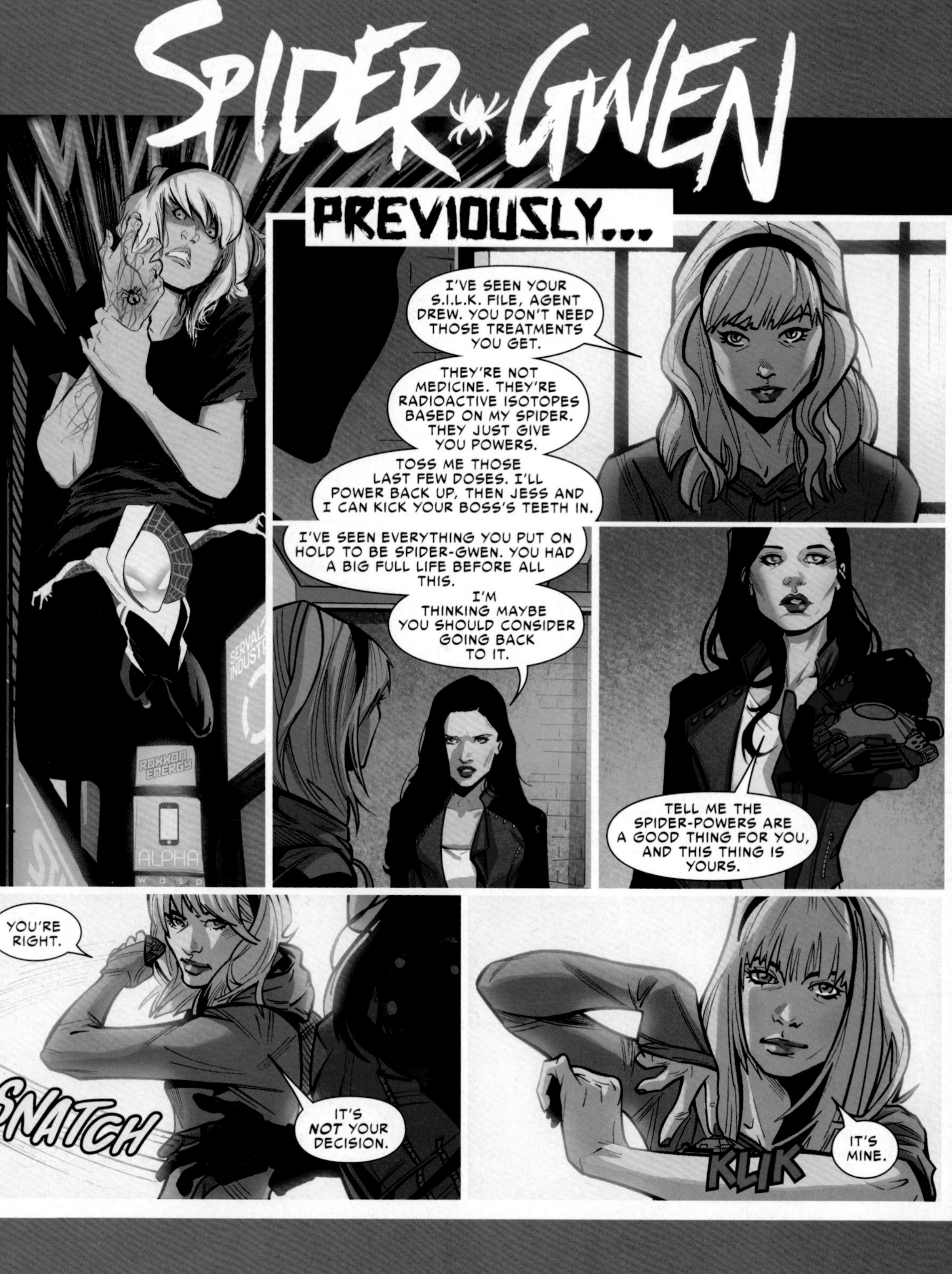
SPIDER-GWEN
PREVIOUSLY...
I'VE SEEN YOUR S.I.L.K. FILE, AGENT DREW. YOU DON'T NEED THOSE TREATMENTS YOU GET.
THEY'RE NOT MEDICINE. THEY'RE RADIOACTIVE ISOTOPES BASED ON MY SPIDER. THEY JUST GIVE YOU POWERS.
TOSS ME THOSE LAST FEW DOSES. I'LL POWER BACK UP, THEN JESS AND I CAN KICK YOUR BOSS'S TEETH IN.
I'VE SEEN EVERYTHING YOU PUT ON HOLD TO BE SPIDER-GWEN. YOU HAD A BIG FULL LIFE BEFORE ALL THIS.
I'M THINKING MAYBE YOU SHOULD CONSIDER GOING BACK TO IT.
TELL ME THE SPIDER-POWERS ARE A GOOD THING FOR YOU, AND THIS THING IS YOURS.
YOU'RE RIGHT.
SNATCH
IT'S NOT YOUR DECISION.
KLIK
IT'S MINE.

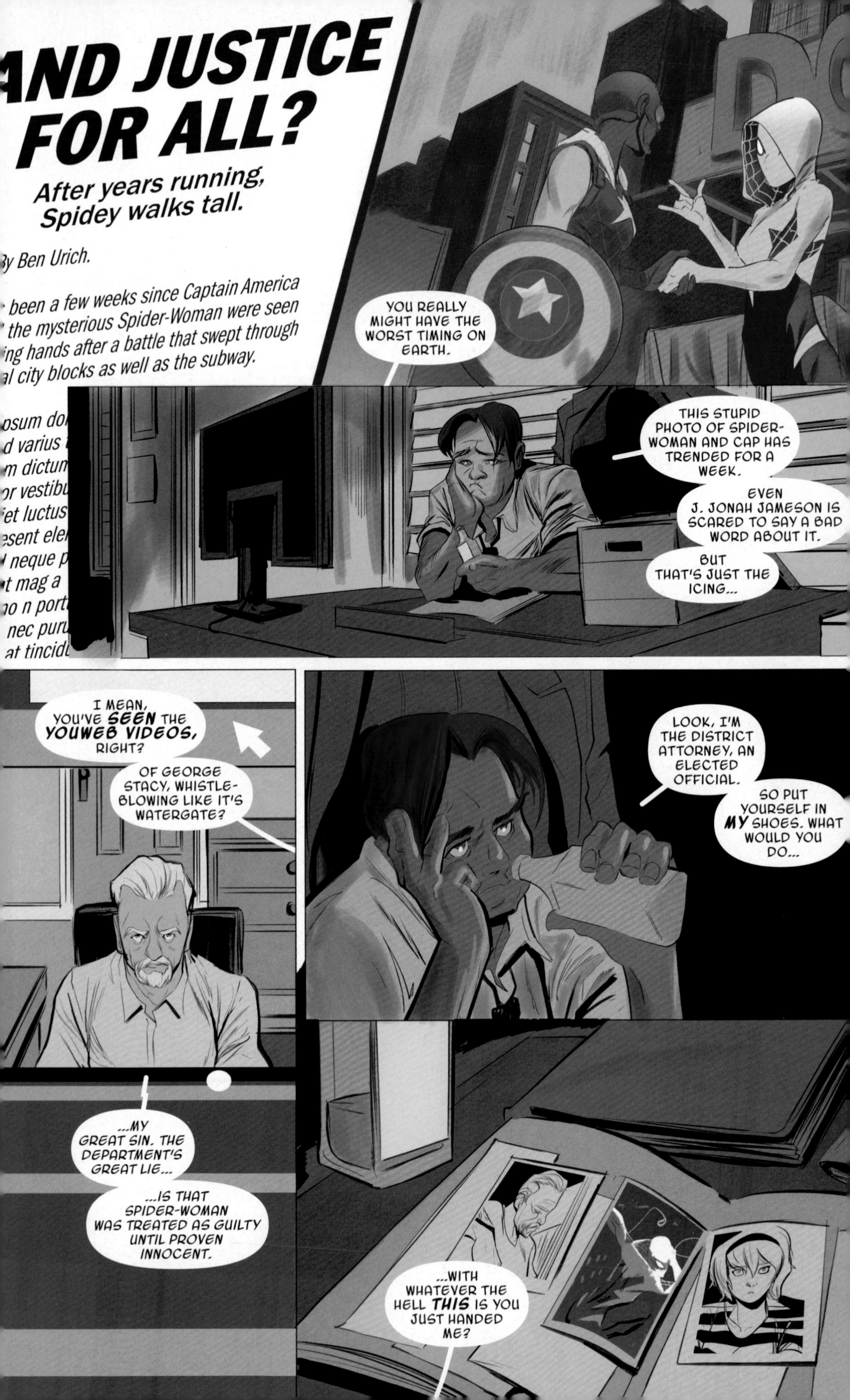
AND JUSTICE FOR ALL?
After years running, Spidey walks tall.
By Ben Urich.
been a few weeks since Captain America
the mysterious Spider-Woman were seen
ing hands after a battle that swept through
city blocks as well as the subway.
YOU REALLY MIGHT HAVE THE WORST TIMING ON EARTH.
THIS STUPID PHOTO OF SPIDER-WOMAN AND CAP HAS TRENDED FOR A WEEK.
EVEN J. JONAH JAMESON IS SCARED TO SAY A BAD WORD ABOUT IT.
BUT THAT'S JUST THE ICING...
I MEAN, YOU'VE SEEN THE YOUWEB VIDEOS, RIGHT?
OF GEORGE STACY, WHISTLE-BLOWING LIKE IT'S WATERGATE?
...MY GREAT SIN. THE DEPARTMENT'S GREAT LIE...
...IS THAT SPIDER-WOMAN WAS TREATED AS GUILTY UNTIL PROVEN INNOCENT.
LOOK, I'M THE DISTRICT ATTORNEY, AN ELECTED OFFICIAL.
SO PUT YOURSELF IN MY SHOES. WHAT WOULD YOU DO...
...WITH WHATEVER THE HELL THIS IS YOU JUST HANDED ME?

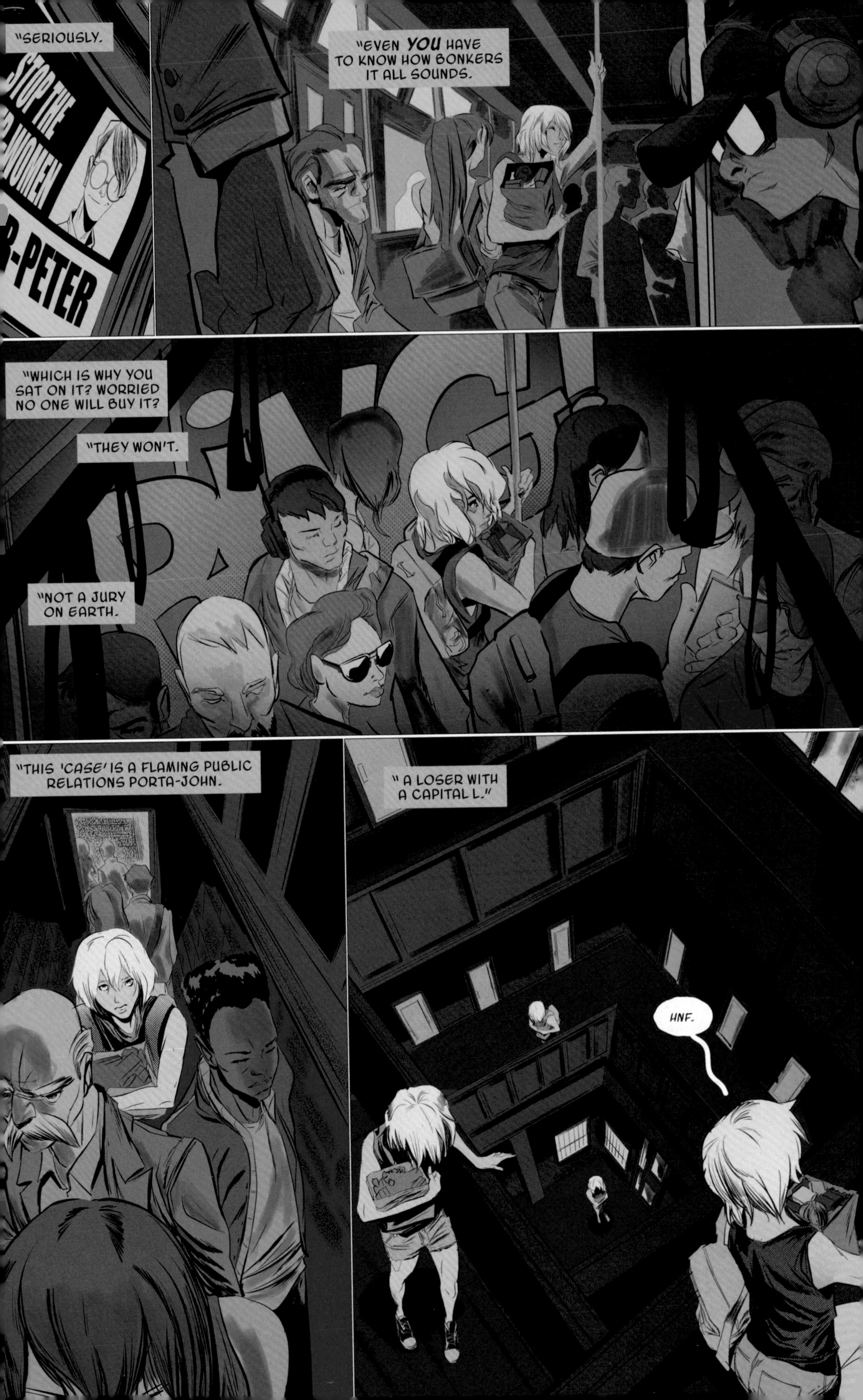
"SERIOUSLY.
STOP THE
WOMEN
-PETER
"EVEN YOU HAVE TO KNOW HOW BONKERS IT ALL SOUNDS.
"WHICH IS WHY YOU SAT ON IT? WORRIED NO ONE WILL BUY IT?
"THEY WON'T.
"NOT A JURY ON EARTH.
"THIS 'CASE' IS A FLAMING PUBLIC RELATIONS PORTA-JOHN.
" A LOSER WITH A CAPITAL L."
HNF.

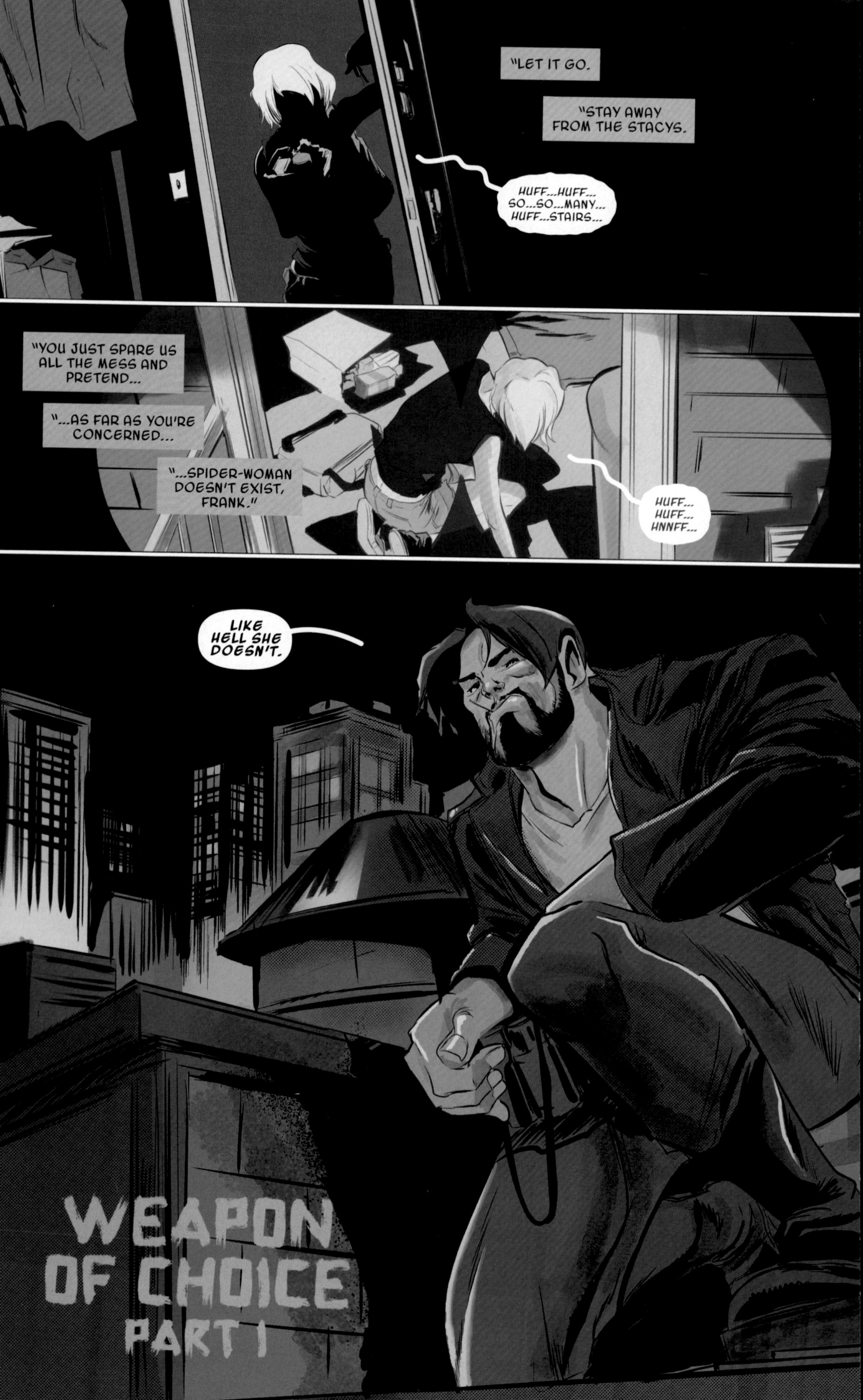
"LET IT GO.
"STAY AWAY FROM THE STACYS.
HUFF...HUFF... SO...SO...MANY... HUFF...STAIRS...
"YOU JUST SPARE US ALL THE MESS AND PRETEND...
"...AS FAR AS YOU'RE CONCERNED...
"...SPIDER-WOMAN DOESN'T EXIST, FRANK."
HUFF... HUFF... HNNFF...
LIKE HELL SHE DOESN'T.
WEAPON OF CHOICE PART 1

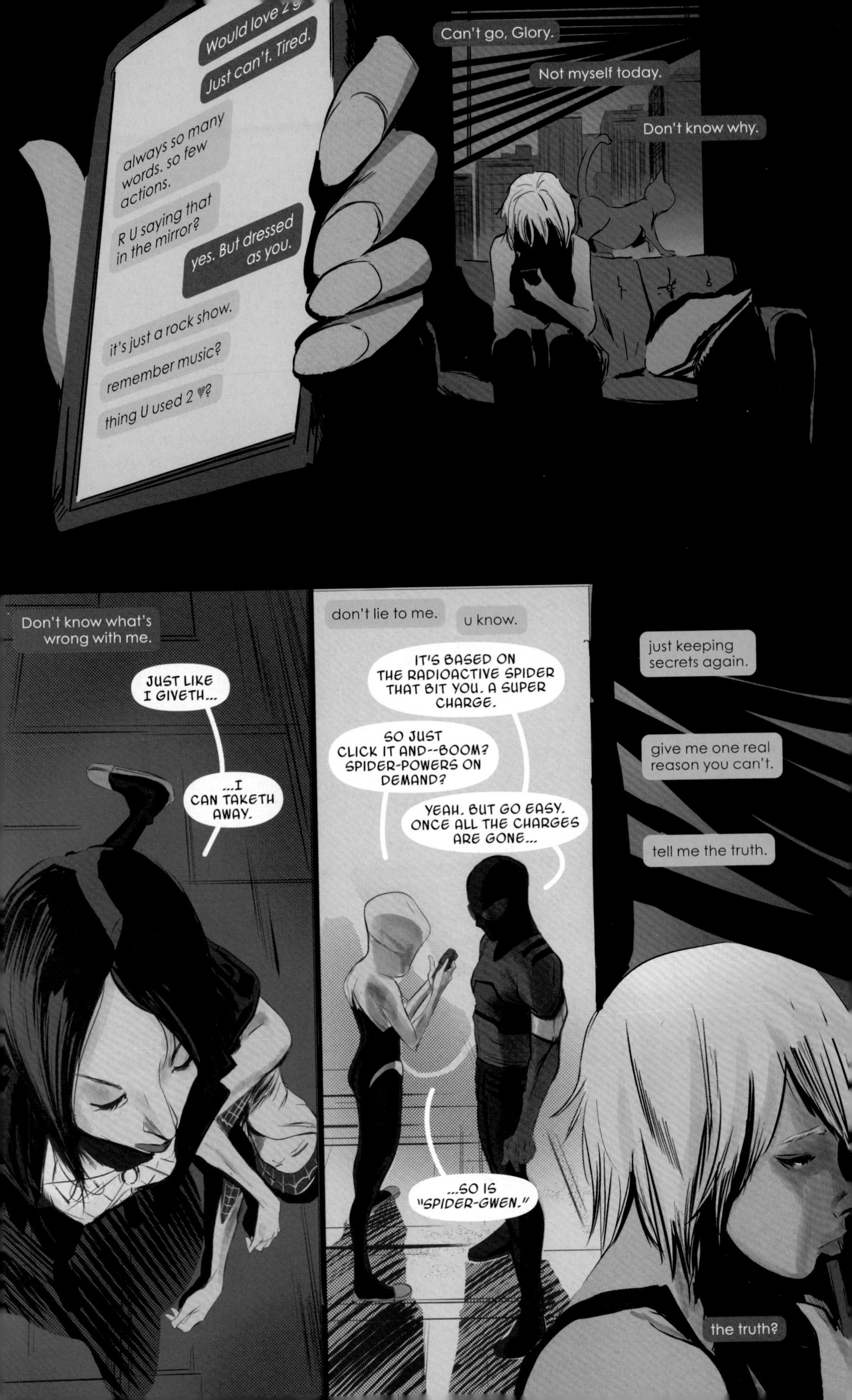
Would love 2 g
Just can't. Tired.
always so many words. so few actions.
R U saying that in the mirror?
yes. But dressed as you.
it's just a rock show.
remember music?
thing U used 2 ♥?
Can't go, Glory.
Not myself today.
Don't know why.
Don't know what's wrong with me.
JUST LIKE I GIVETH...
...I CAN TAKETH AWAY.
don't lie to me.
u know.
IT'S BASED ON THE RADIOACTIVE SPIDER THAT BIT YOU. A SUPER CHARGE.
SO JUST CLICK IT AND--BOOM? SPIDER-POWERS ON DEMAND?
YEAH. BUT GO EASY. ONCE ALL THE CHARGES ARE GONE...
...SO IS "SPIDER-GWEN."
just keeping secrets again.
give me one real reason you can't.
tell me the truth.
the truth?

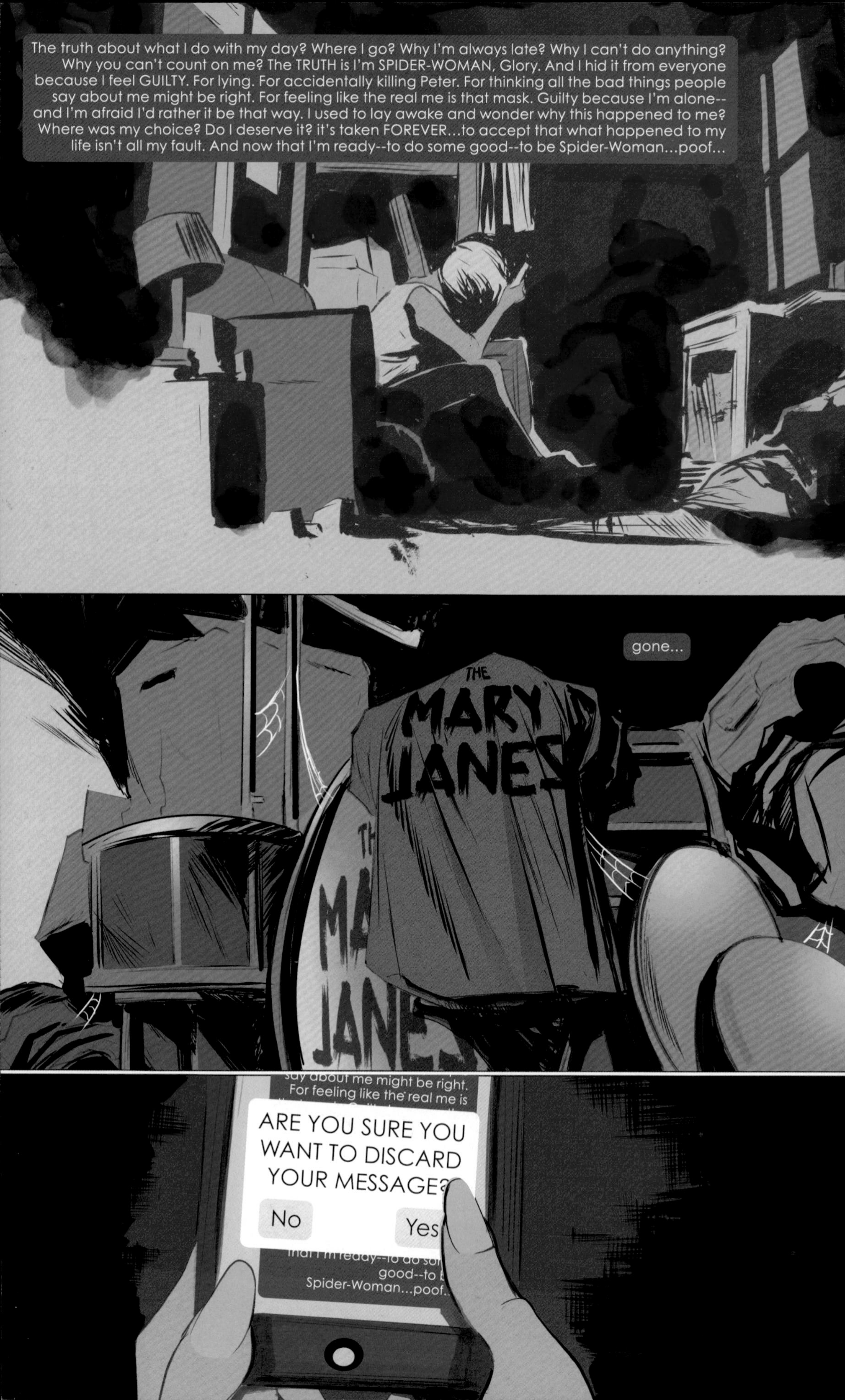
The truth about what I do with my day? Where I go? Why I'm always late? Why I can't do anything? Why you can't count on me? The TRUTH is I'm SPIDER-WOMAN, Glory. And I hid it from everyone because I feel GUILTY. For lying. For accidentally killing Peter. For thinking all the bad things people say about me might be right. For feeling like the real me is that mask. Guilty because I'm alone--and I'm afraid I'd rather it be that way. I used to lay awake and wonder why this happened to me? Where was my choice? Do I deserve it? it's taken FOREVER...to accept that what happened to my life isn't all my fault. And now that I'm ready--to do some good--to be Spider-Woman...poof...
gone...
THE MARY JANES
say about me might be right. For feeling like the real me is
ARE YOU SURE YOU WANT TO DISCARD YOUR MESSAGE?
No
Yes
good--to b
Spider-Woman...poof...

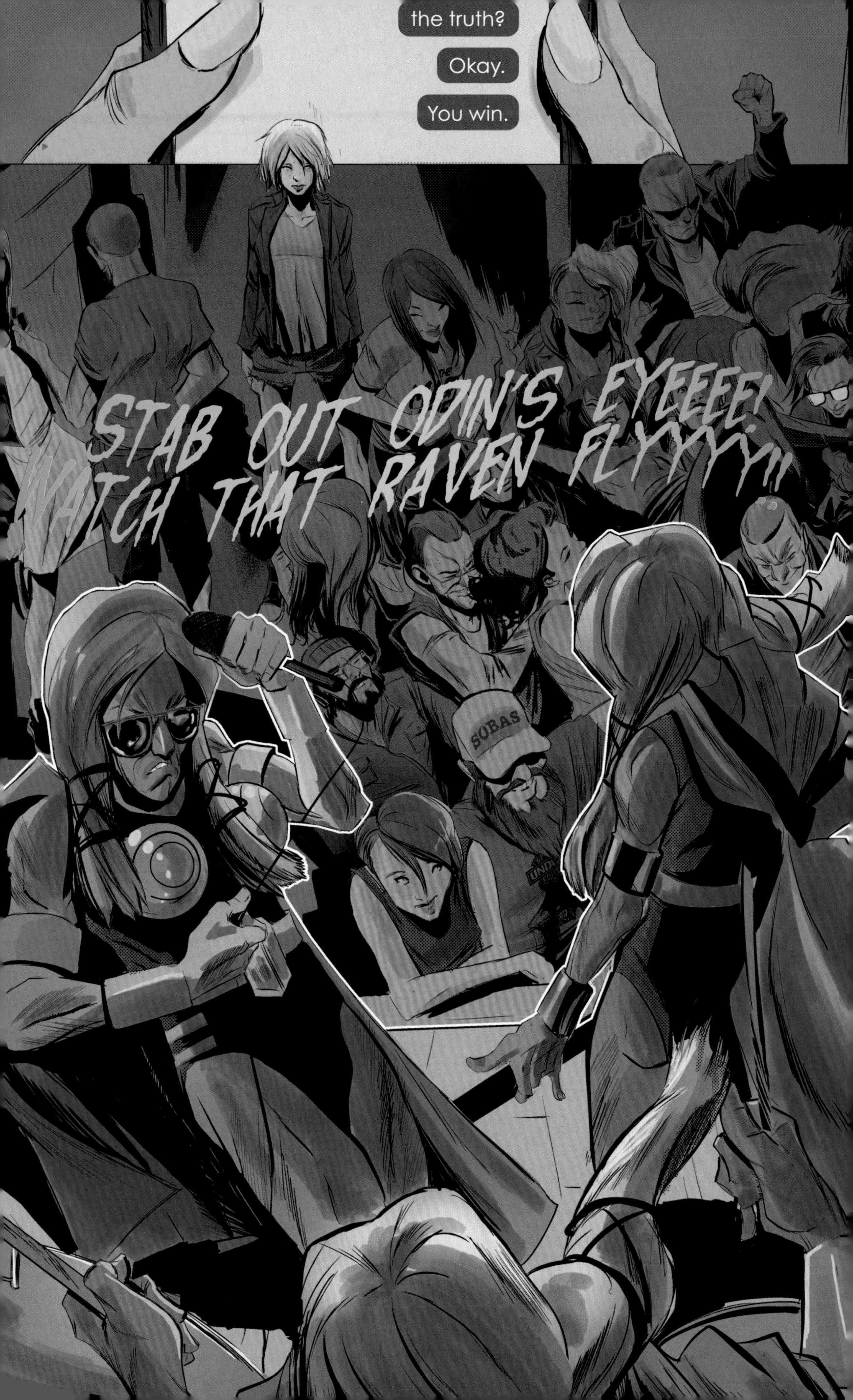
the truth?
Okay.
You win.
STAB OUT ODIN'S EYEEEE!
WATCH THAT RAVEN FLYYYY!!
SOBAS

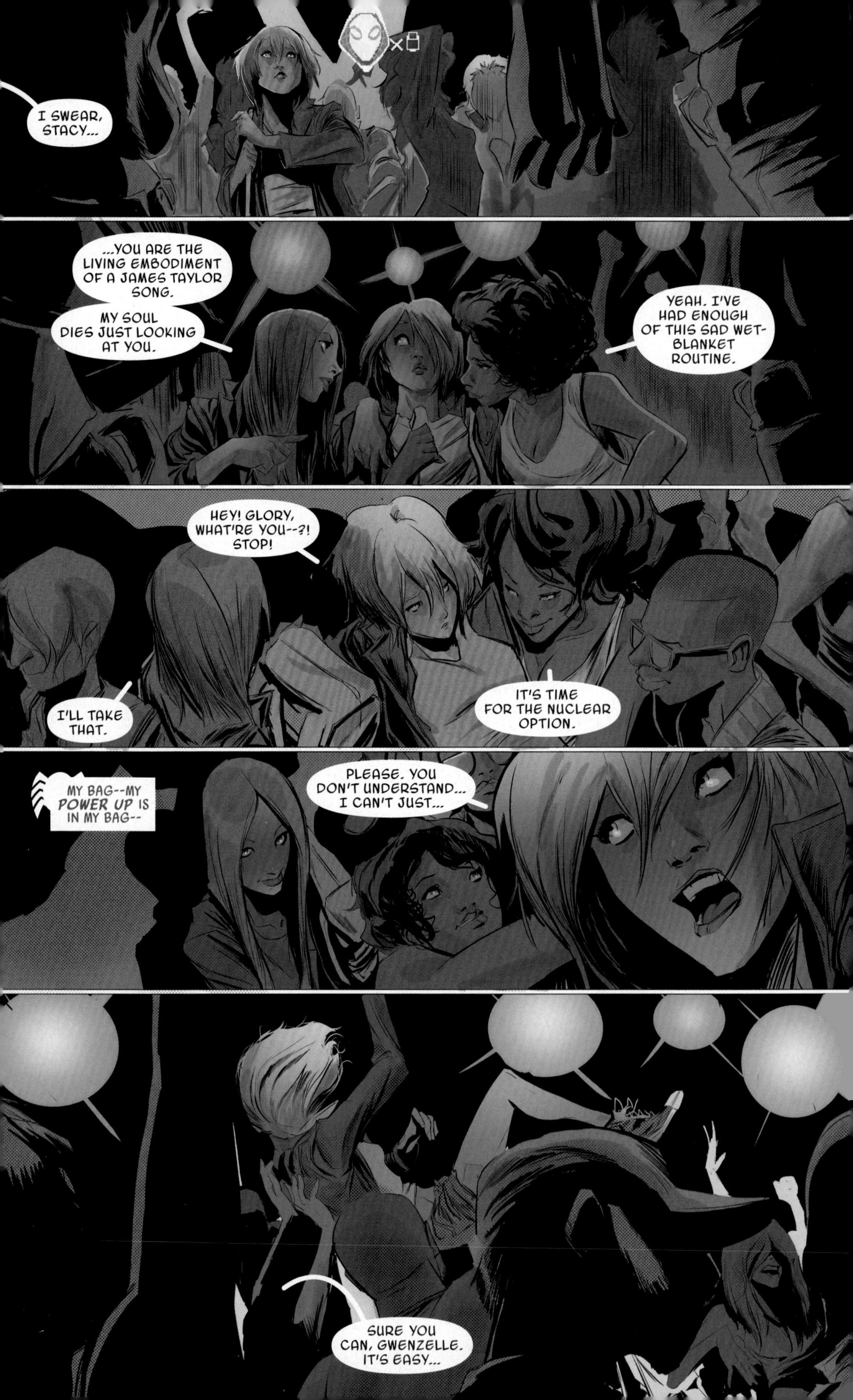
×8
I SWEAR, STACY...
...YOU ARE THE LIVING EMBODIMENT OF A JAMES TAYLOR SONG.
MY SOUL DIES JUST LOOKING AT YOU.
YEAH. I'VE HAD ENOUGH OF THIS SAD WET-BLANKET ROUTINE.
HEY! GLORY, WHAT'RE YOU--?! STOP!
I'LL TAKE THAT.
IT'S TIME FOR THE NUCLEAR OPTION.
MY BAG--MY POWER UP IS IN MY BAG--
PLEASE. YOU DON'T UNDERSTAND... I CAN'T JUST...
SURE YOU CAN, GWENZELLE. IT'S EASY...

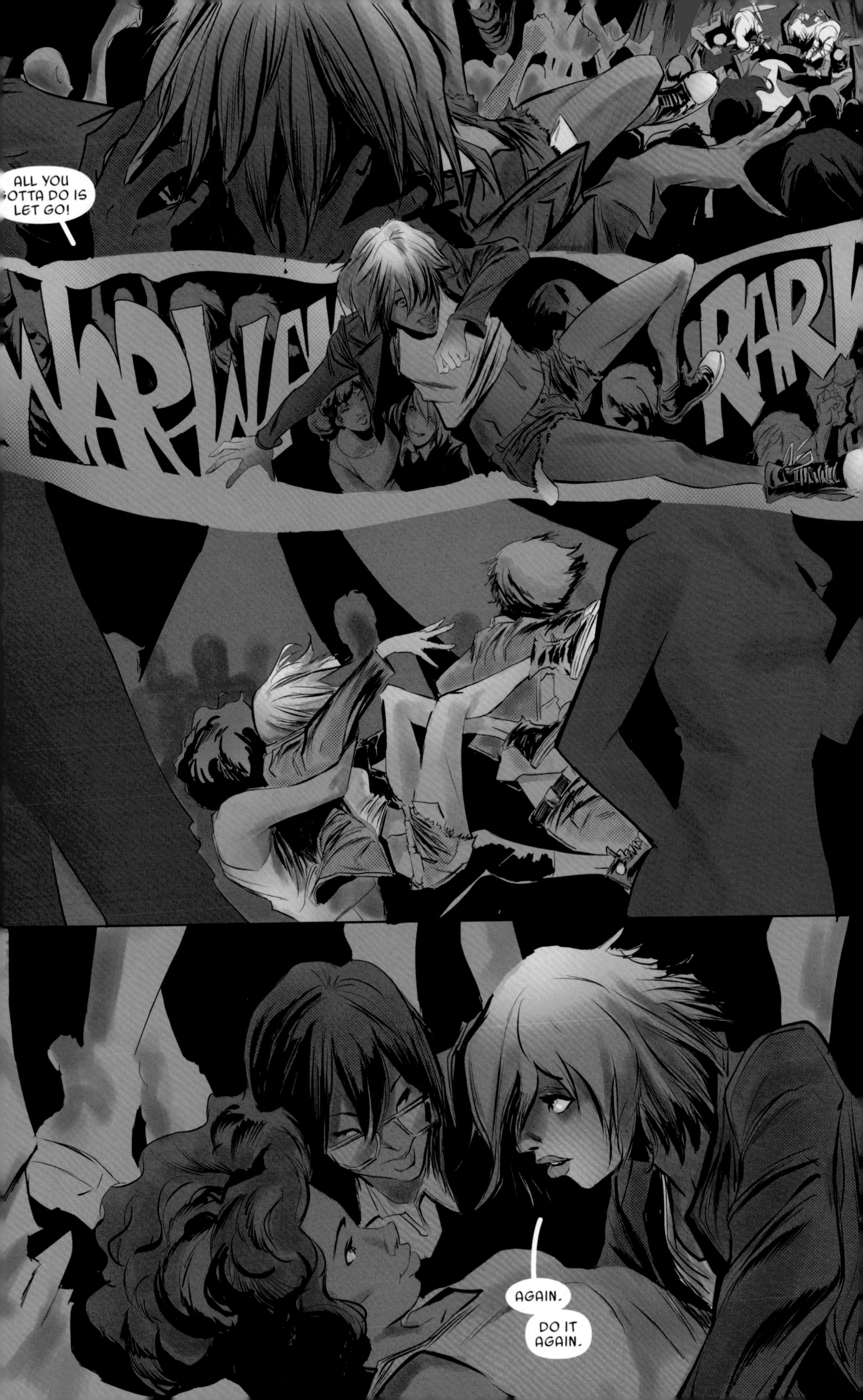
ALL YOU GOTTA DO IS LET GO!
AGAIN.
DO IT AGAIN.

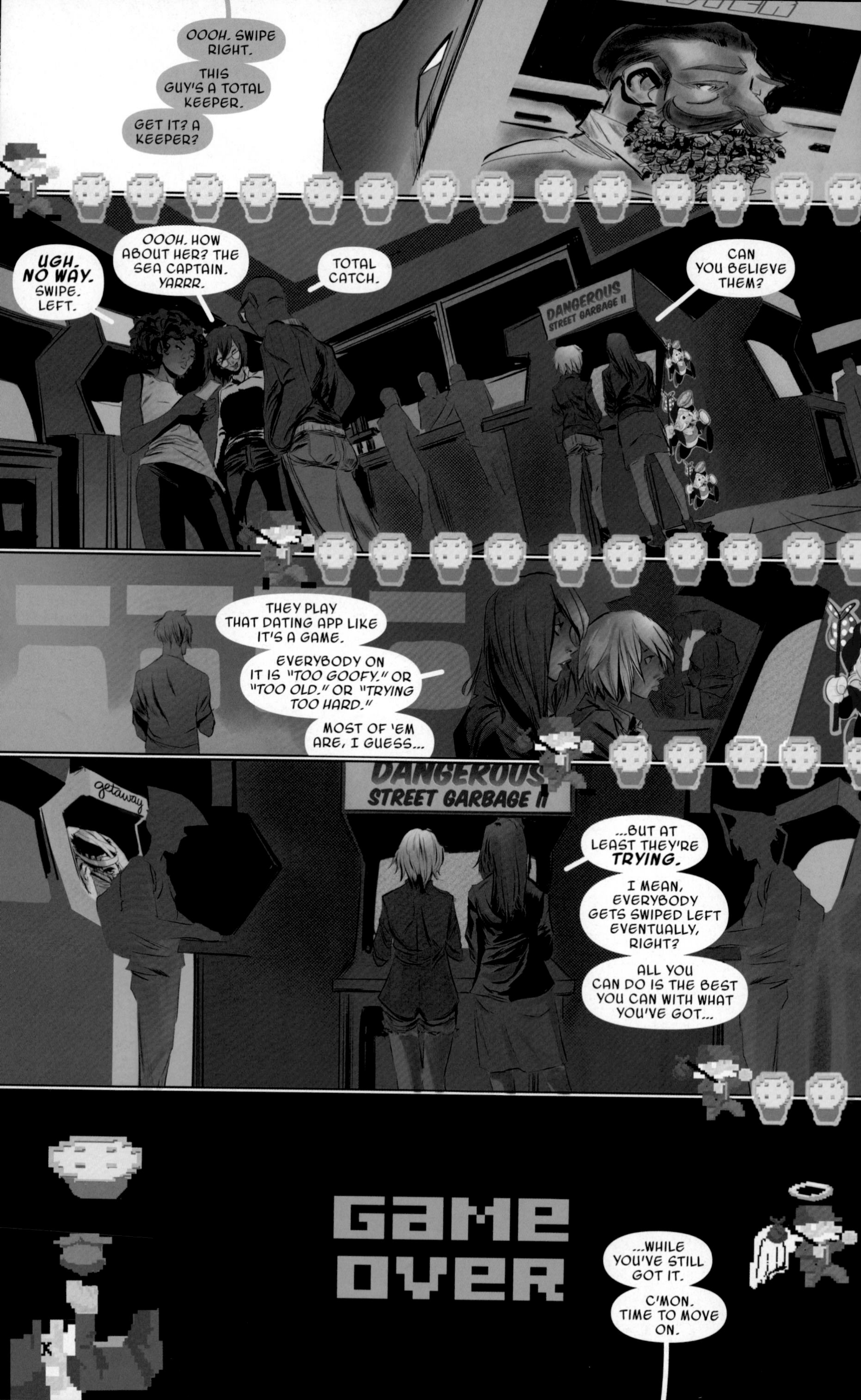
OOOH. SWIPE RIGHT.
THIS GUY'S A TOTAL KEEPER.
GET IT? A KEEPER?
UGH. NO WAY. SWIPE. LEFT.
OOOH. HOW ABOUT HER? THE SEA CAPTAIN. YARRR.
TOTAL CATCH.
CAN YOU BELIEVE THEM?
DANGEROUS STREET GARBAGE II
THEY PLAY THAT DATING APP LIKE IT'S A GAME.
EVERYBODY ON IT IS "TOO GOOFY." OR "TOO OLD." OR "TRYING TOO HARD."
MOST OF 'EM ARE, I GUESS...
getaway
DANGEROUS STREET GARBAGE II
...BUT AT LEAST THEY'RE TRYING.
I MEAN, EVERYBODY GETS SWIPED LEFT EVENTUALLY, RIGHT?
ALL YOU CAN DO IS THE BEST YOU CAN WITH WHAT YOU'VE GOT...
GAME OVER
...WHILE YOU'VE STILL GOT IT.
C'MON. TIME TO MOVE ON.

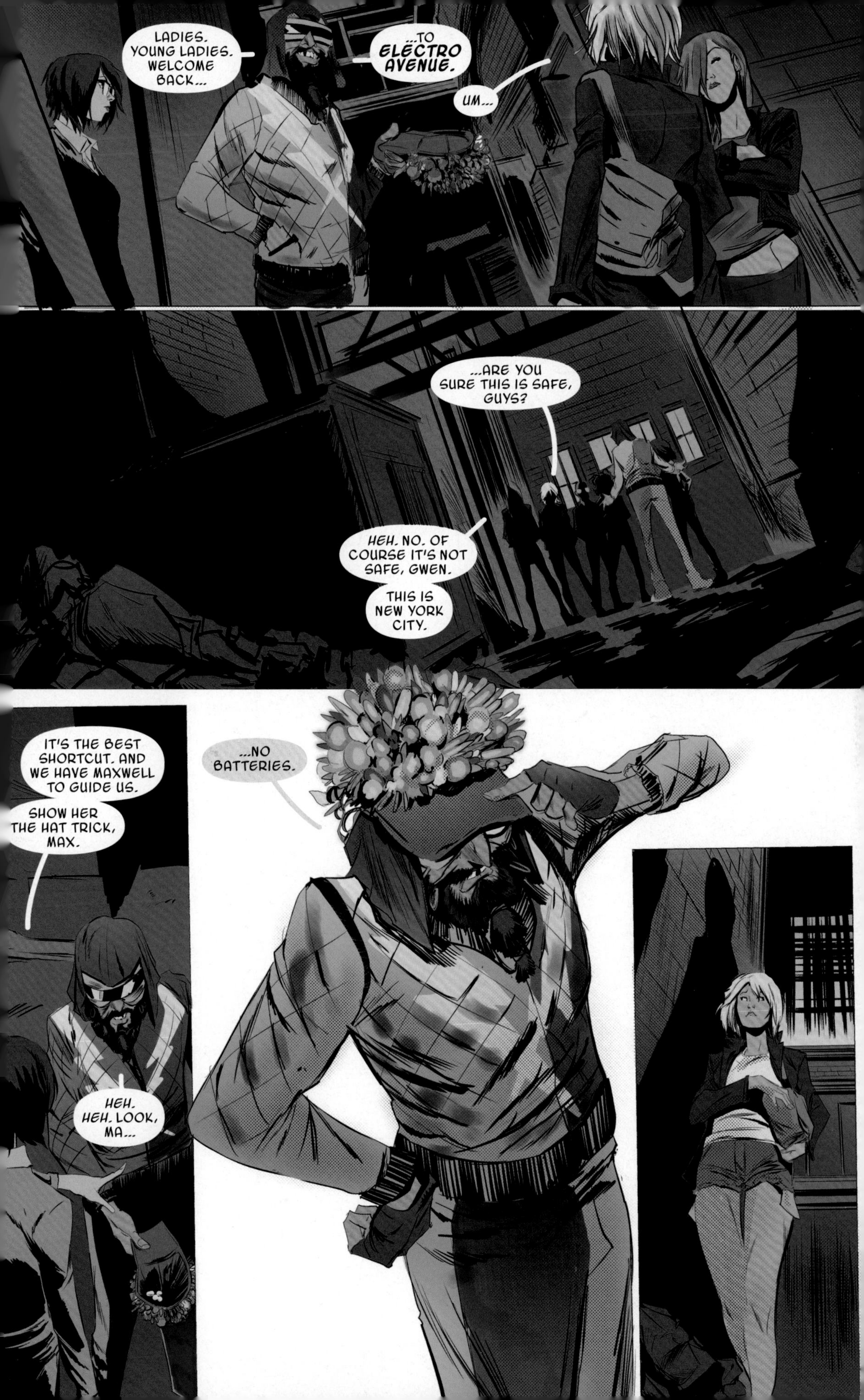
LADIES. YOUNG LADIES. WELCOME BACK...
...TO ELECTRO AVENUE.
UM...
...ARE YOU SURE THIS IS SAFE, GUYS?
HEH. NO. OF COURSE IT'S NOT SAFE, GWEN.
THIS IS NEW YORK CITY.
IT'S THE BEST SHORTCUT. AND WE HAVE MAXWELL TO GUIDE US.
SHOW HER THE HAT TRICK, MAX.
...NO BATTERIES.
HEH. HEH. LOOK, MA...

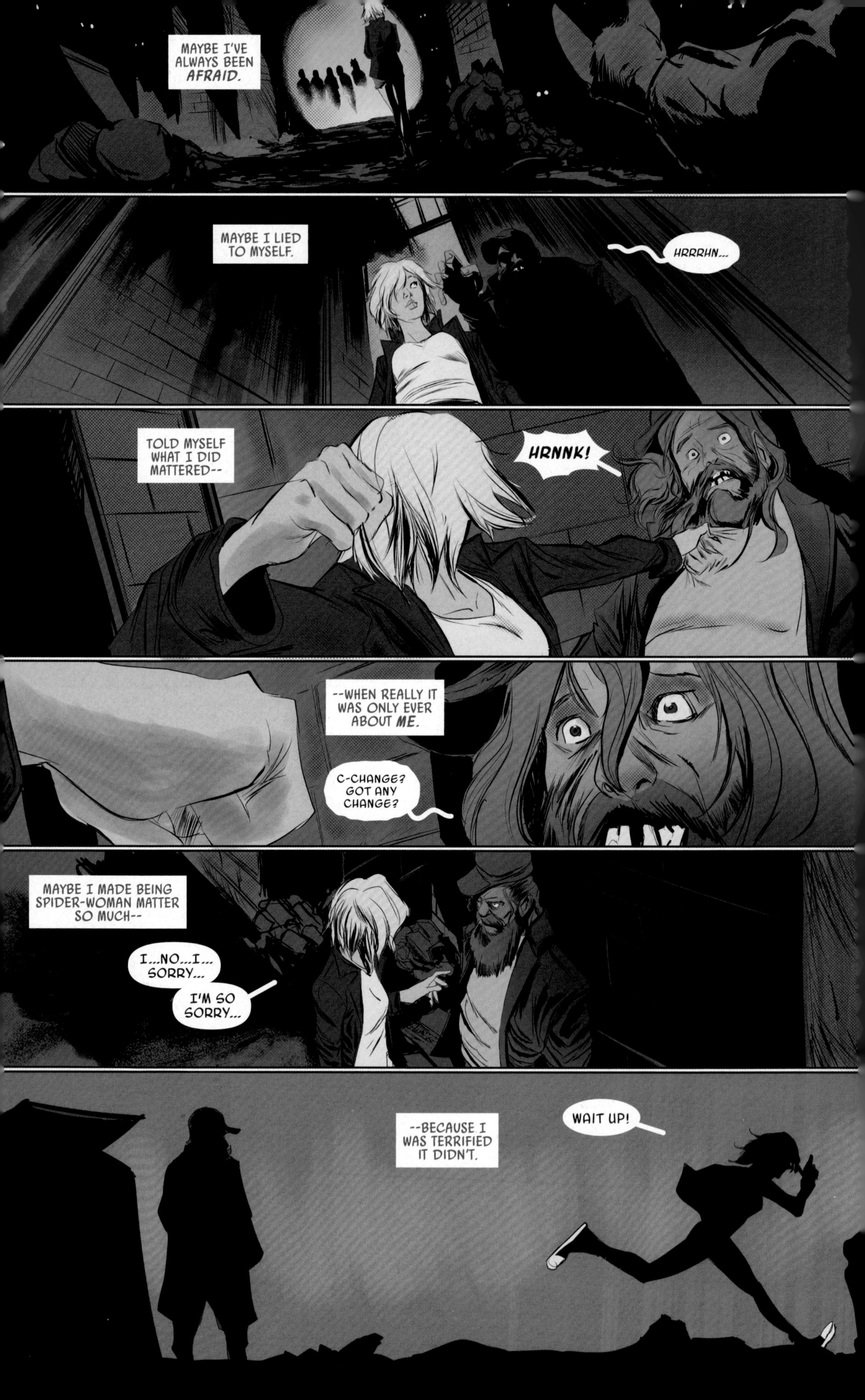
MAYBE I'VE ALWAYS BEEN AFRAID.
MAYBE I LIED TO MYSELF.
HRRRHN...
TOLD MYSELF WHAT I DID MATTERED--
HRNNK!
--WHEN REALLY IT WAS ONLY EVER ABOUT ME.
C-CHANGE? GOT ANY CHANGE?
MAYBE I MADE BEING SPIDER-WOMAN MATTER SO MUCH--
I...NO...I... SORRY...
I'M SO SORRY...
--BECAUSE I WAS TERRIFIED IT DIDN'T.
WAIT UP!

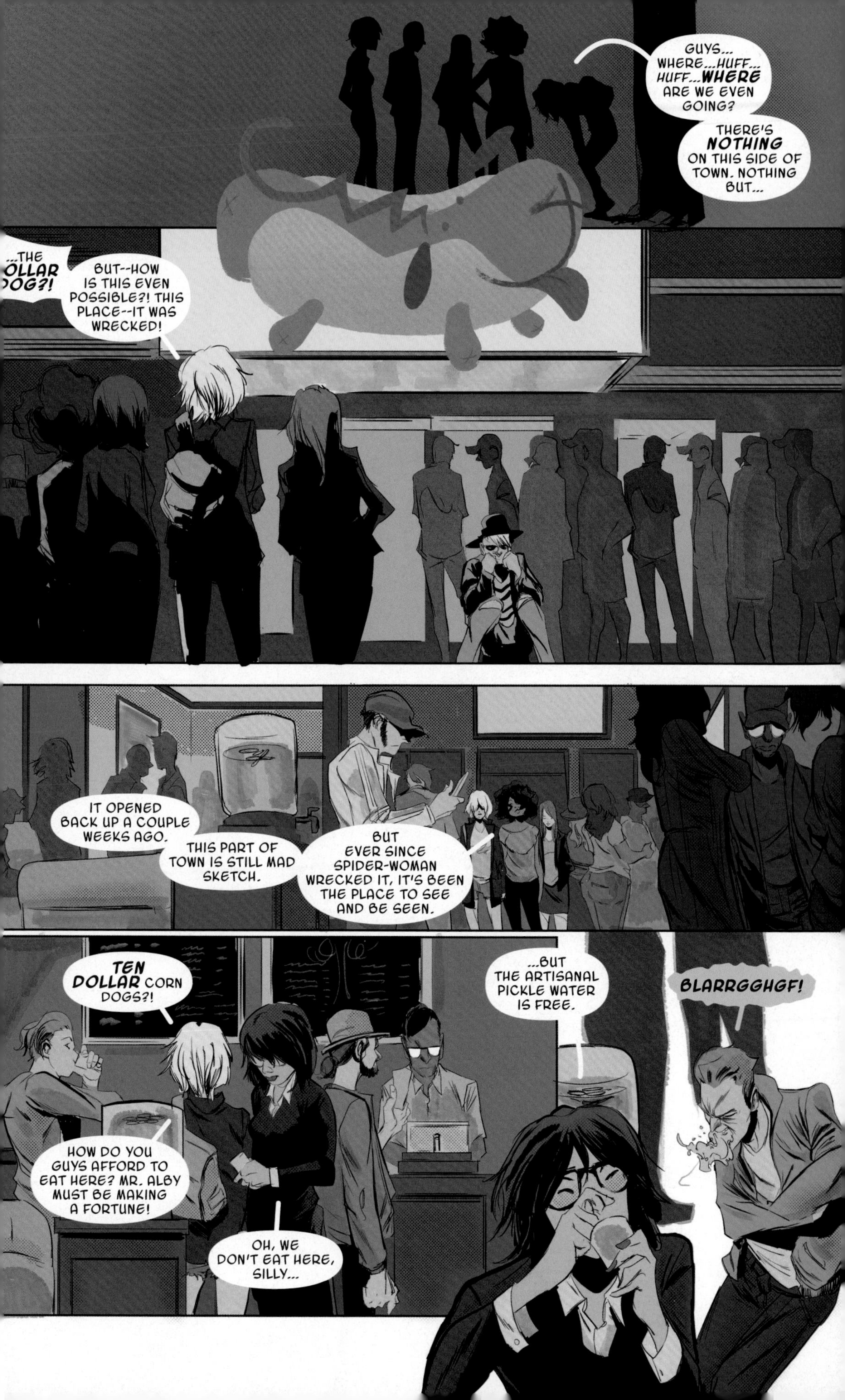
GUYS... WHERE...HUFF... HUFF...WHERE ARE WE EVEN GOING?
THERE'S NOTHING ON THIS SIDE OF TOWN. NOTHING BUT...
...THE DOLLAR DOG?!
BUT--HOW IS THIS EVEN POSSIBLE?! THIS PLACE--IT WAS WRECKED!
IT OPENED BACK UP A COUPLE WEEKS AGO.
THIS PART OF TOWN IS STILL MAD SKETCH.
BUT EVER SINCE SPIDER-WOMAN WRECKED IT, IT'S BEEN THE PLACE TO SEE AND BE SEEN.
TEN DOLLAR CORN DOGS?!
HOW DO YOU GUYS AFFORD TO EAT HERE? MR. ALBY MUST BE MAKING A FORTUNE!
OH, WE DON'T EAT HERE, SILLY...
...BUT THE ARTISANAL PICKLE WATER IS FREE.
BLARRGGHGF!

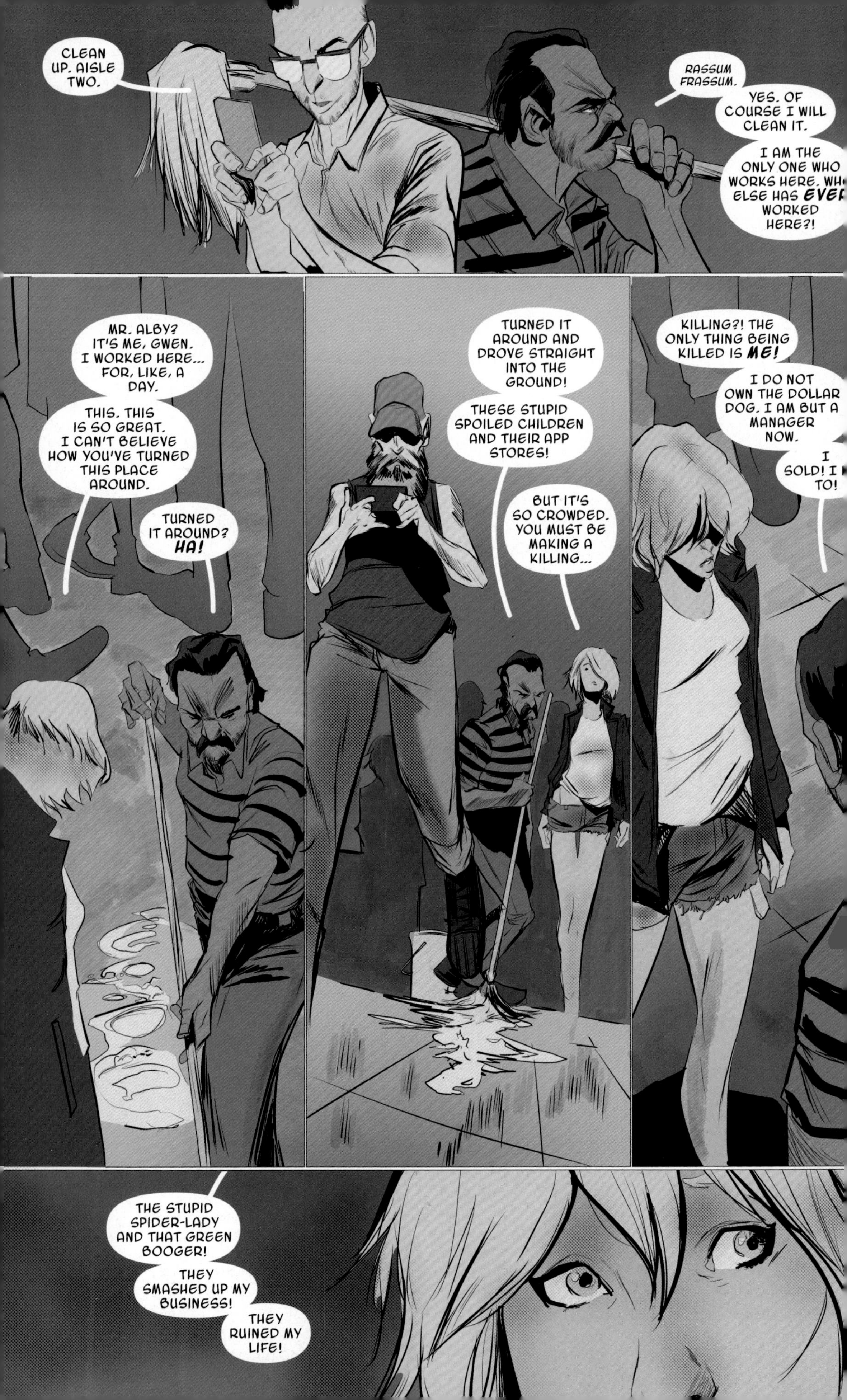

CLEAN UP. AISLE TWO.
RASSUM FRASSUM.
YES. OF COURSE I WILL CLEAN IT.
I AM THE ONLY ONE WHO WORKS HERE. WH ELSE HAS EVER WORKED HERE?!
MR. ALBY? IT'S ME, GWEN. I WORKED HERE... FOR, LIKE, A DAY.
THIS. THIS IS SO GREAT. I CAN'T BELIEVE HOW YOU'VE TURNED THIS PLACE AROUND.
TURNED IT AROUND? HA!
TURNED IT AROUND AND DROVE STRAIGHT INTO THE GROUND!
THESE STUPID SPOILED CHILDREN AND THEIR APP STORES!
BUT IT'S SO CROWDED. YOU MUST BE MAKING A KILLING...
KILLING?! THE ONLY THING BEING KILLED IS ME!
I DO NOT OWN THE DOLLAR DOG. I AM BUT A MANAGER NOW.
I SOLD! I TO!
THE STUPID SPIDER-LADY AND THAT GREEN BOOGER!
THEY SMASHED UP MY BUSINESS!
THEY RUINED MY LIFE!

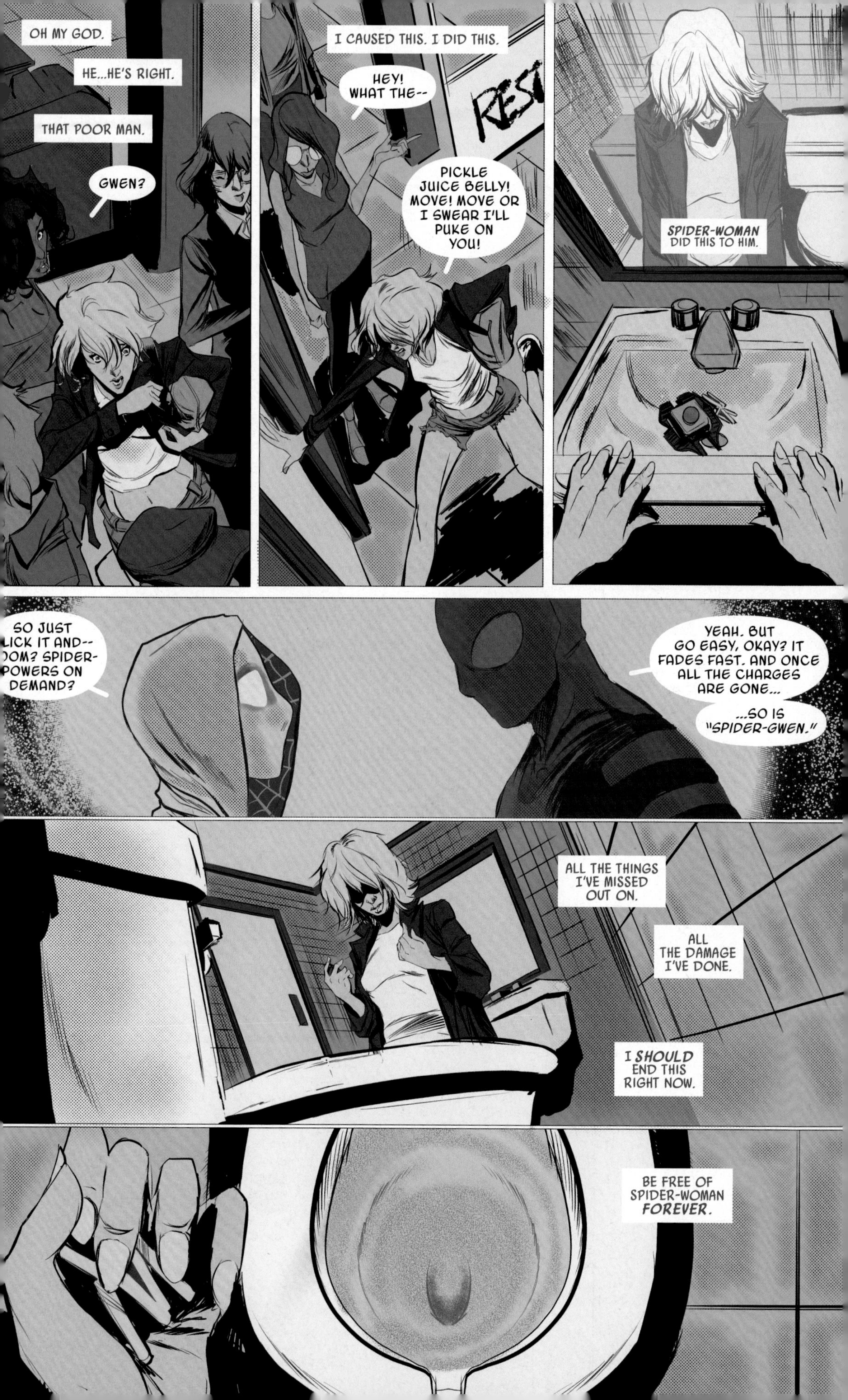
OH MY GOD.
HE...HE'S RIGHT.
THAT POOR MAN.
GWEN?
I CAUSED THIS. I DID THIS.
HEY! WHAT THE--
PICKLE JUICE BELLY! MOVE! MOVE OR I SWEAR I'LL PUKE ON YOU!
SPIDER-WOMAN DID THIS TO HIM.
SO JUST LICK IT AND-- OOM? SPIDER-POWERS ON DEMAND?
YEAH. BUT GO EASY, OKAY? IT FADES FAST. AND ONCE ALL THE CHARGES ARE GONE...
...SO IS "SPIDER-GWEN."
ALL THE THINGS I'VE MISSED OUT ON.
ALL THE DAMAGE I'VE DONE.
I SHOULD END THIS RIGHT NOW.
BE FREE OF SPIDER-WOMAN FOREVER.

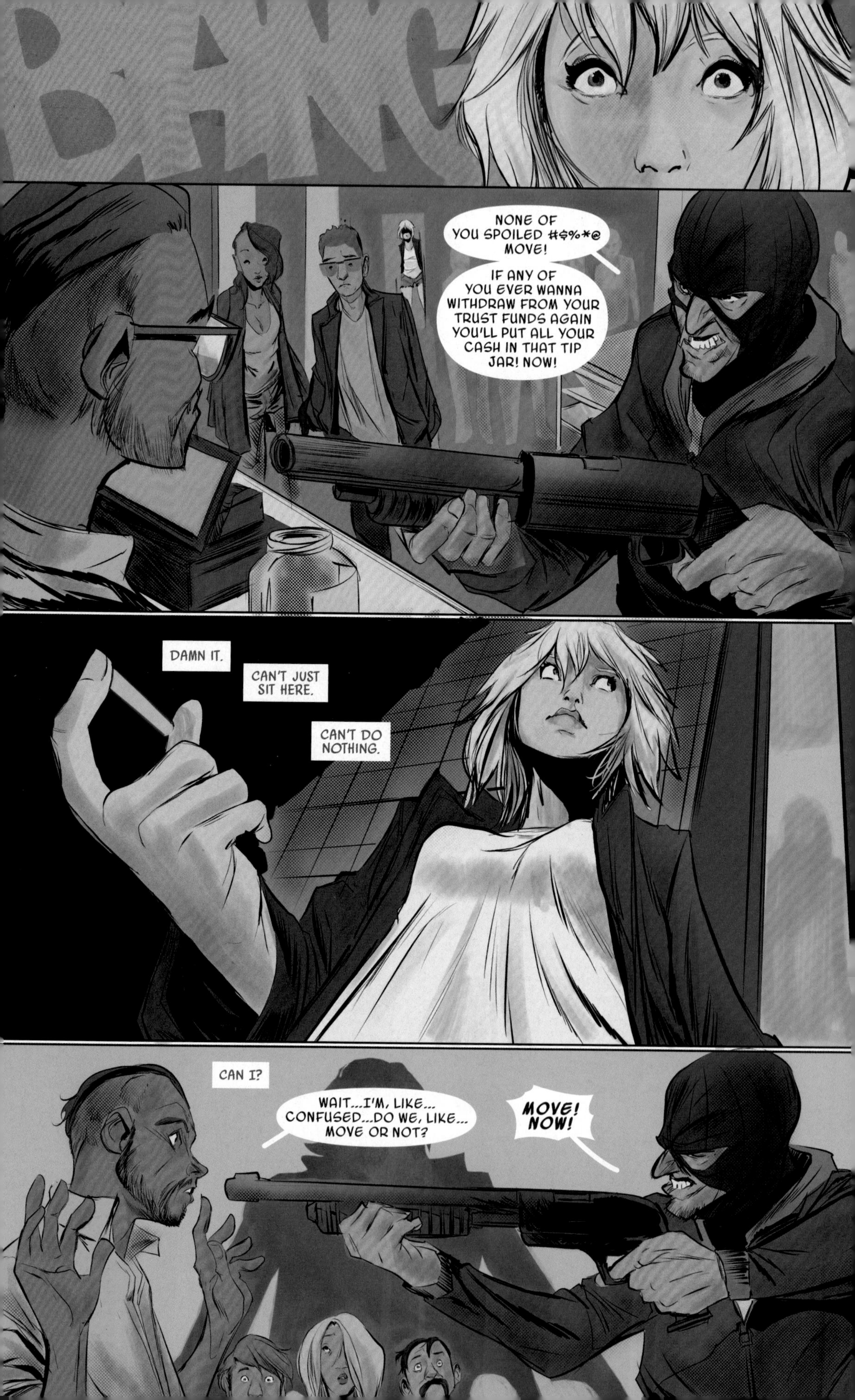
NONE OF YOU SPOILED #$%*@ MOVE!
IF ANY OF YOU EVER WANNA WITHDRAW FROM YOUR TRUST FUNDS AGAIN YOU'LL PUT ALL YOUR CASH IN THAT TIP JAR! NOW!
DAMN IT.
CAN'T JUST SIT HERE.
CAN'T DO NOTHING.
CAN I?
WAIT...I'M, LIKE... CONFUSED...DO WE, LIKE... MOVE OR NOT?
MOVE! NOW!

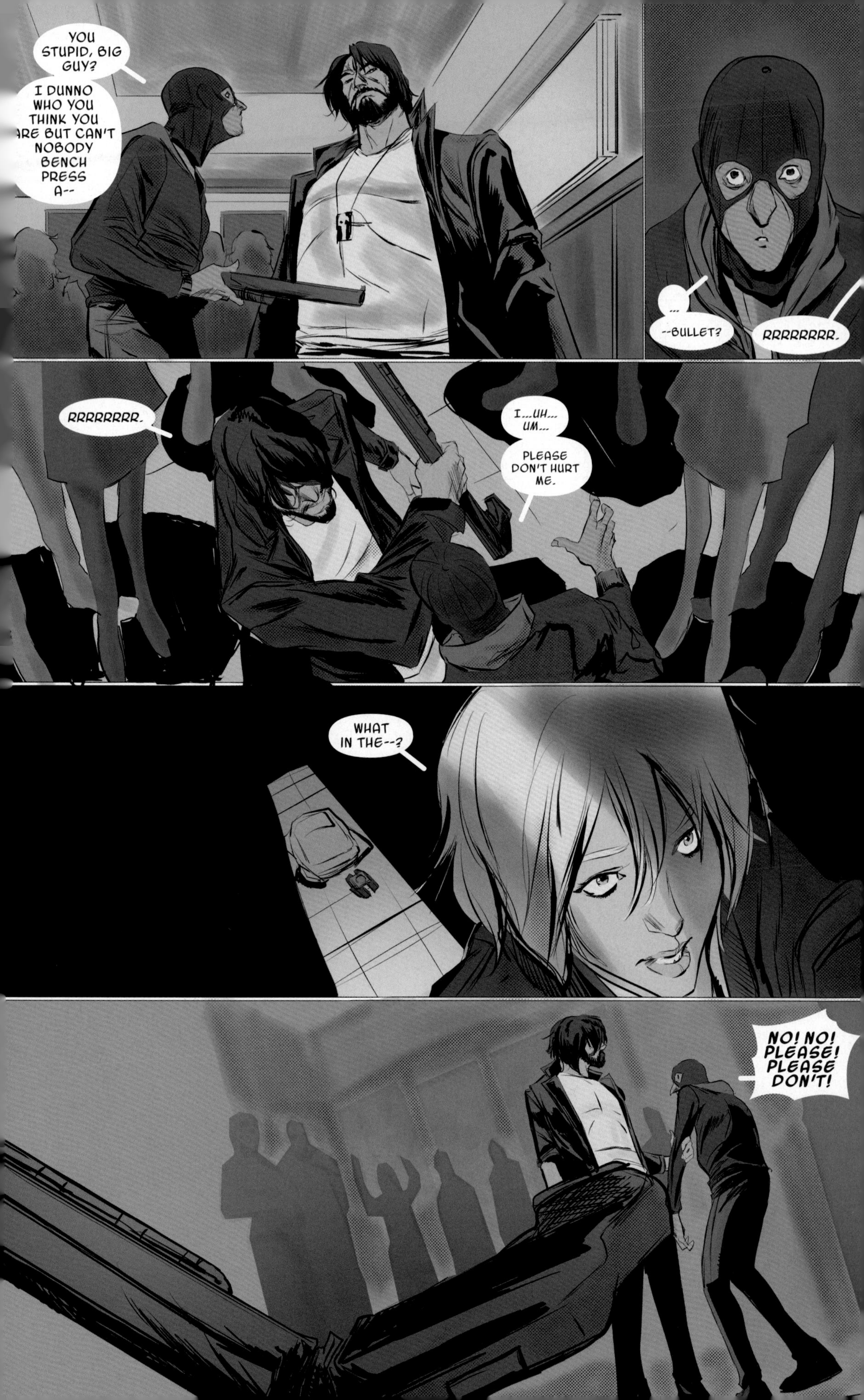
YOU STUPID, BIG GUY?
I DUNNO WHO YOU THINK YOU ARE BUT CAN'T NOBODY BENCH PRESS A--
...
--BULLET?
RRRRRRRR.
RRRRRRRR.
I...UH... UM...
PLEASE DON'T HURT ME.
WHAT IN THE--?
NO! NO! PLEASE! PLEASE DON'T!

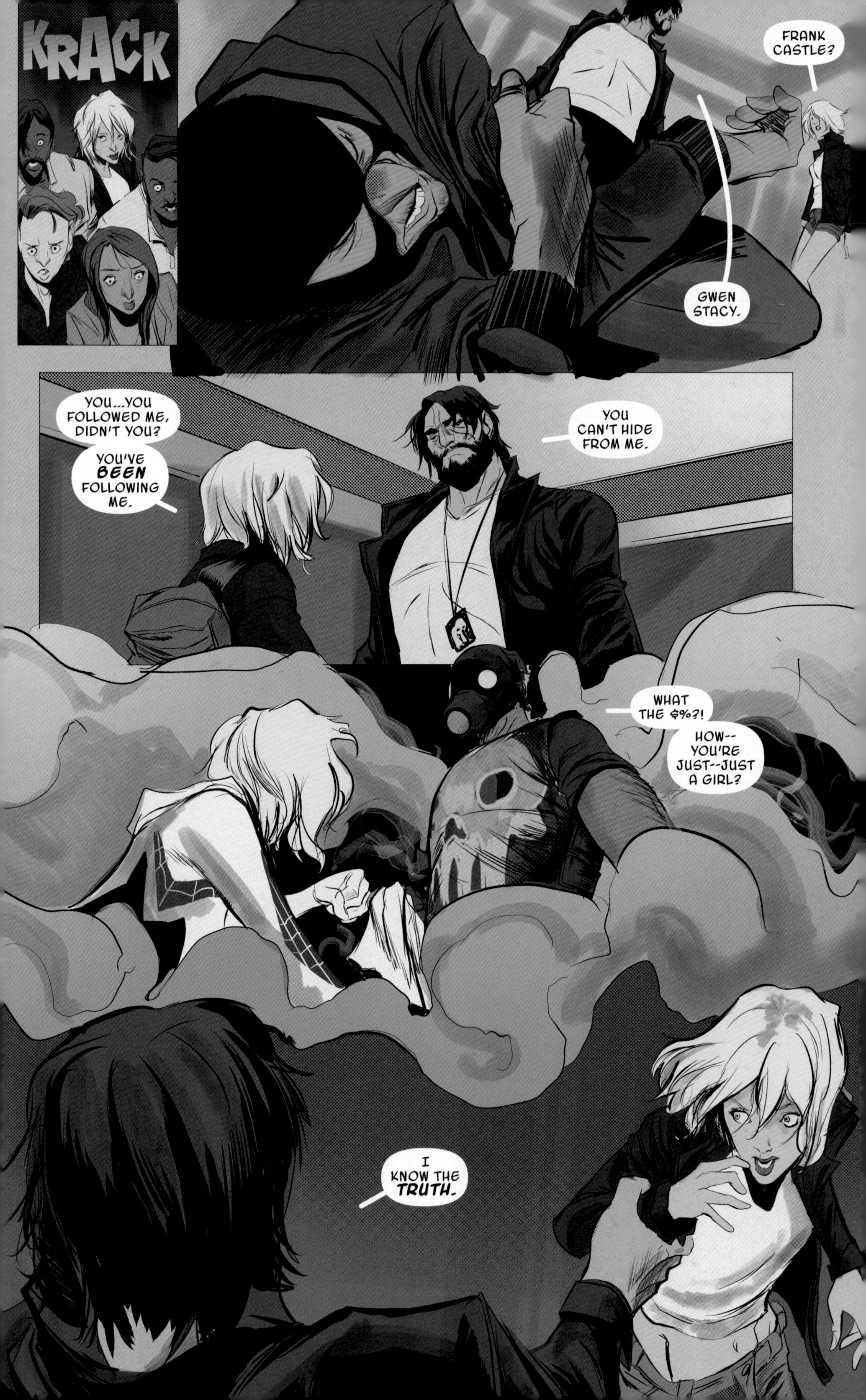
KRACK
FRANK CASTLE?
GWEN STACY.
YOU...YOU FOLLOWED ME, DIDN'T YOU?
YOU'VE **BEEN** FOLLOWING ME.
YOU CAN'T HIDE FROM ME.
WHAT THE $%?!
HOW--YOU'RE JUST--JUST A GIRL?
I KNOW THE **TRUTH**.

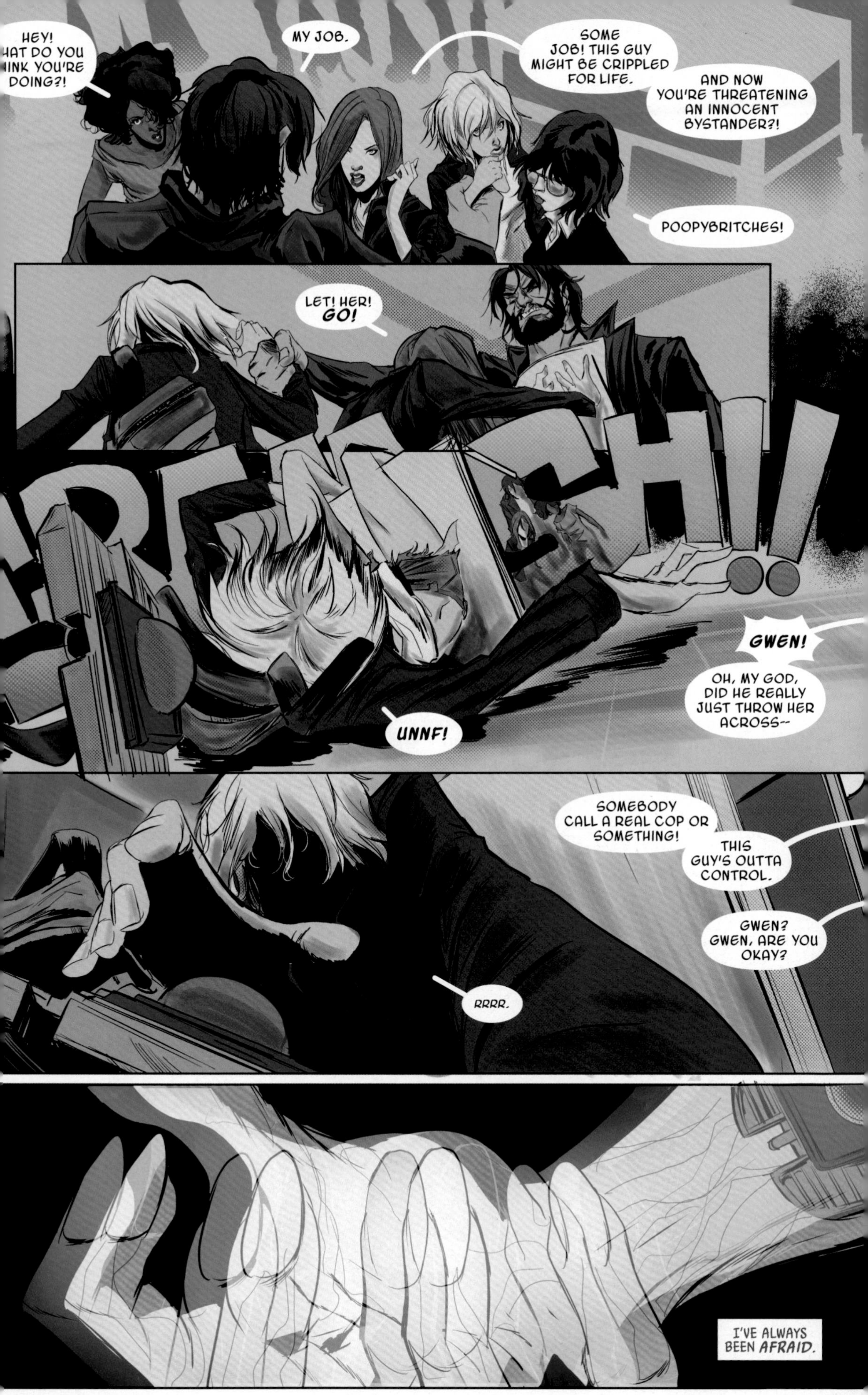

HEY! HAT DO YOU INK YOU'RE DOING?!
MY JOB.
SOME JOB! THIS GUY MIGHT BE CRIPPLED FOR LIFE.
AND NOW YOU'RE THREATENING AN INNOCENT BYSTANDER?!
POOPYBRITCHES!
LET! HER! GO!
GWEN!
OH, MY GOD, DID HE REALLY JUST THROW HER ACROSS--
UNNF!
SOMEBODY CALL A REAL COP OR SOMETHING!
THIS GUY'S OUTTA CONTROL.
GWEN? GWEN, ARE YOU OKAY?
RRRR.
I'VE ALWAYS BEEN AFRAID.

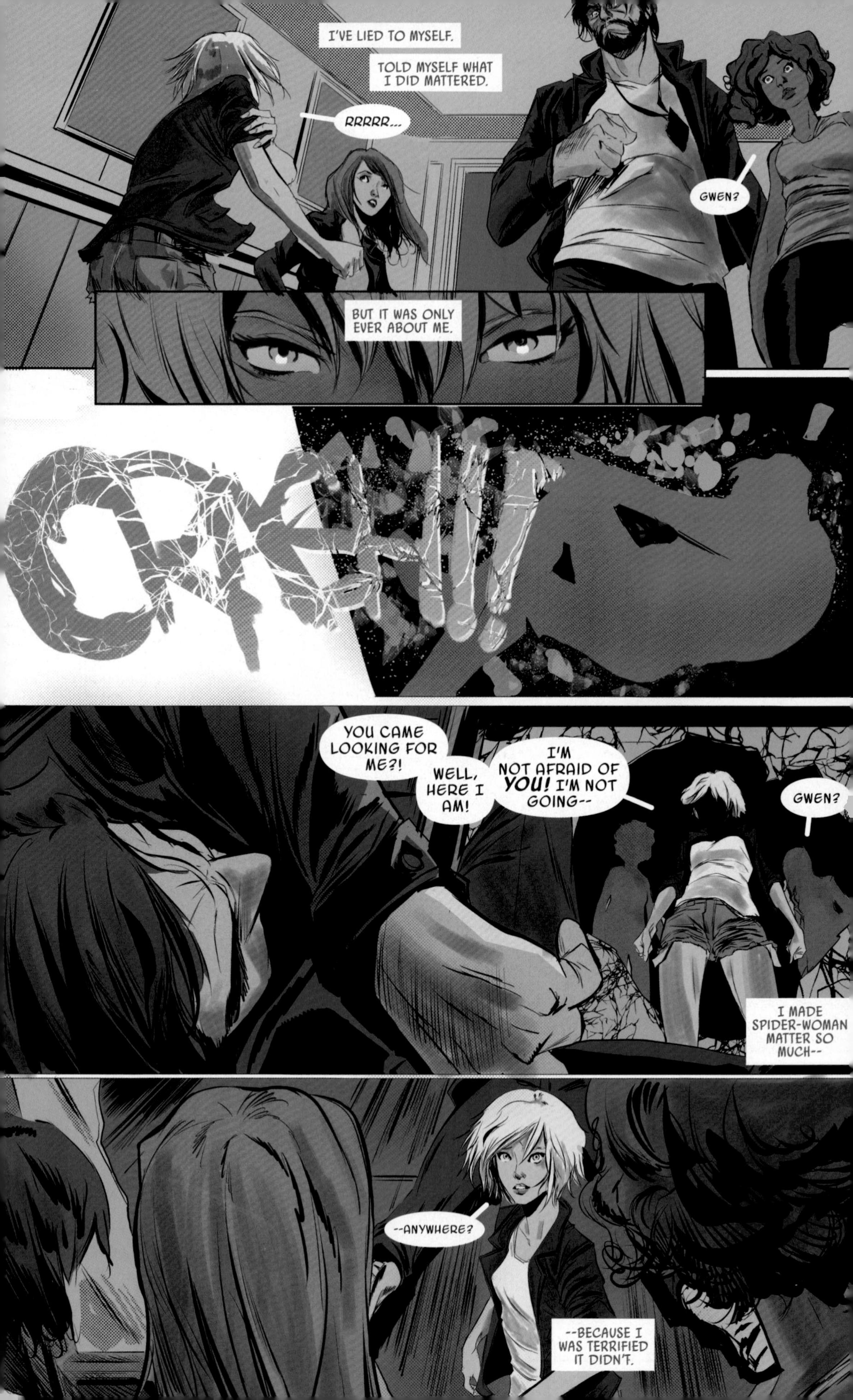
I'VE LIED TO MYSELF.
TOLD MYSELF WHAT I DID MATTERED.
RRRRR...
GWEN?
BUT IT WAS ONLY EVER ABOUT ME.
CRK
YOU CAME LOOKING FOR ME?!
WELL, HERE I AM!
I'M NOT AFRAID OF YOU! I'M NOT GOING--
GWEN?
I MADE SPIDER-WOMAN MATTER SO MUCH--
--ANYWHERE?
--BECAUSE I WAS TERRIFIED IT DIDN'T.

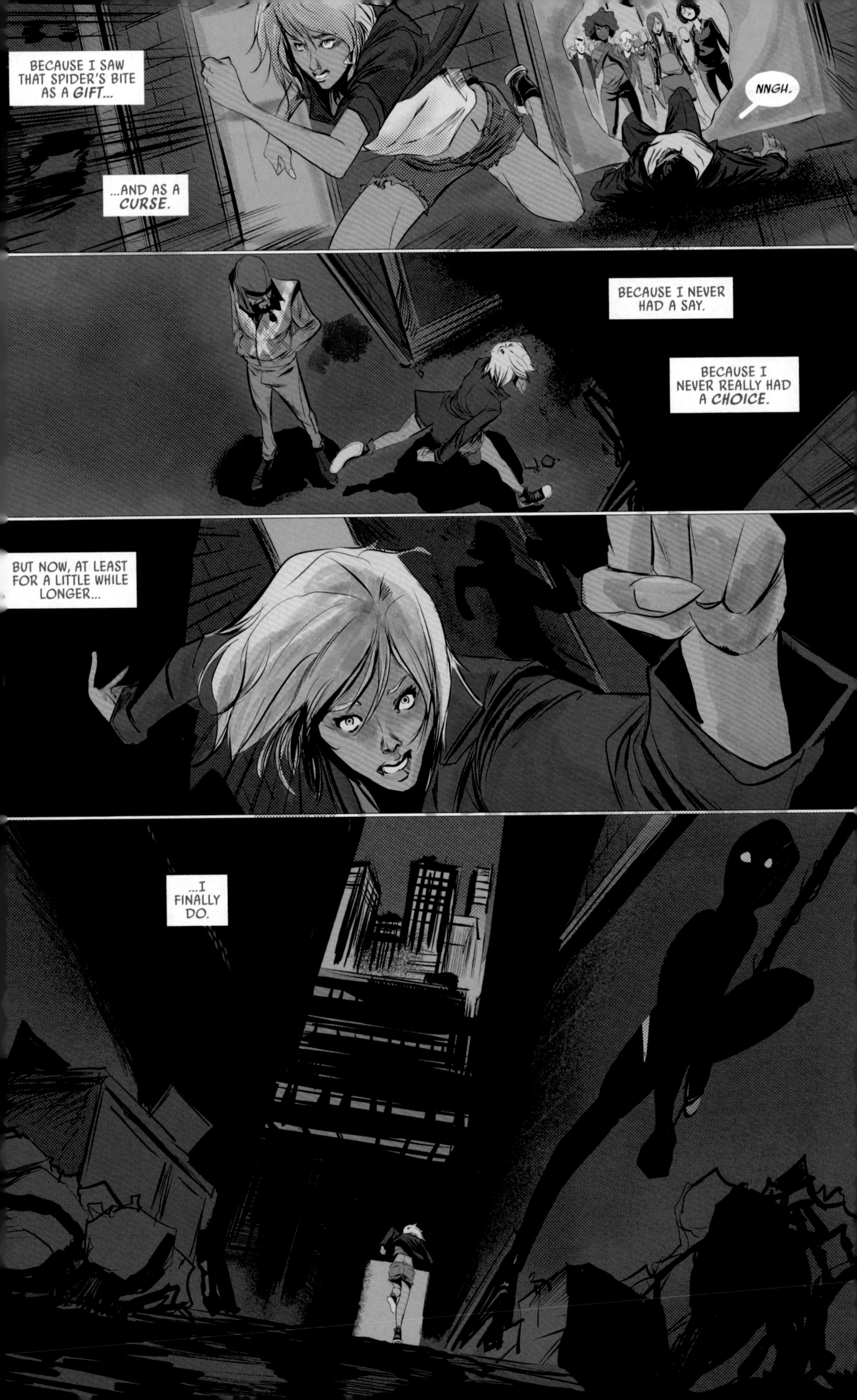
BECAUSE I SAW THAT SPIDER'S BITE AS A GIFT...
...AND AS A CURSE.
NNGH.
BECAUSE I NEVER HAD A SAY.
BECAUSE I NEVER REALLY HAD A CHOICE.
BUT NOW, AT LEAST FOR A LITTLE WHILE LONGER...
...I FINALLY DO.

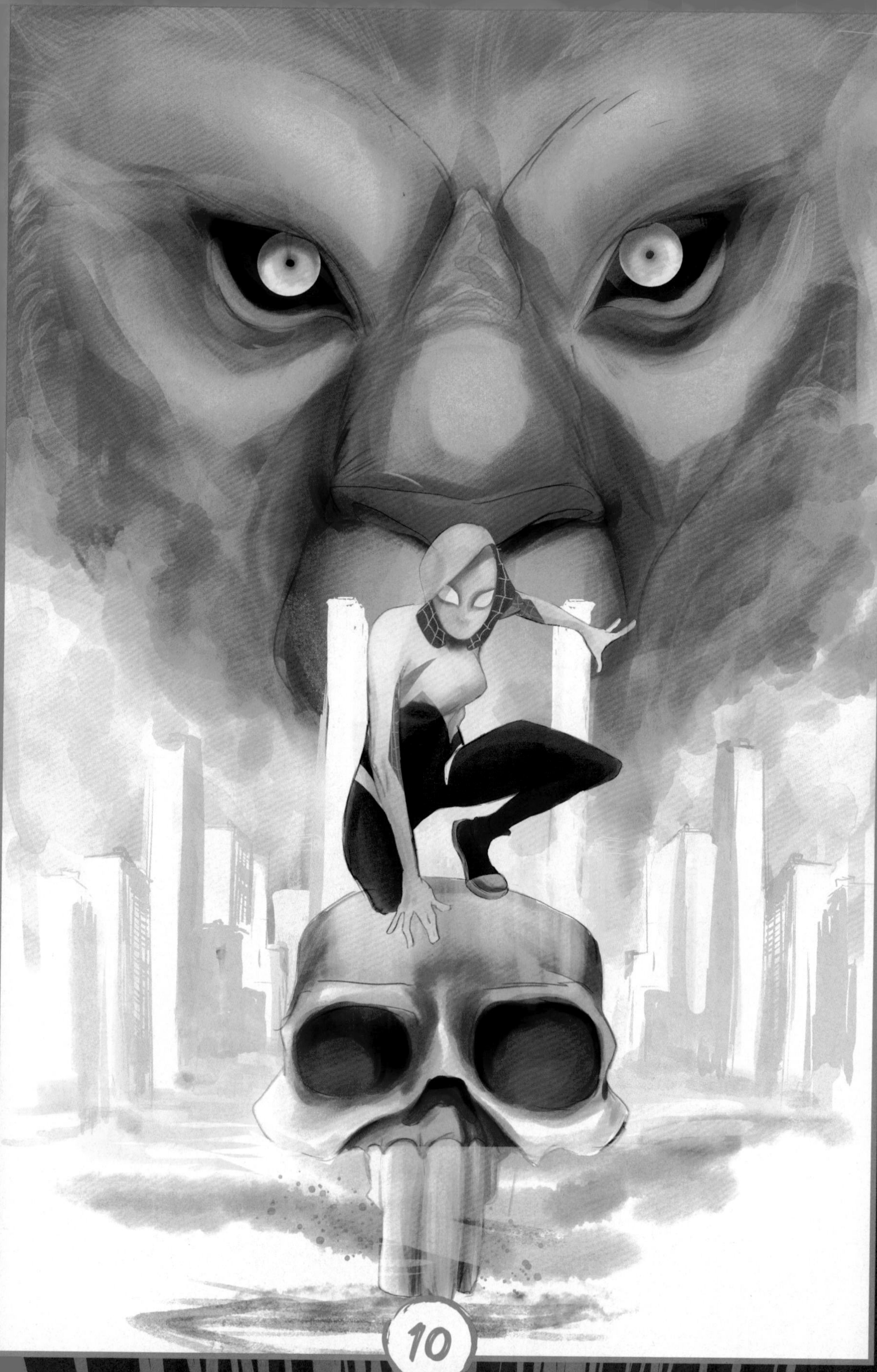
10

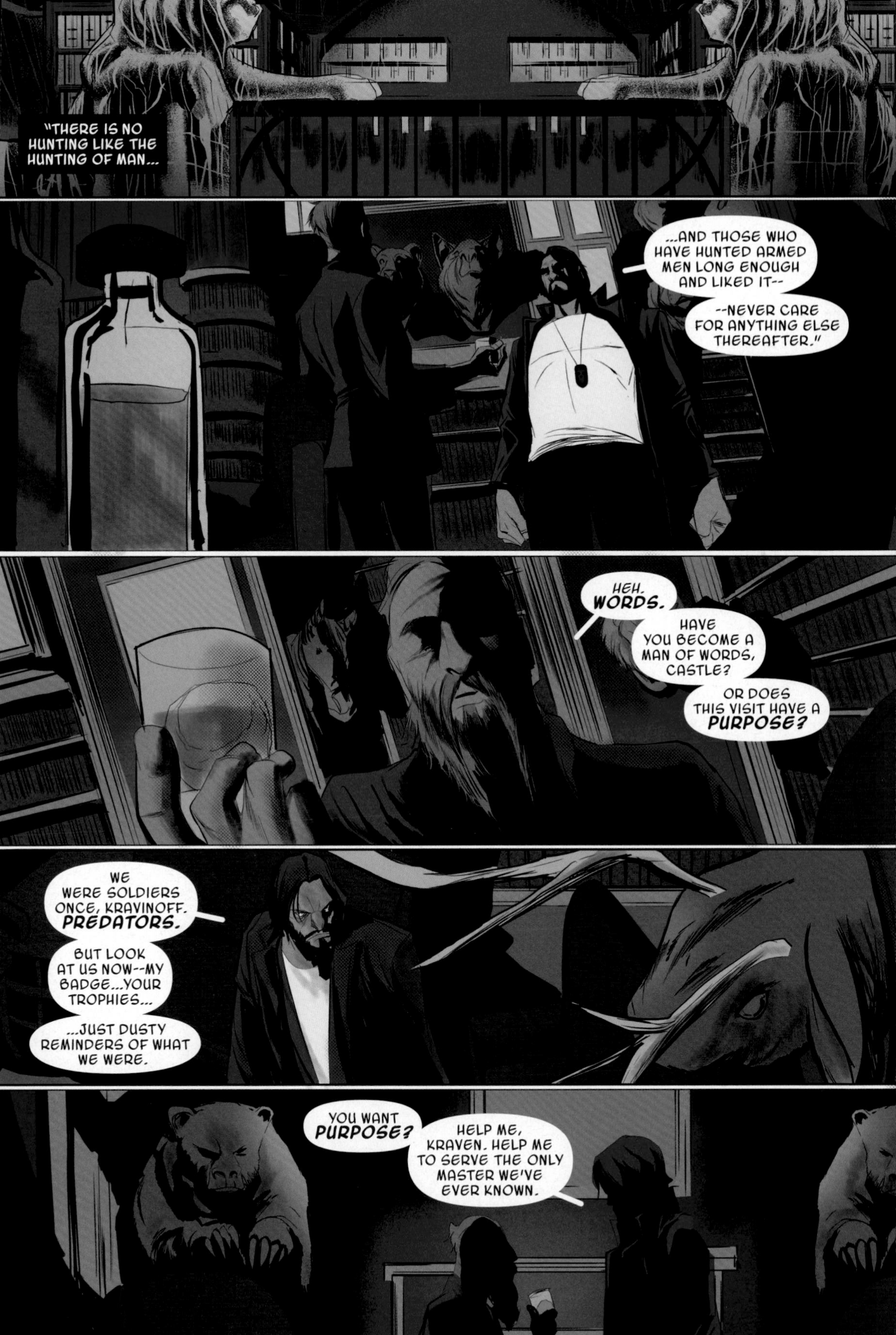

"THERE IS NO HUNTING LIKE THE HUNTING OF MAN...
...AND THOSE WHO HAVE HUNTED ARMED MEN LONG ENOUGH AND LIKED IT--
--NEVER CARE FOR ANYTHING ELSE THEREAFTER."
HEH. WORDS.
HAVE YOU BECOME A MAN OF WORDS, CASTLE?
OR DOES THIS VISIT HAVE A PURPOSE?
WE WERE SOLDIERS ONCE, KRAVINOFF. PREDATORS.
BUT LOOK AT US NOW--MY BADGE...YOUR TROPHIES...
...JUST DUSTY REMINDERS OF WHAT WE WERE.
YOU WANT PURPOSE?
HELP ME, KRAVEN. HELP ME TO SERVE THE ONLY MASTER WE'VE EVER KNOWN.

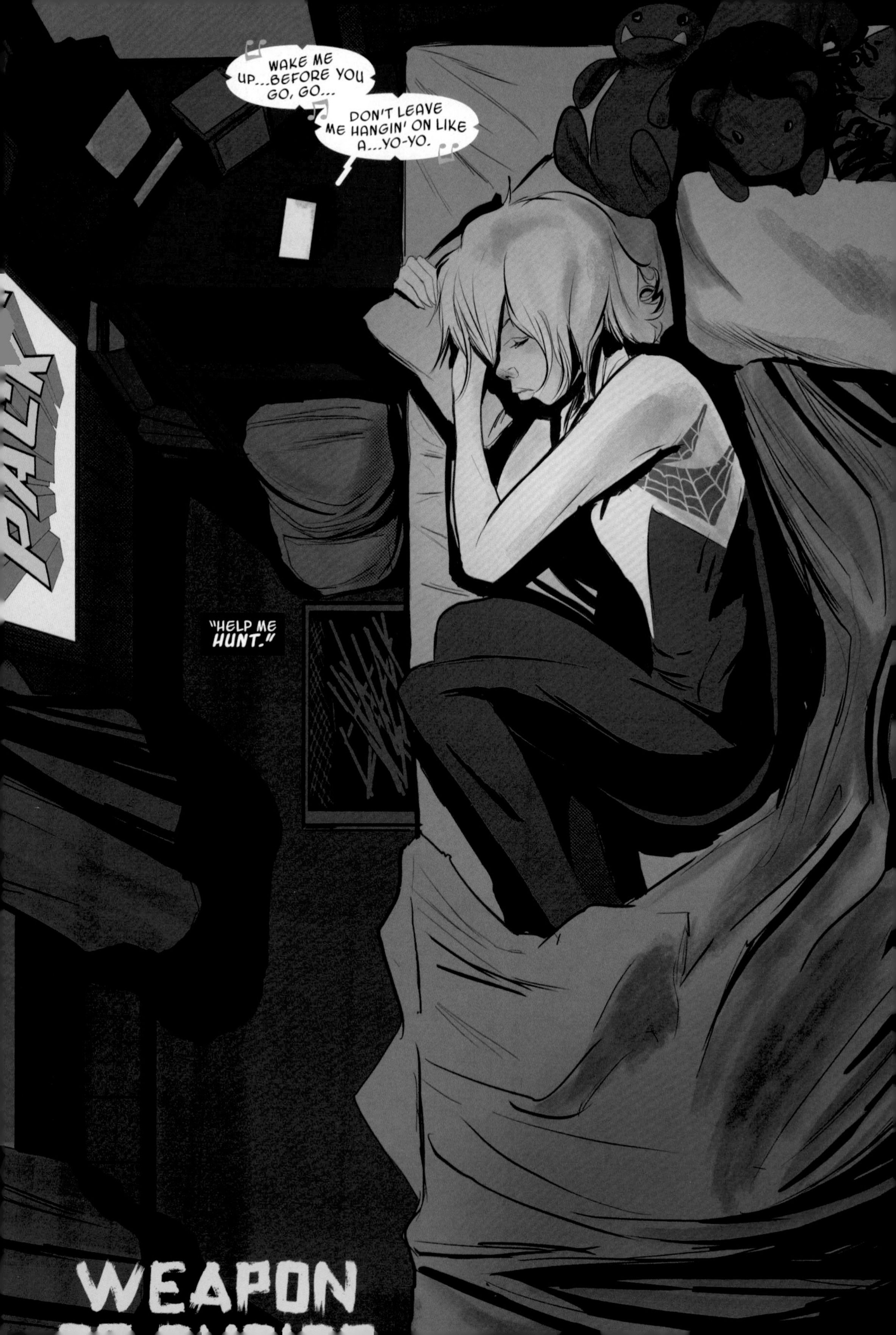
WAKE ME UP...BEFORE YOU GO, GO...
DON'T LEAVE ME HANGIN' ON LIKE A...YO-YO.
"HELP ME HUNT."
WEAPON

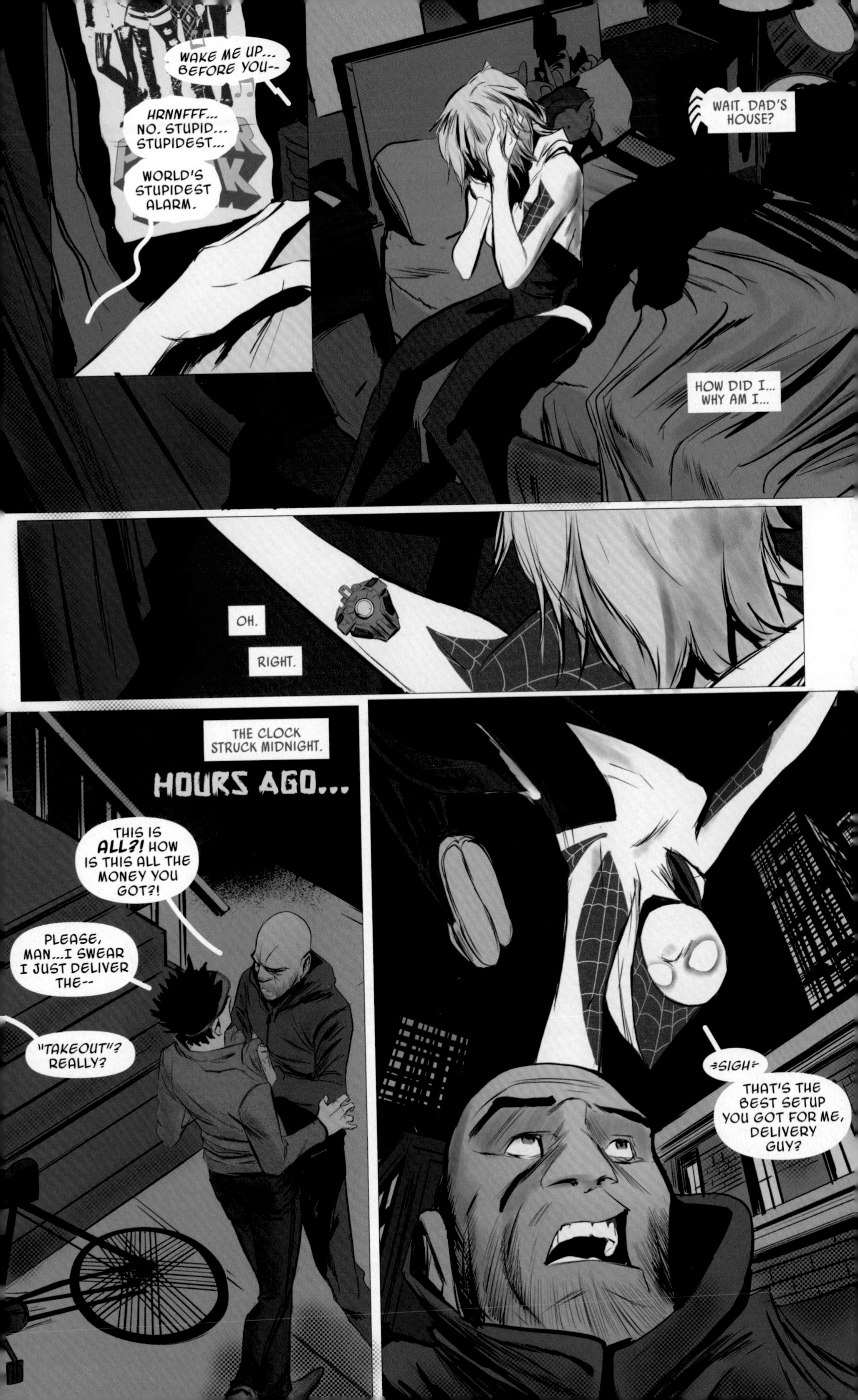
WAKE ME UP... BEFORE YOU--
HRNNFFF... NO. STUPID... STUPIDEST...
WORLD'S STUPIDEST ALARM.
WAIT. DAD'S HOUSE?
HOW DID I... WHY AM I...
OH.
RIGHT.
THE CLOCK STRUCK MIDNIGHT.
HOURS AGO...
THIS IS ALL?! HOW IS THIS ALL THE MONEY YOU GOT?!
PLEASE, MAN...I SWEAR I JUST DELIVER THE--
"TAKEOUT"? REALLY?
=SIGH=
THAT'S THE BEST SETUP YOU GOT FOR ME, DELIVERY GUY?

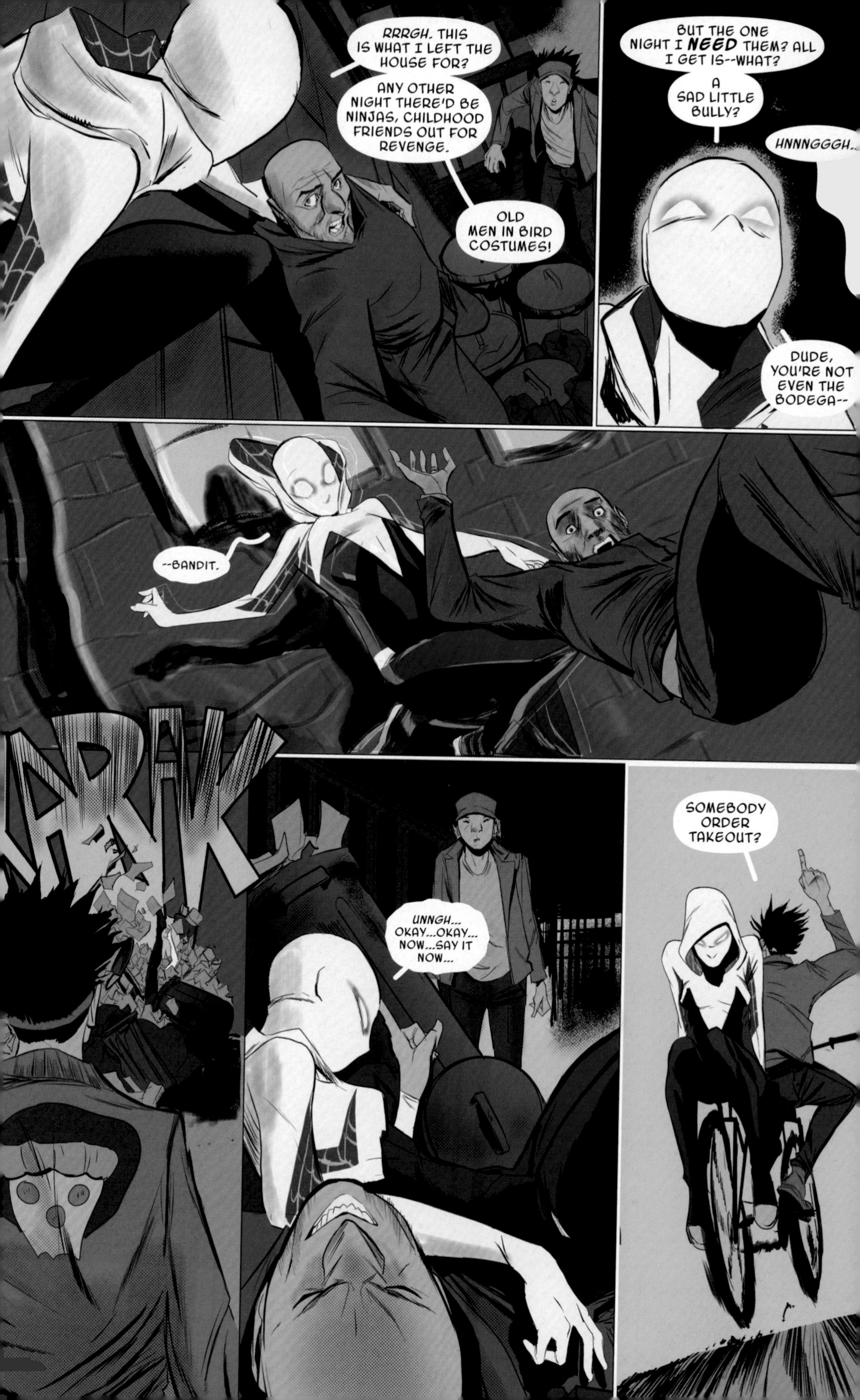
RRRGH. THIS IS WHAT I LEFT THE HOUSE FOR?
ANY OTHER NIGHT THERE'D BE NINJAS, CHILDHOOD FRIENDS OUT FOR REVENGE.
OLD MEN IN BIRD COSTUMES!
BUT THE ONE NIGHT I NEED THEM? ALL I GET IS--WHAT?
A SAD LITTLE BULLY?
HNNNGGGH..
DUDE, YOU'RE NOT EVEN THE BODEGA--
--BANDIT.
KRAK
UNNGH... OKAY...OKAY... NOW...SAY IT NOW...
SOMEBODY ORDER TAKEOUT?

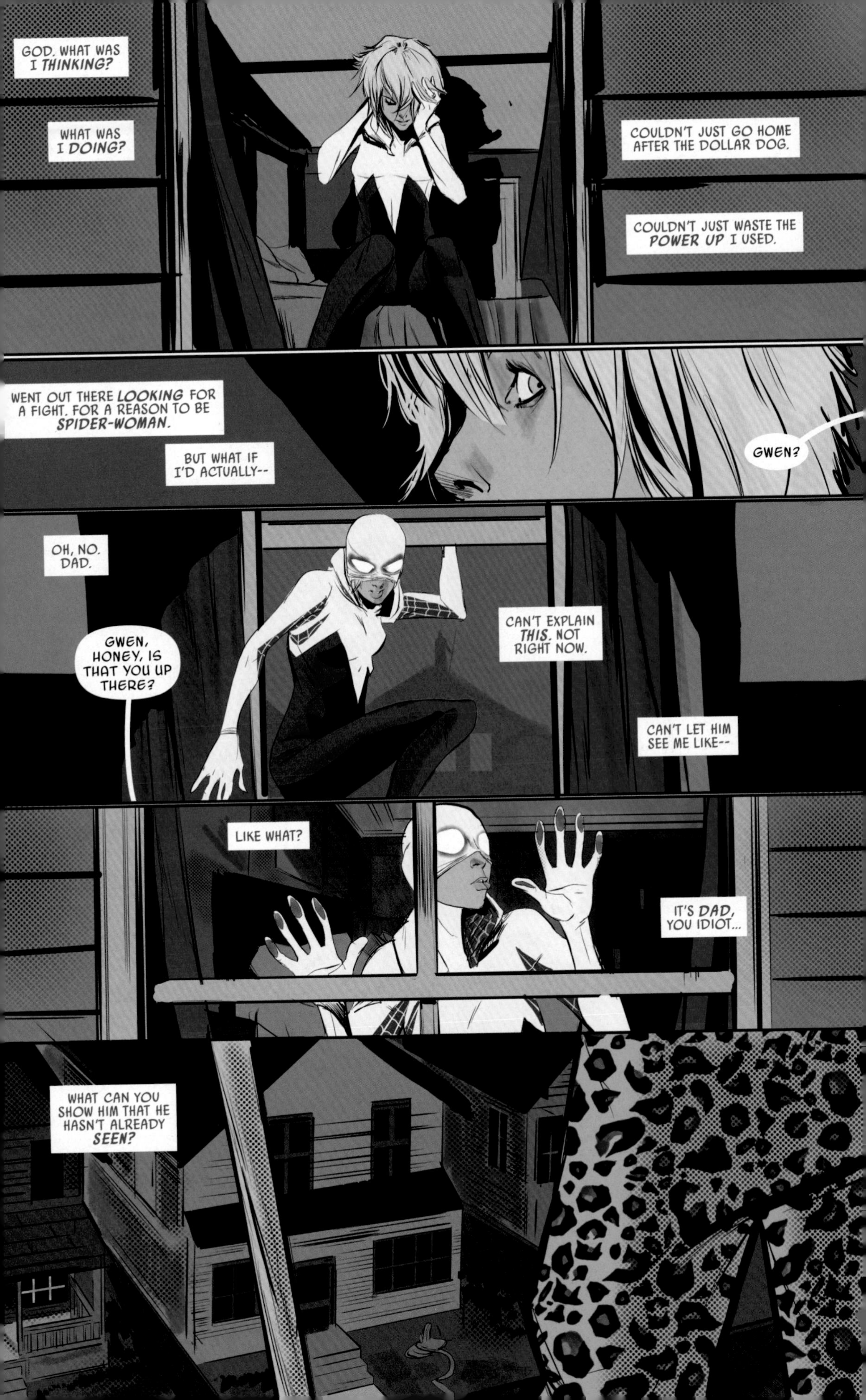
GOD. WHAT WAS I THINKING?
WHAT WAS I DOING?
COULDN'T JUST GO HOME AFTER THE DOLLAR DOG.
COULDN'T JUST WASTE THE POWER UP I USED.
WENT OUT THERE LOOKING FOR A FIGHT. FOR A REASON TO BE SPIDER-WOMAN.
BUT WHAT IF I'D ACTUALLY--
GWEN?
OH, NO. DAD.
GWEN, HONEY, IS THAT YOU UP THERE?
CAN'T EXPLAIN THIS. NOT RIGHT NOW.
CAN'T LET HIM SEE ME LIKE--
LIKE WHAT?
IT'S DAD, YOU IDIOT...
WHAT CAN YOU SHOW HIM THAT HE HASN'T ALREADY SEEN?

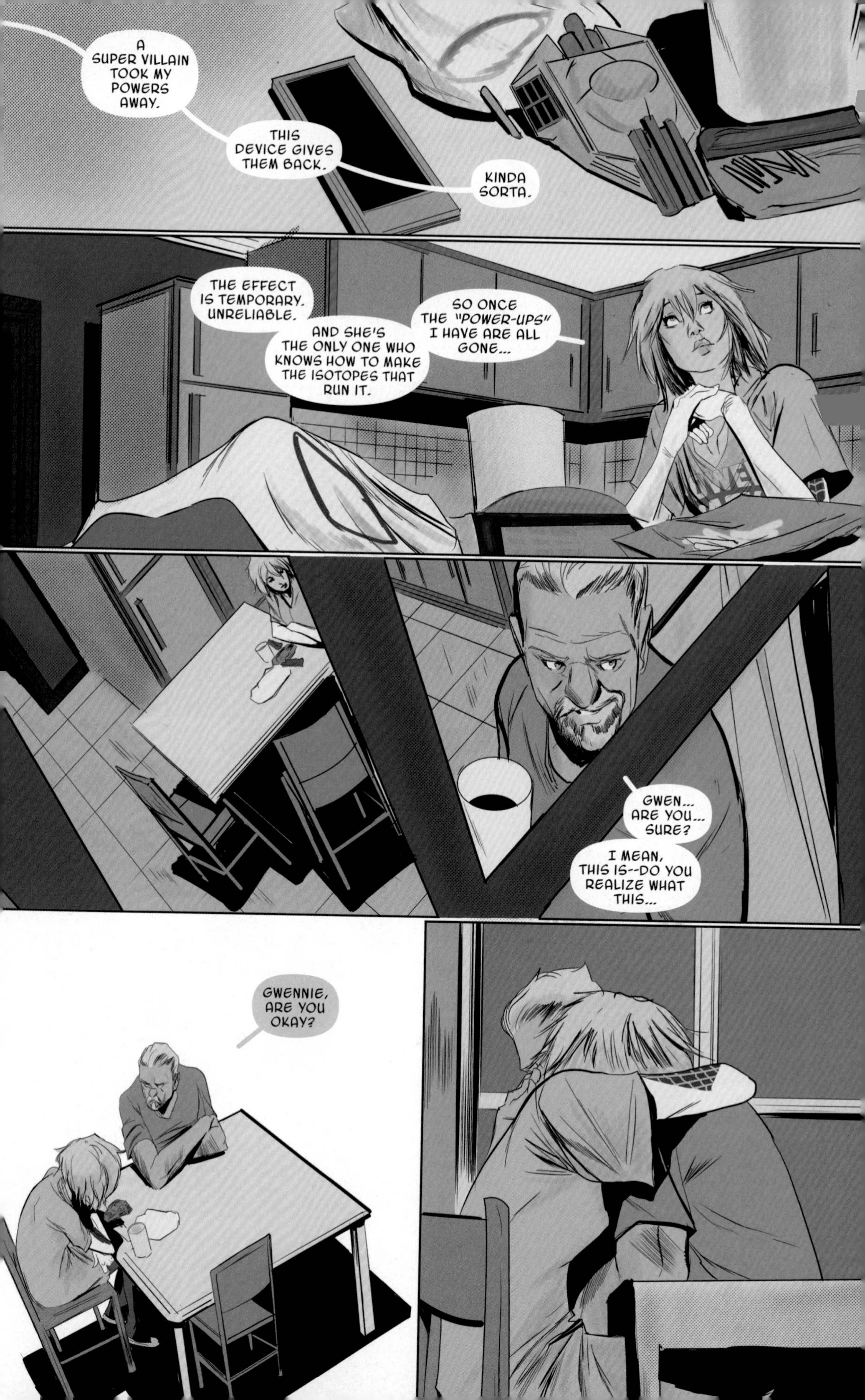
A SUPER VILLAIN TOOK MY POWERS AWAY.
THIS DEVICE GIVES THEM BACK.
KINDA SORTA.
THE EFFECT IS TEMPORARY. UNRELIABLE.
AND SHE'S THE ONLY ONE WHO KNOWS HOW TO MAKE THE ISOTOPES THAT RUN IT.
SO ONCE THE "POWER-UPS" I HAVE ARE ALL GONE...
GWEN... ARE YOU... SURE?
I MEAN, THIS IS--DO YOU REALIZE WHAT THIS...
GWENNIE, ARE YOU OKAY?

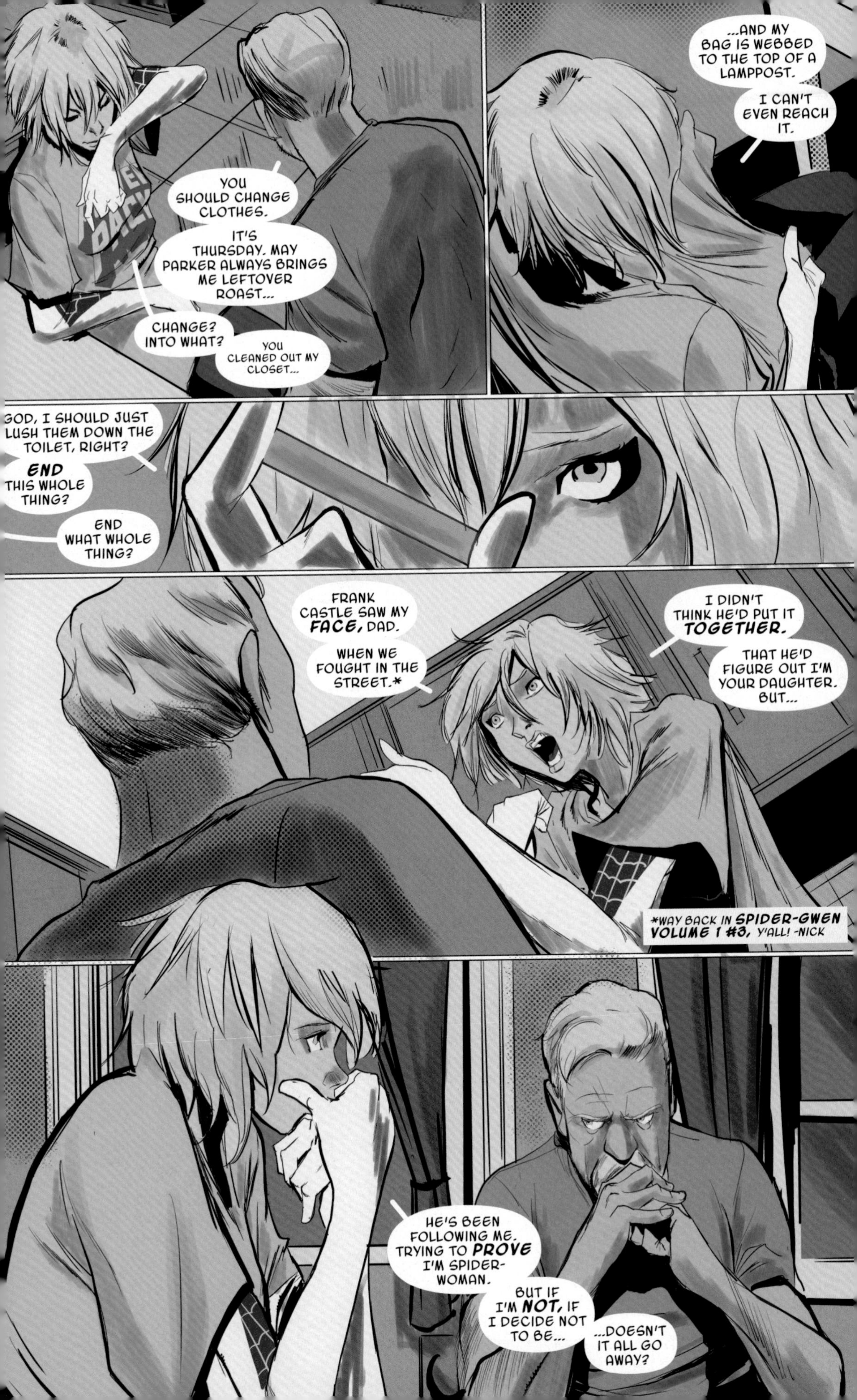
YOU SHOULD CHANGE CLOTHES.
IT'S THURSDAY. MAY PARKER ALWAYS BRINGS ME LEFTOVER ROAST...
CHANGE? INTO WHAT?
YOU CLEANED OUT MY CLOSET...
...AND MY BAG IS WEBBED TO THE TOP OF A LAMPPOST.
I CAN'T EVEN REACH IT.
GOD, I SHOULD JUST LUSH THEM DOWN THE TOILET, RIGHT?
END THIS WHOLE THING?
END WHAT WHOLE THING?
FRANK CASTLE SAW MY FACE, DAD.
WHEN WE FOUGHT IN THE STREET.*
I DIDN'T THINK HE'D PUT IT TOGETHER.
THAT HE'D FIGURE OUT I'M YOUR DAUGHTER. BUT...
*WAY BACK IN SPIDER-GWEN VOLUME 1 #3, Y'ALL! -NICK
HE'S BEEN FOLLOWING ME. TRYING TO PROVE I'M SPIDER-WOMAN.
BUT IF I'M NOT, IF I DECIDE NOT TO BE...
...DOESN'T IT ALL GO AWAY?

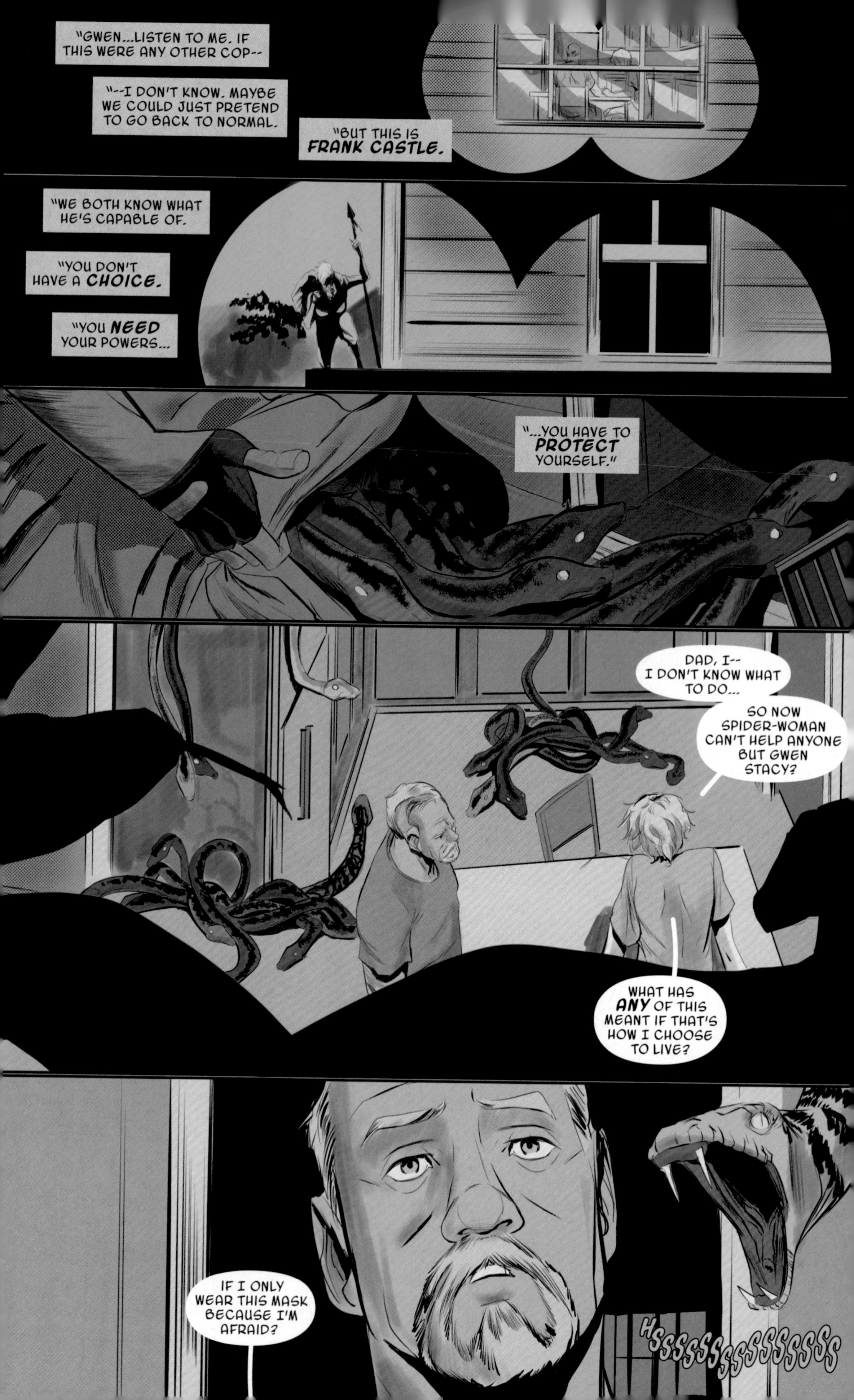
"GWEN...LISTEN TO ME. IF THIS WERE ANY OTHER COP--
"--I DON'T KNOW. MAYBE WE COULD JUST PRETEND TO GO BACK TO NORMAL.
"BUT THIS IS FRANK CASTLE.
"WE BOTH KNOW WHAT HE'S CAPABLE OF.
"YOU DON'T HAVE A CHOICE.
"YOU NEED YOUR POWERS...
"...YOU HAVE TO PROTECT YOURSELF."
DAD, I-- I DON'T KNOW WHAT TO DO...
SO NOW SPIDER-WOMAN CAN'T HELP ANYONE BUT GWEN STACY?
WHAT HAS ANY OF THIS MEANT IF THAT'S HOW I CHOOSE TO LIVE?
IF I ONLY WEAR THIS MASK BECAUSE I'M AFRAID?
HSSSSSSSSSSSSSSSS

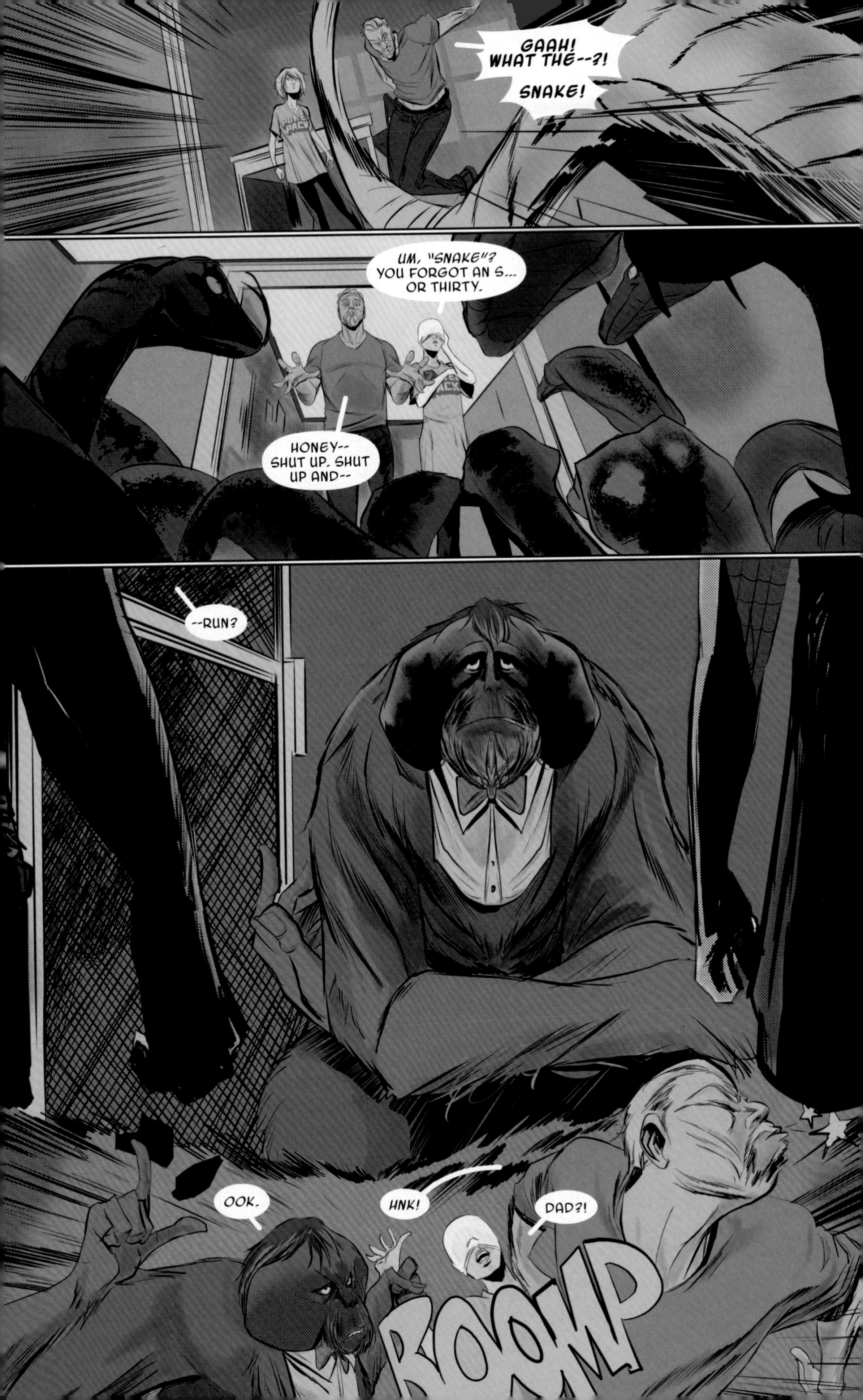
GAAH! WHAT THE--?!
SNAKE!
UM, "SNAKE"? YOU FORGOT AN S... OR THIRTY.
HONEY-- SHUT UP. SHUT UP AND--
--RUN?
OOK.
HNK!
DAD?!
BOOMP

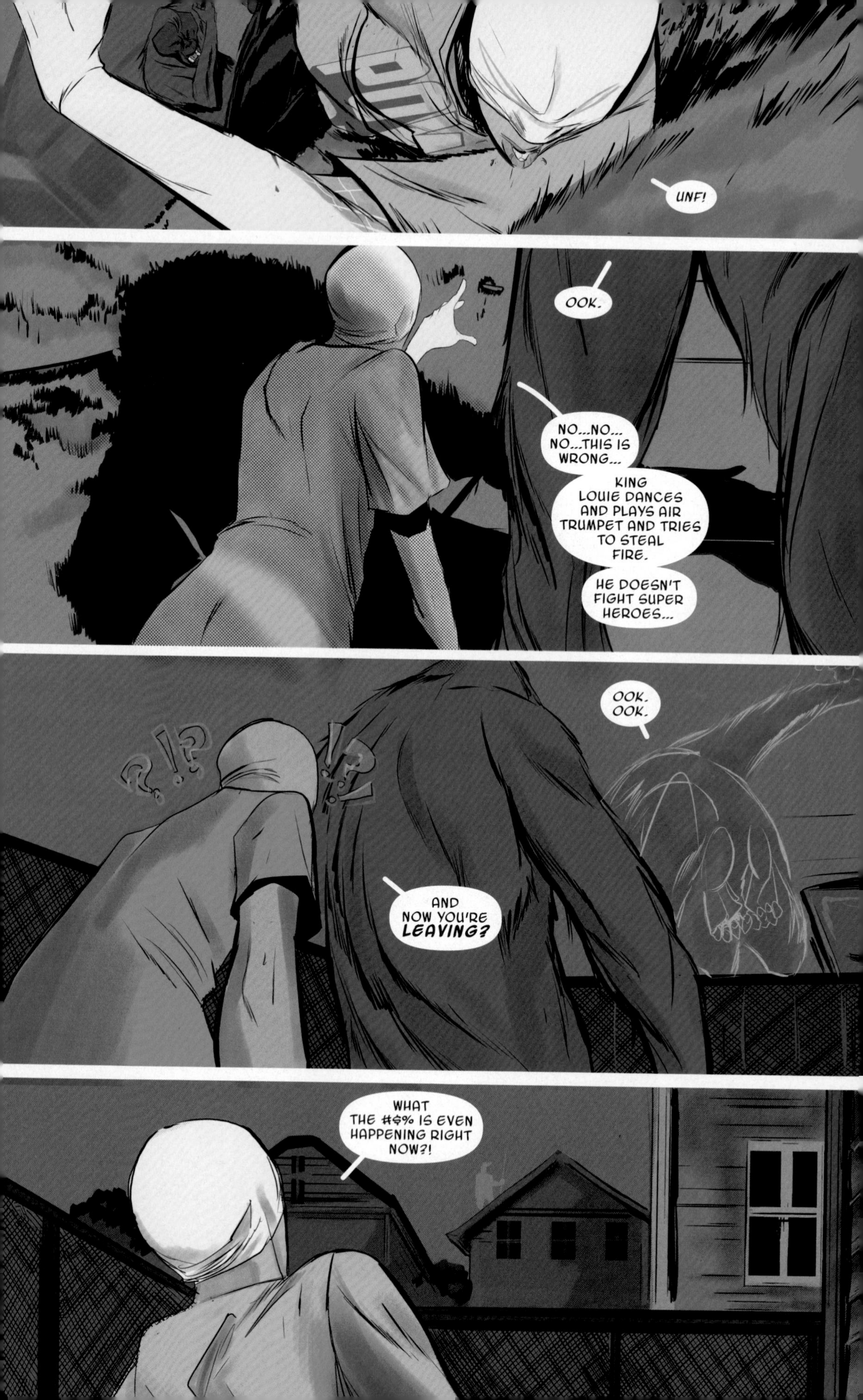
UNF!
OOK.
NO...NO... NO...THIS IS WRONG...
KING LOUIE DANCES AND PLAYS AIR TRUMPET AND TRIES TO STEAL FIRE.
HE DOESN'T FIGHT SUPER HEROES...
OOK. OOK.
?!?
!?!
AND NOW YOU'RE LEAVING?
WHAT THE #$% IS EVEN HAPPENING RIGHT NOW?!

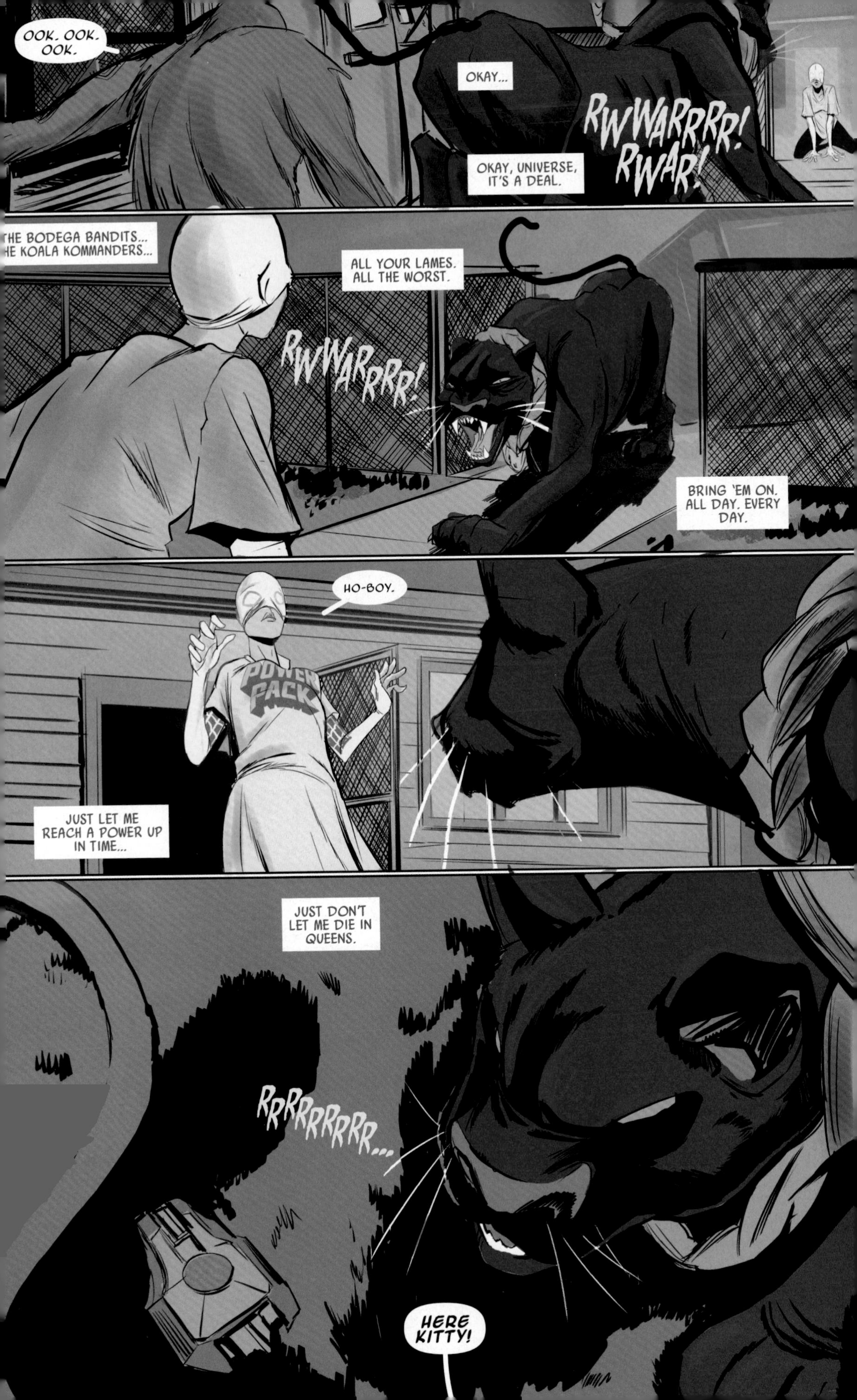
OOK. OOK. OOK.
OKAY...
RWWARRRR! RWAR!
OKAY, UNIVERSE, IT'S A DEAL.
THE BODEGA BANDITS... THE KOALA KOMMANDERS...
ALL YOUR LAMES. ALL THE WORST.
RWWARRRR!
BRING 'EM ON. ALL DAY. EVERY DAY.
HO-BOY.
POWER PACK
JUST LET ME REACH A POWER UP IN TIME...
JUST DON'T LET ME DIE IN QUEENS.
RRRRRRRR...
HERE KITTY!

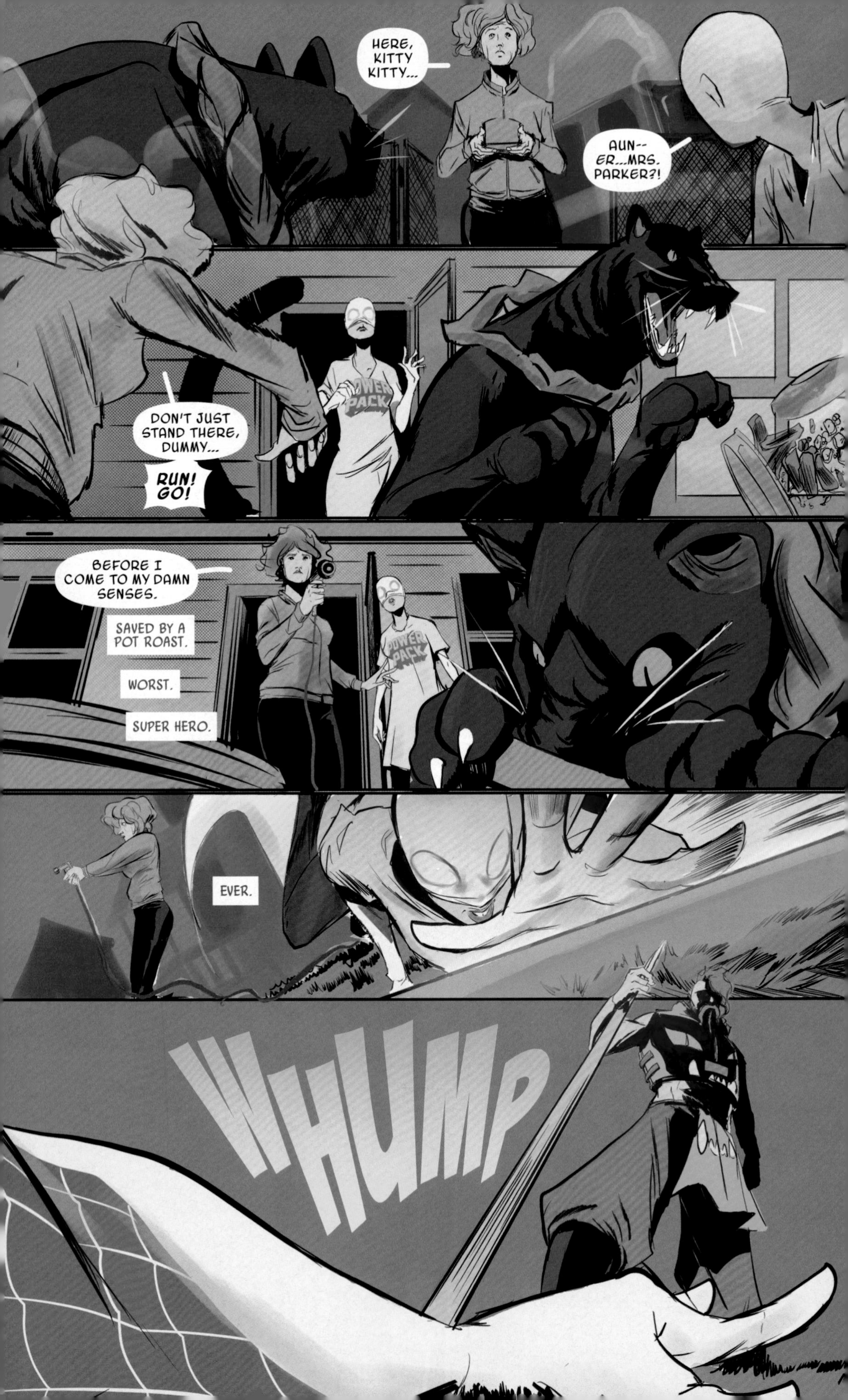
HERE, KITTY KITTY...
AUN-- ER...MRS. PARKER?!
DON'T JUST STAND THERE, DUMMY...
RUN! GO!
BEFORE I COME TO MY DAMN SENSES.
SAVED BY A POT ROAST.
WORST.
SUPER HERO.
EVER.
WHUMP

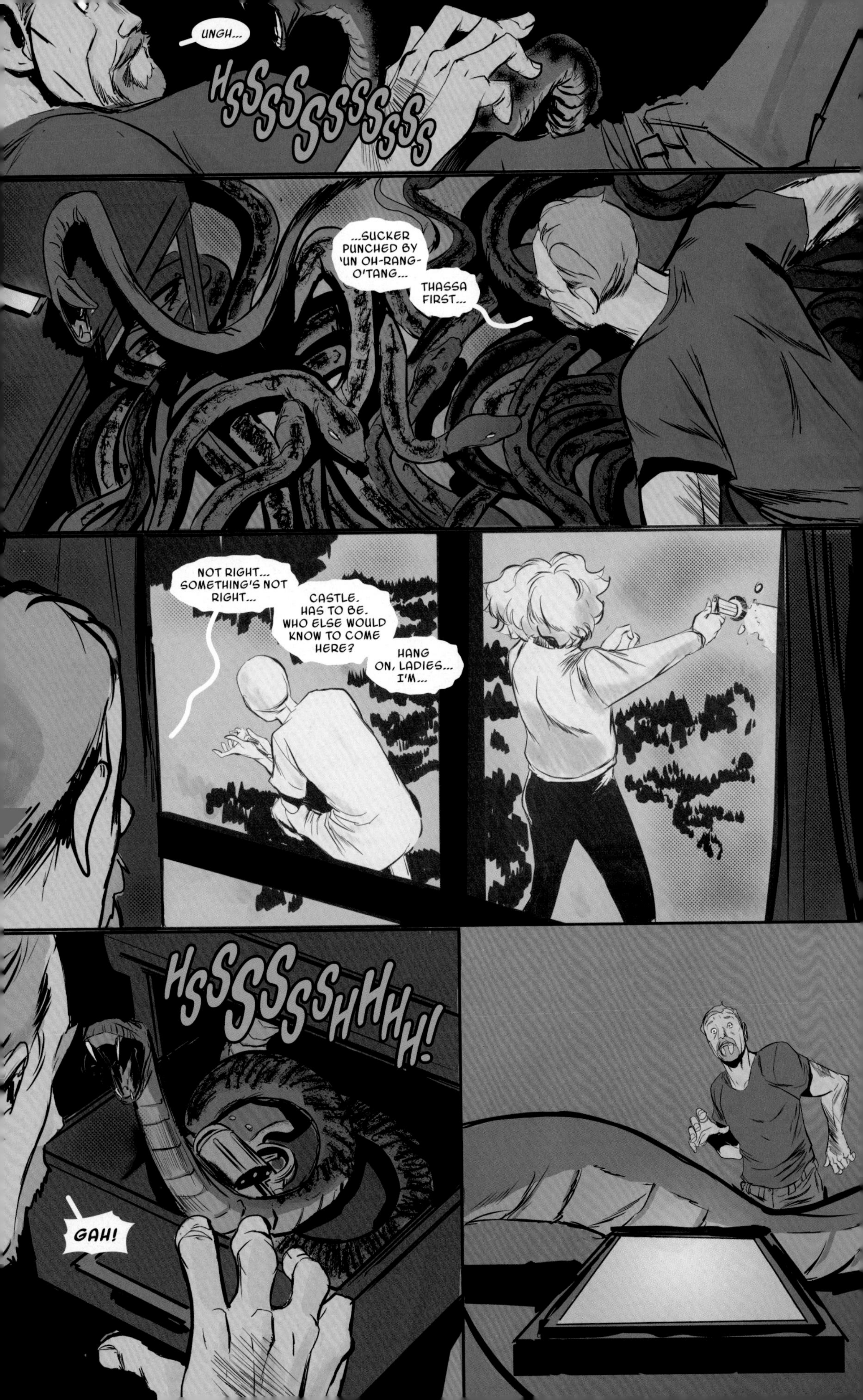
UNGH...
HSSSSSSSSSSSS
...SUCKER PUNCHED BY 'UN OH-RANG-O'TANG...
THASSA FIRST...
NOT RIGHT... SOMETHING'S NOT RIGHT...
CASTLE. HAS TO BE. WHO ELSE WOULD KNOW TO COME HERE?
HANG ON, LADIES... I'M...
HSSSSSSHHHH!
GAH!

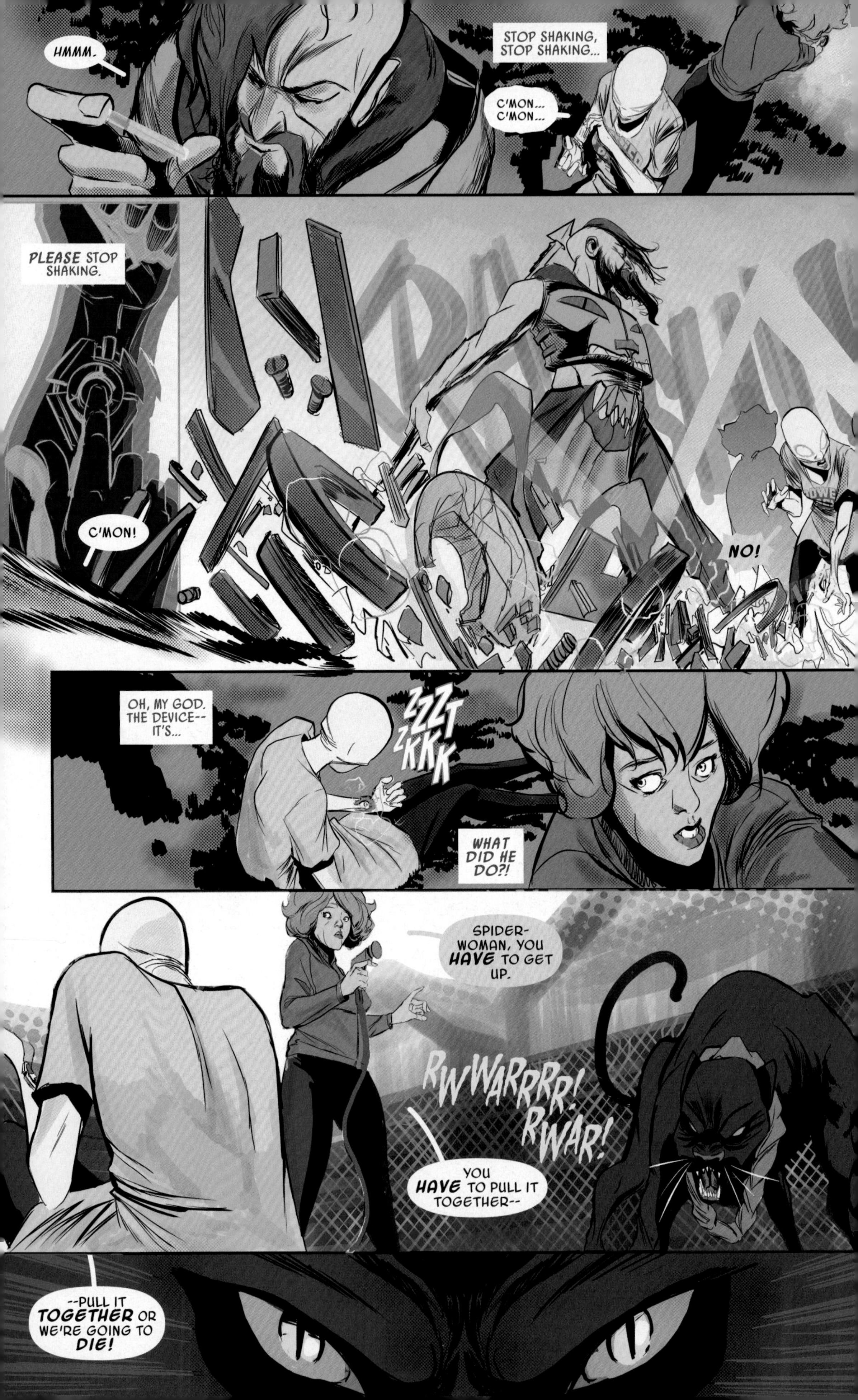
HMMM.
STOP SHAKING, STOP SHAKING...
C'MON... C'MON...
PLEASE STOP SHAKING.
C'MON!
NO!
OH, MY GOD. THE DEVICE-- IT'S...
ZZZT ZKKK
WHAT DID HE DO?!
SPIDER-WOMAN, YOU HAVE TO GET UP.
RWWARRRR! RWAR!
YOU HAVE TO PULL IT TOGETHER--
--PULL IT TOGETHER OR WE'RE GOING TO DIE!

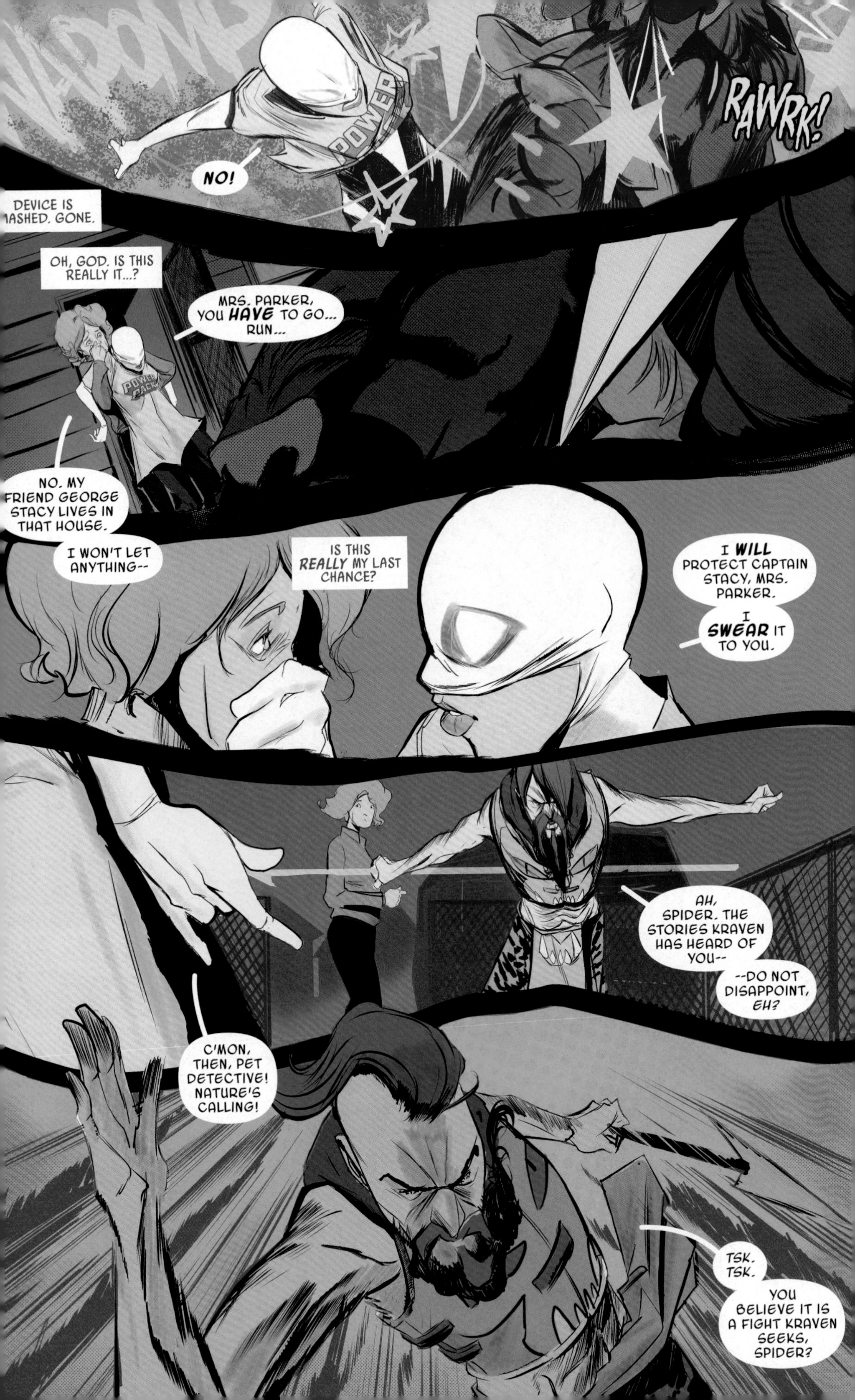

RAWRK!
NO!
DEVICE IS
MASHED. GONE.
OH, GOD. IS THIS REALLY IT...?
MRS. PARKER, YOU HAVE TO GO... RUN...
NO. MY FRIEND GEORGE STACY LIVES IN THAT HOUSE.
I WON'T LET ANYTHING--
IS THIS REALLY MY LAST CHANCE?
I WILL PROTECT CAPTAIN STACY, MRS. PARKER.
I SWEAR IT TO YOU.
AH, SPIDER. THE STORIES KRAVEN HAS HEARD OF YOU--
--DO NOT DISAPPOINT, EH?
C'MON, THEN, PET DETECTIVE! NATURE'S CALLING!
TSK. TSK.
YOU BELIEVE IT IS A FIGHT KRAVEN SEEKS, SPIDER?

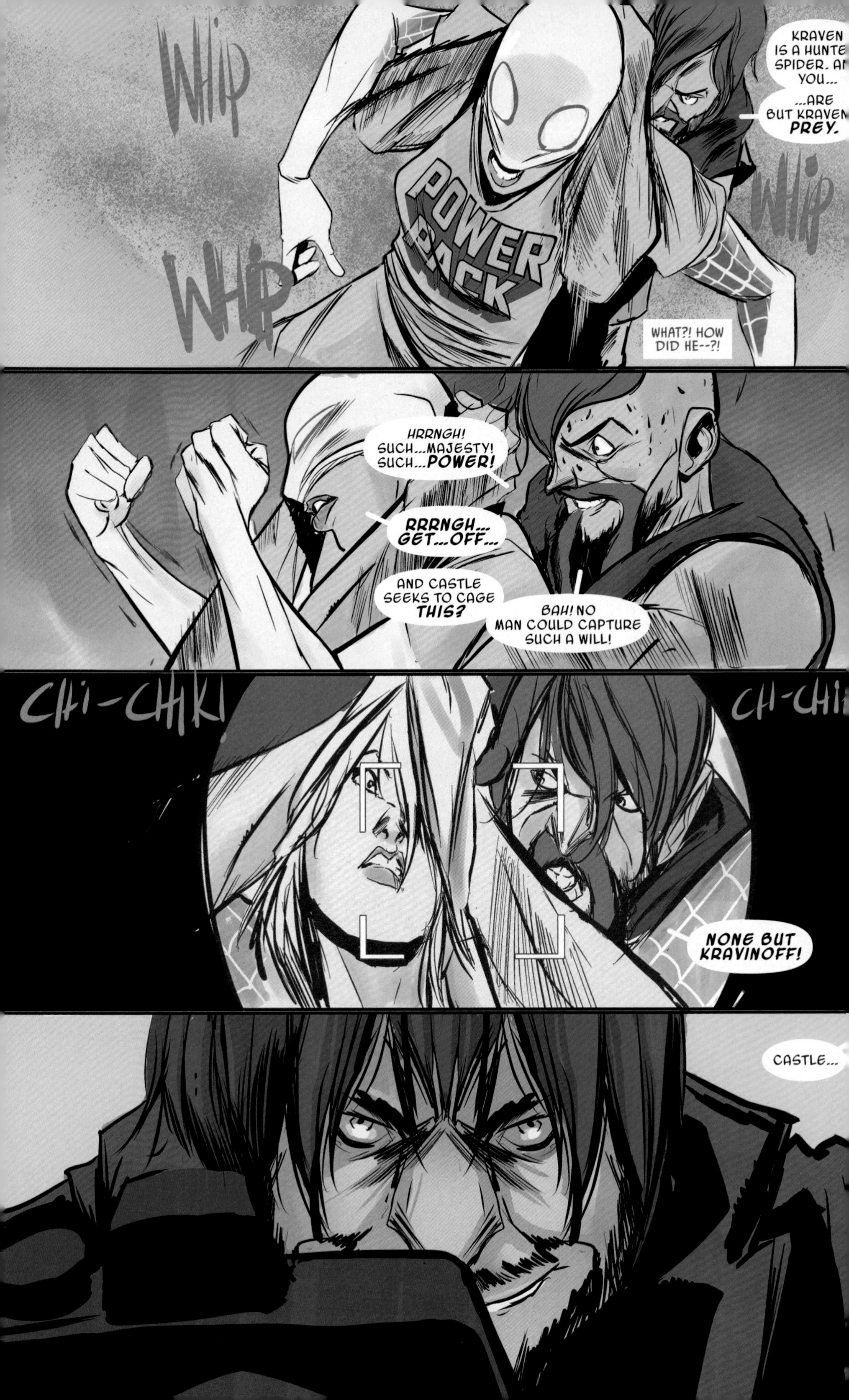
WHIP
KRAVEN IS A HUNTE
SPIDER. AN
YOU...
...ARE BUT KRAVEN
PREY.
WHIP
WHIP
POWER PACK
WHAT?! HOW DID HE--?!
HRRNGH! SUCH...MAJESTY! SUCH...POWER!
RRRNGH... GET...OFF...
AND CASTLE SEEKS TO CAGE THIS?
BAH! NO MAN COULD CAPTURE SUCH A WILL!
CHI-CHIK
CHI-CHI
NONE BUT KRAVINOFF!
CASTLE...

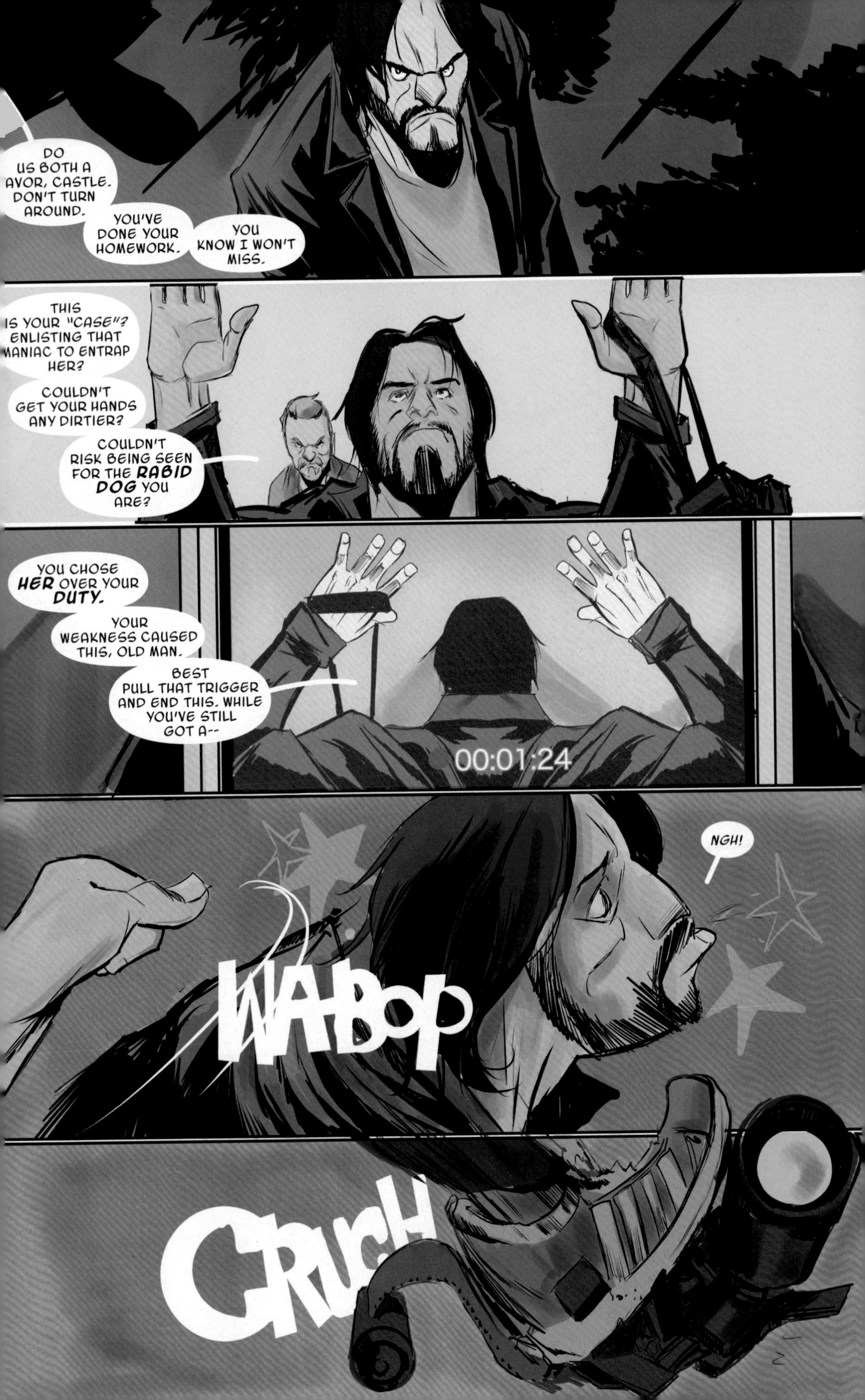
DO US BOTH A AVOR, CASTLE. DON'T TURN AROUND.
YOU'VE DONE YOUR HOMEWORK.
YOU KNOW I WON'T MISS.
THIS IS YOUR "CASE"? ENLISTING THAT MANIAC TO ENTRAP HER?
COULDN'T GET YOUR HANDS ANY DIRTIER?
COULDN'T RISK BEING SEEN FOR THE RABID DOG YOU ARE?
YOU CHOSE HER OVER YOUR DUTY.
YOUR WEAKNESS CAUSED THIS, OLD MAN.
BEST PULL THAT TRIGGER AND END THIS. WHILE YOU'VE STILL GOT A--
00:01:24
NGH!
WABOP
CRUCH

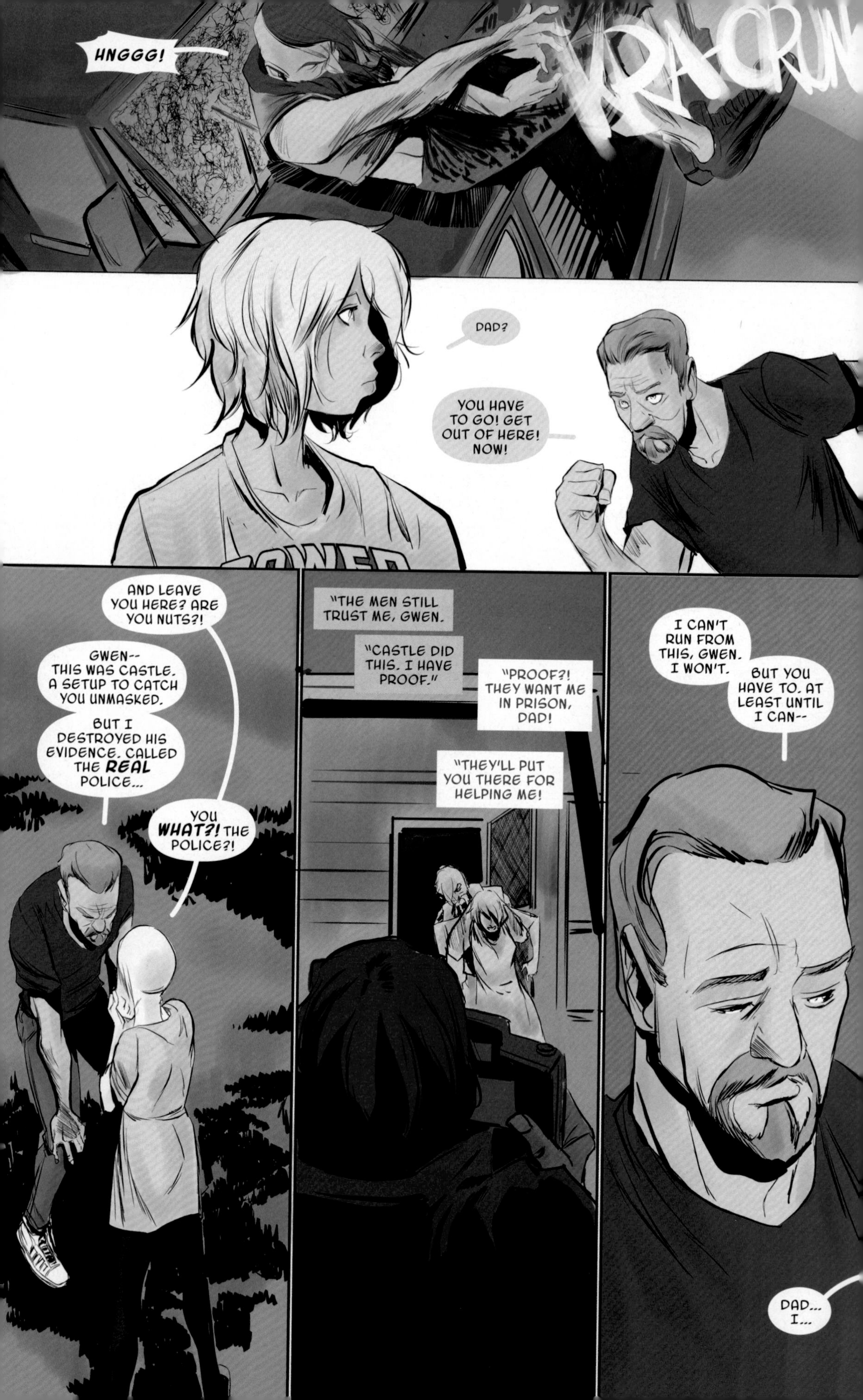
HNGGG!
KRA-CRUN
DAD?
YOU HAVE TO GO! GET OUT OF HERE! NOW!
AND LEAVE YOU HERE? ARE YOU NUTS?!
GWEN-- THIS WAS CASTLE. A SETUP TO CATCH YOU UNMASKED.
BUT I DESTROYED HIS EVIDENCE. CALLED THE REAL POLICE...
YOU WHAT?! THE POLICE?!
"THE MEN STILL TRUST ME, GWEN.
"CASTLE DID THIS. I HAVE PROOF."
"PROOF?! THEY WANT ME IN PRISON, DAD!
"THEY'LL PUT YOU THERE FOR HELPING ME!
I CAN'T RUN FROM THIS, GWEN. I WON'T.
BUT YOU HAVE TO. AT LEAST UNTIL I CAN--
DAD... I...

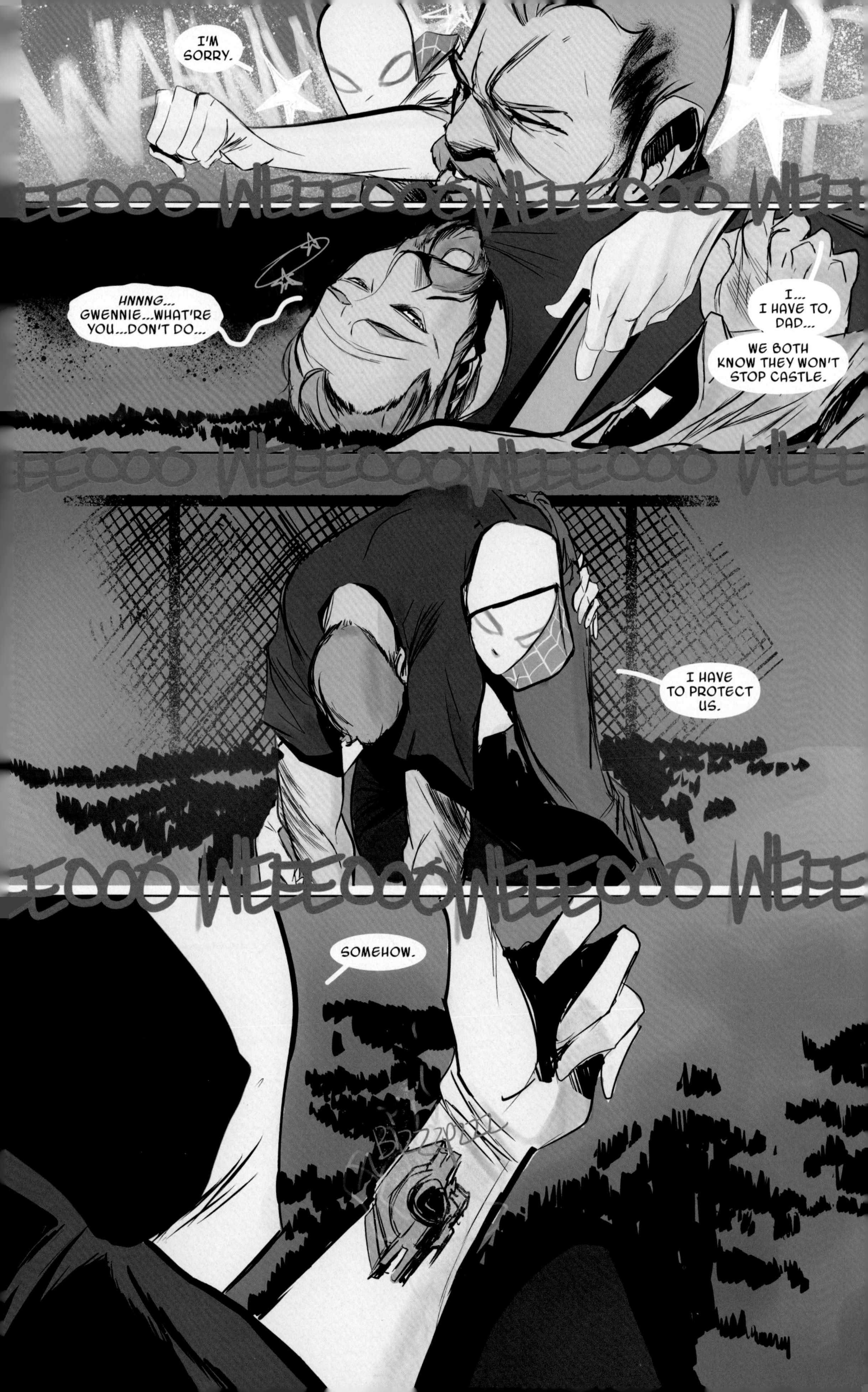
I'M SORRY.
EEOOO WEEEOOO WEEEOOO WEEE
HNNNG... GWENNIE...WHAT'RE YOU...DON'T DO...
I... I HAVE TO, DAD...
WE BOTH KNOW THEY WON'T STOP CASTLE.
EEOOO WEEEOOO WEEEOOO WEEE
I HAVE TO PROTECT US.
EEOOO WEEEOOO WEEEOOO WEEE
SOMEHOW.

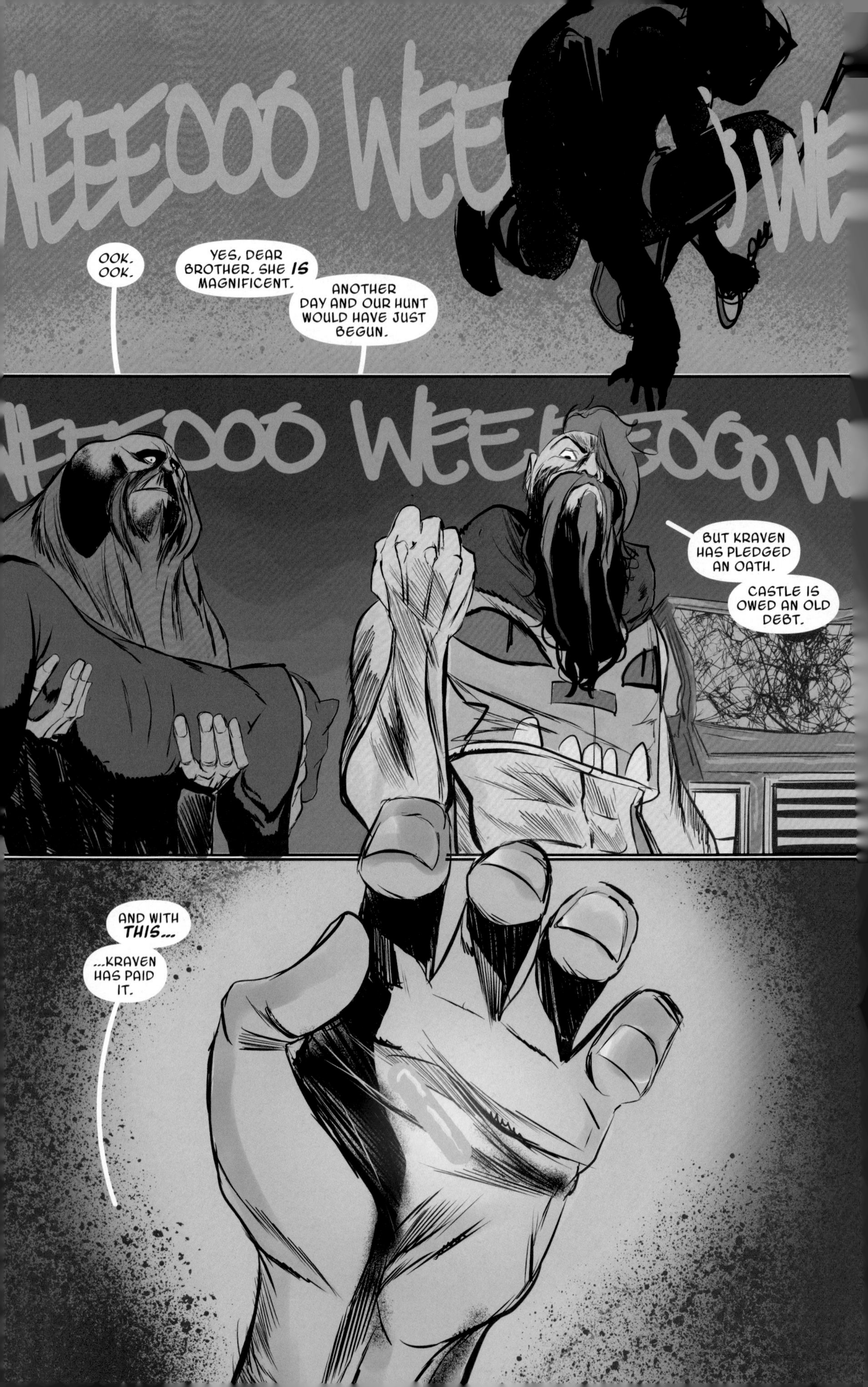
WEEEOOO WEEEOOO WE
OOK. OOK.
YES, DEAR BROTHER. SHE *IS* MAGNIFICENT.
ANOTHER DAY AND OUR HUNT WOULD HAVE JUST BEGUN.
WEEEOOO WEEEOOO W
BUT KRAVEN HAS PLEDGED AN OATH.
CASTLE IS OWED AN OLD DEBT.
AND WITH *THIS*...
...KRAVEN HAS PAID IT.

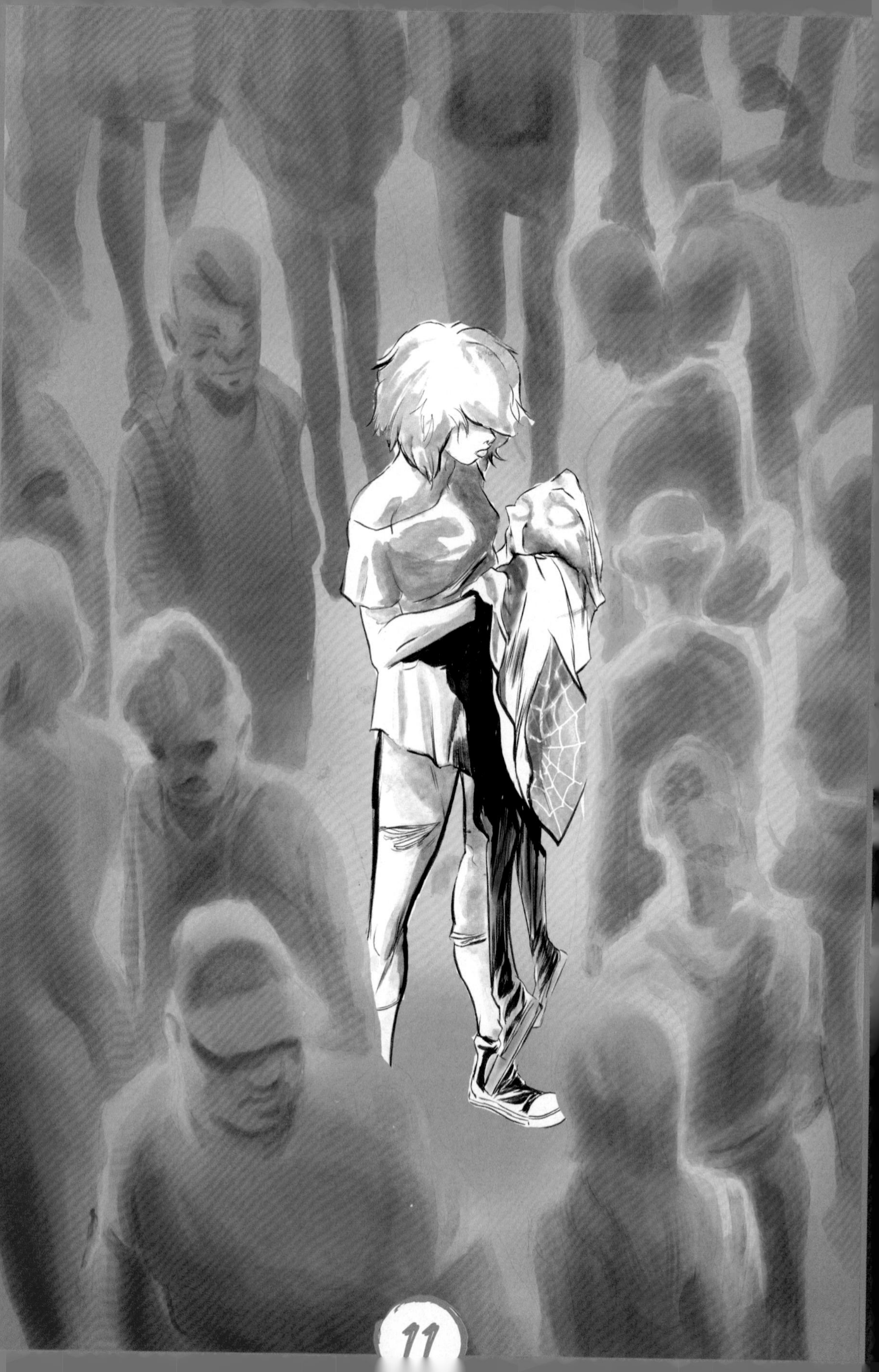

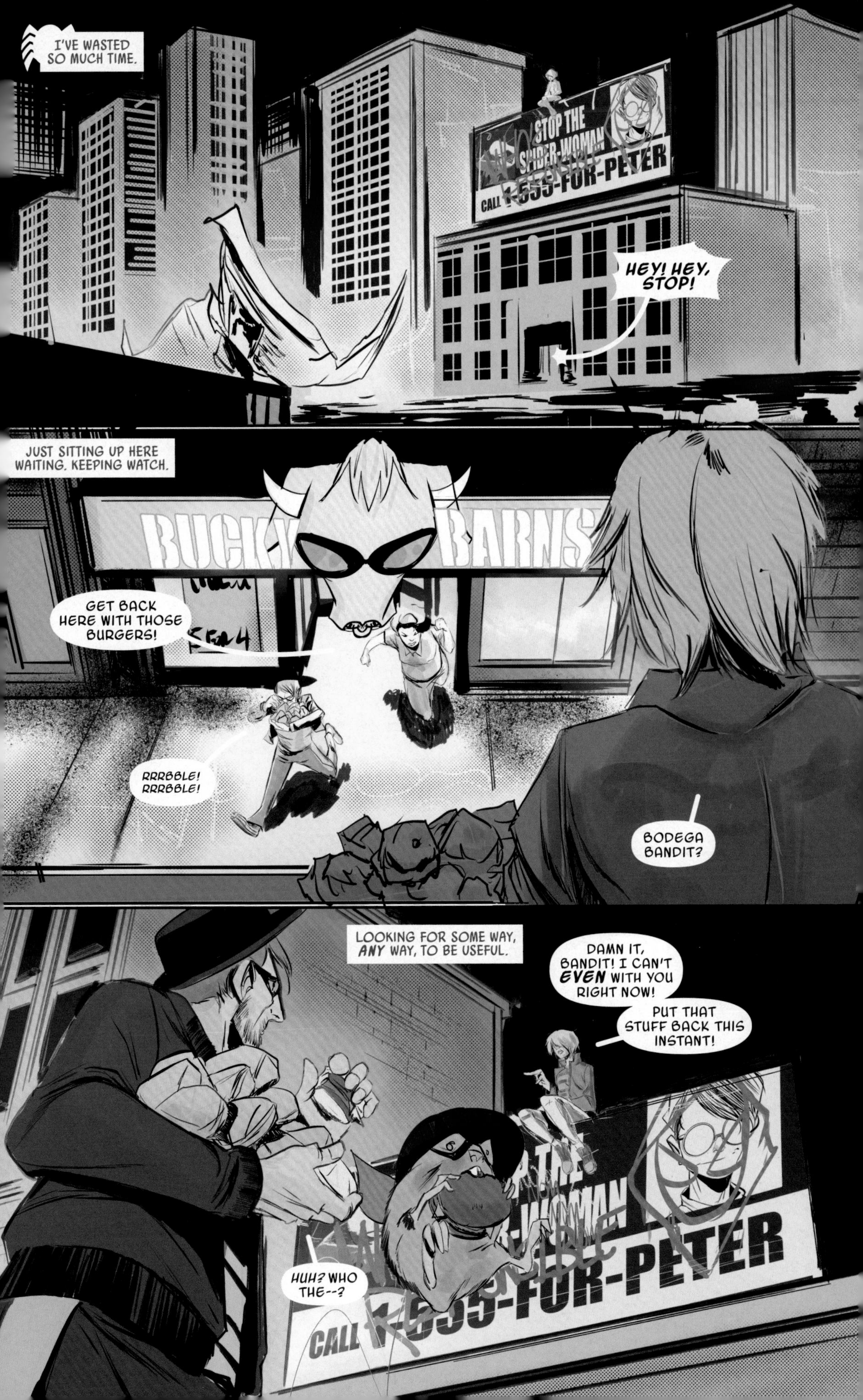

I'VE WASTED SO MUCH TIME.
STOP THE SPIDER-WOMAN
CALL 1-555-FOR-PETER
HEY! HEY, STOP!
JUST SITTING UP HERE WAITING. KEEPING WATCH.
BUCKY BARNS
GET BACK HERE WITH THOSE BURGERS!
RRRBBLE! RRRBBLE!
BODEGA BANDIT?
LOOKING FOR SOME WAY, ANY WAY, TO BE USEFUL.
DAMN IT, BANDIT! I CAN'T EVEN WITH YOU RIGHT NOW!
PUT THAT STUFF BACK THIS INSTANT!
HUH? WHO THE--?
CALL 1-555-FOR-PETER

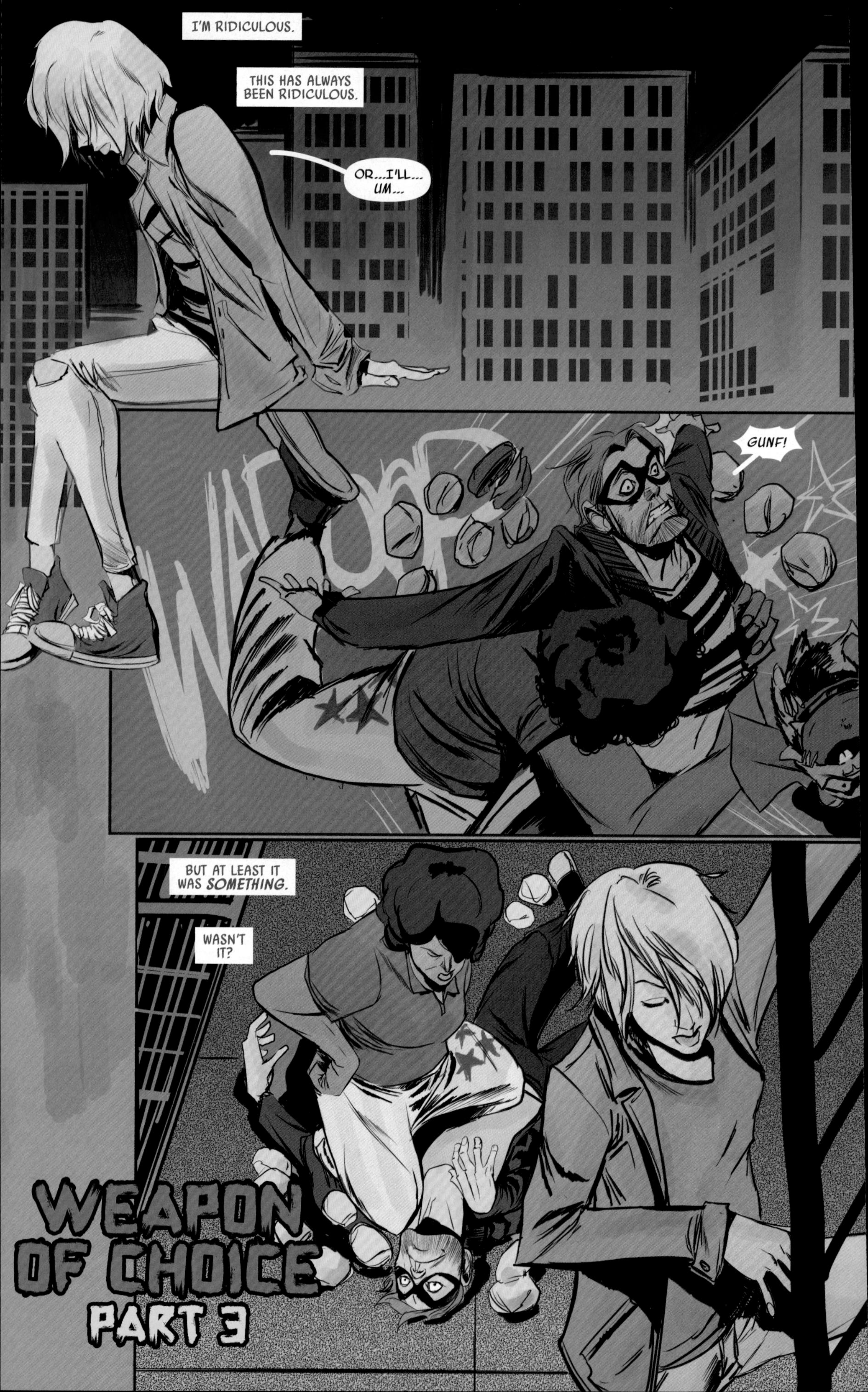
I'M RIDICULOUS.
THIS HAS ALWAYS BEEN RIDICULOUS.
OR...I'LL... UM...
WADOOP
GUNF!
BUT AT LEAST IT WAS SOMETHING.
WASN'T IT?
WEAPON OF CHOICE
PART 3

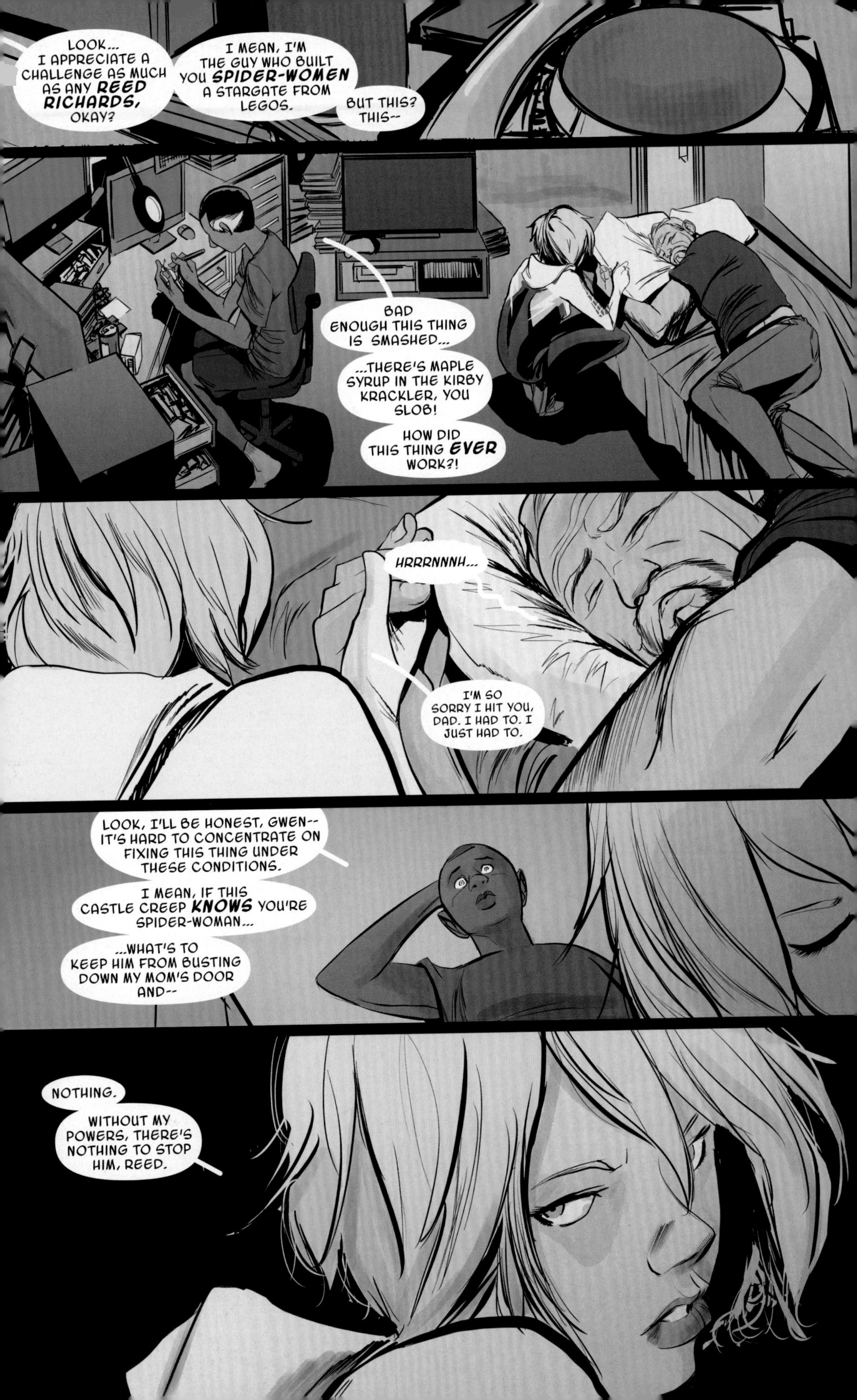
LOOK... I APPRECIATE A CHALLENGE AS MUCH AS ANY REED RICHARDS, OKAY?
I MEAN, I'M THE GUY WHO BUILT YOU SPIDER-WOMEN A STARGATE FROM LEGOS.
BUT THIS? THIS--
BAD ENOUGH THIS THING IS SMASHED...
...THERE'S MAPLE SYRUP IN THE KIRBY KRACKLER, YOU SLOB!
HOW DID THIS THING EVER WORK?!
HRRRNNNH...
I'M SO SORRY I HIT YOU, DAD. I HAD TO. I JUST HAD TO.
LOOK, I'LL BE HONEST, GWEN-- IT'S HARD TO CONCENTRATE ON FIXING THIS THING UNDER THESE CONDITIONS.
I MEAN, IF THIS CASTLE CREEP KNOWS YOU'RE SPIDER-WOMAN...
...WHAT'S TO KEEP HIM FROM BUSTING DOWN MY MOM'S DOOR AND--
NOTHING.
WITHOUT MY POWERS, THERE'S NOTHING TO STOP HIM, REED.

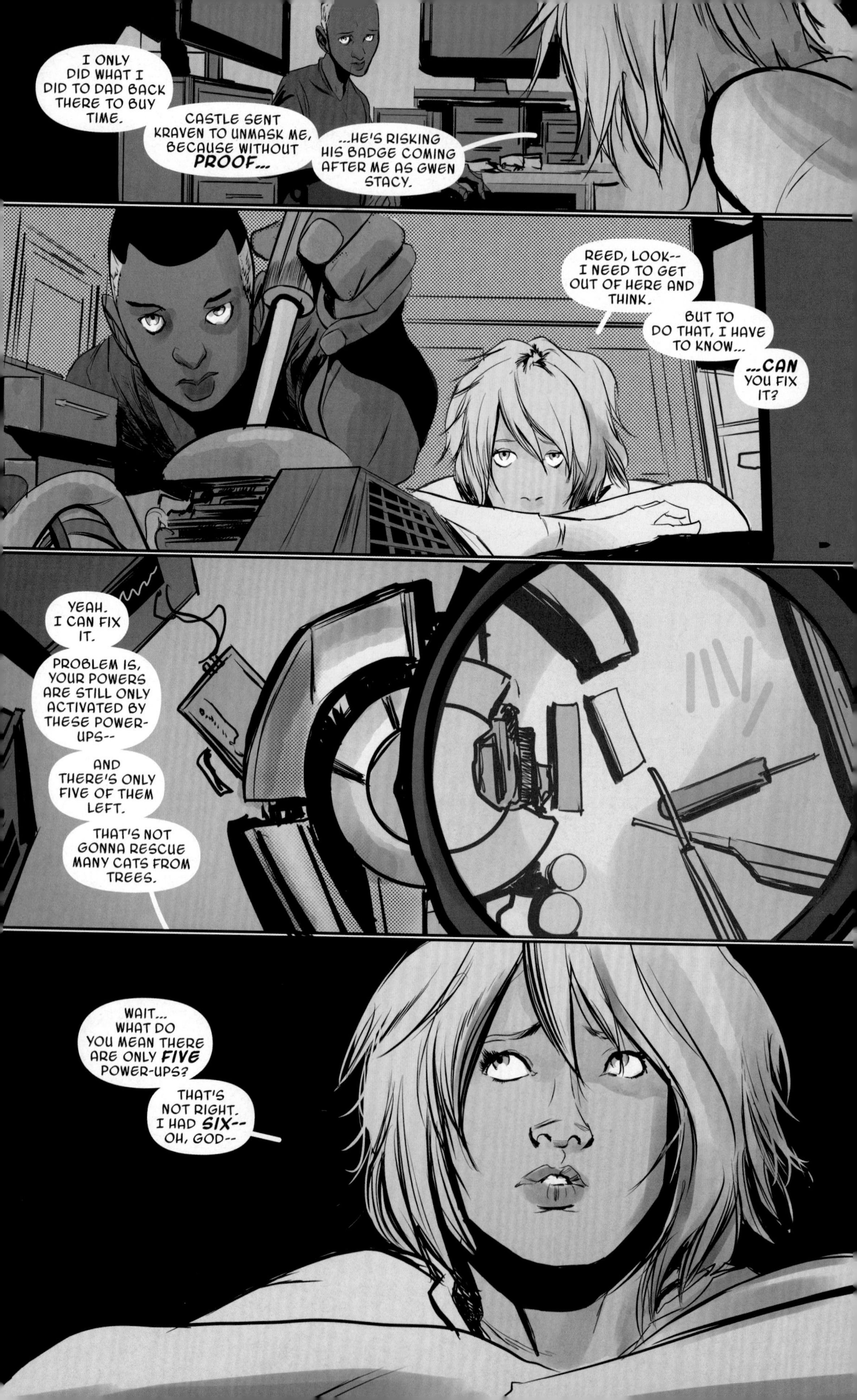
I ONLY DID WHAT I DID TO DAD BACK THERE TO BUY TIME.
CASTLE SENT KRAVEN TO UNMASK ME, BECAUSE WITHOUT PROOF...
...HE'S RISKING HIS BADGE COMING AFTER ME AS GWEN STACY.
REED, LOOK-- I NEED TO GET OUT OF HERE AND THINK.
BUT TO DO THAT, I HAVE TO KNOW...
...CAN YOU FIX IT?
YEAH. I CAN FIX IT.
PROBLEM IS, YOUR POWERS ARE STILL ONLY ACTIVATED BY THESE POWER-UPS--
AND THERE'S ONLY FIVE OF THEM LEFT.
THAT'S NOT GONNA RESCUE MANY CATS FROM TREES.
WAIT... WHAT DO YOU MEAN THERE ARE ONLY FIVE POWER-UPS?
THAT'S NOT RIGHT. I HAD SIX-- OH, GOD--

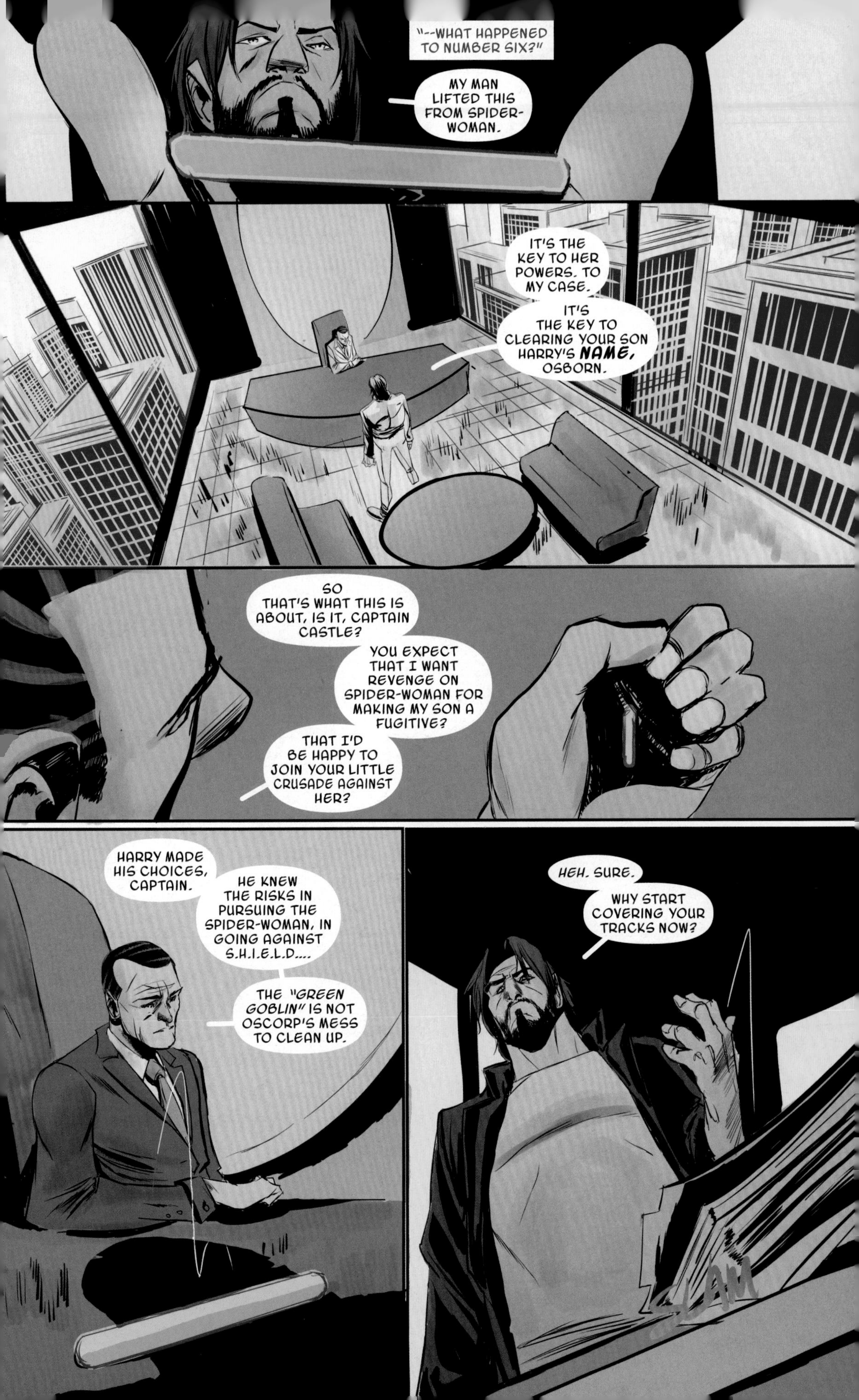
"--WHAT HAPPENED TO NUMBER SIX?"
MY MAN LIFTED THIS FROM SPIDER-WOMAN.
IT'S THE KEY TO HER POWERS. TO MY CASE.
IT'S THE KEY TO CLEARING YOUR SON HARRY'S NAME, OSBORN.
SO THAT'S WHAT THIS IS ABOUT, IS IT, CAPTAIN CASTLE?
YOU EXPECT THAT I WANT REVENGE ON SPIDER-WOMAN FOR MAKING MY SON A FUGITIVE?
THAT I'D BE HAPPY TO JOIN YOUR LITTLE CRUSADE AGAINST HER?
HARRY MADE HIS CHOICES, CAPTAIN.
HE KNEW THE RISKS IN PURSUING THE SPIDER-WOMAN, IN GOING AGAINST S.H.I.E.L.D....
THE "GREEN GOBLIN" IS NOT OSCORP'S MESS TO CLEAN UP.
HEH. SURE.
WHY START COVERING YOUR TRACKS NOW?
SLAM

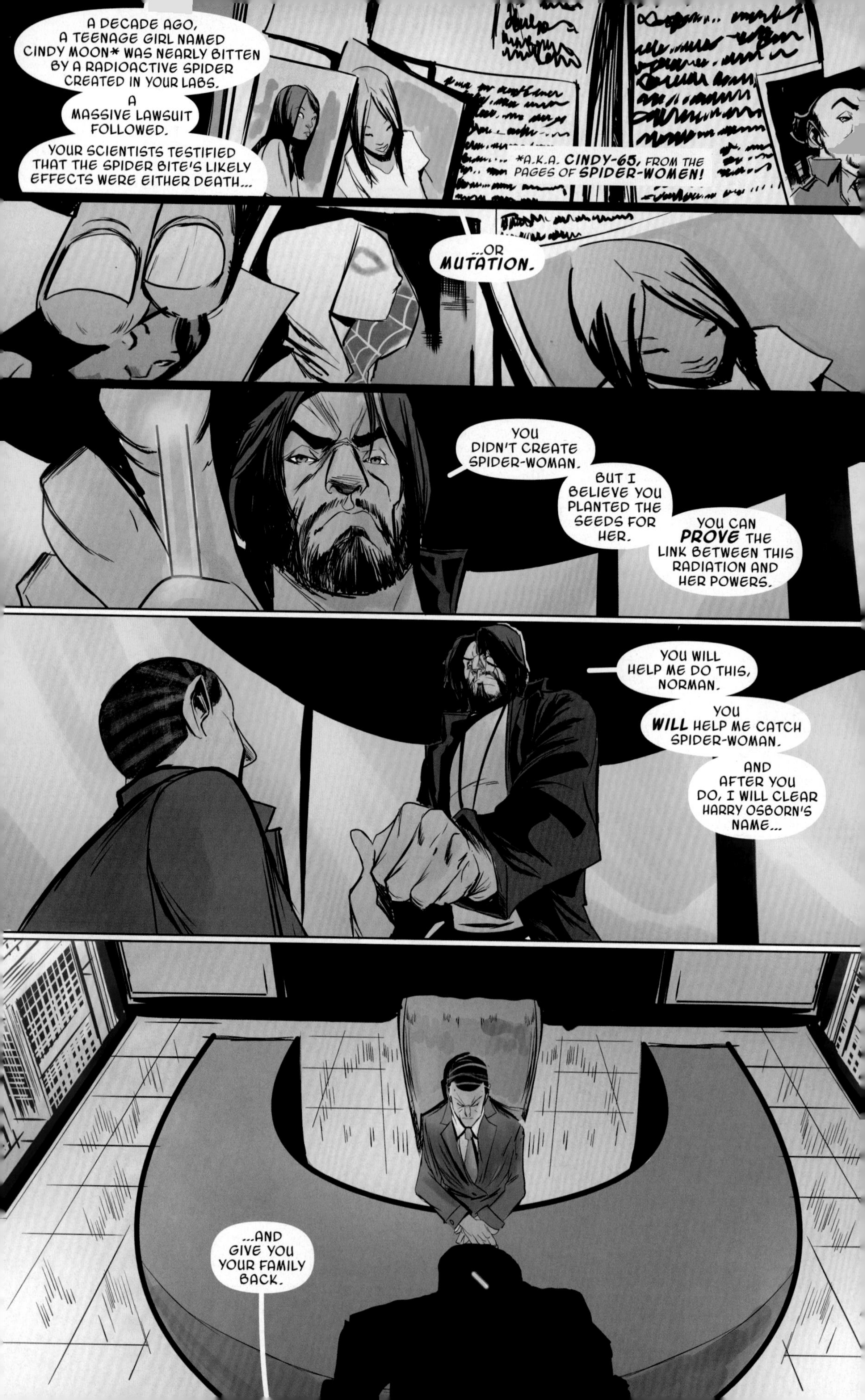
A DECADE AGO, A TEENAGE GIRL NAMED CINDY MOON* WAS NEARLY BITTEN BY A RADIOACTIVE SPIDER CREATED IN YOUR LABS.
A MASSIVE LAWSUIT FOLLOWED.
YOUR SCIENTISTS TESTIFIED THAT THE SPIDER BITE'S LIKELY EFFECTS WERE EITHER DEATH...
*A.K.A. CINDY-65, FROM THE PAGES OF SPIDER-WOMEN!
...OR MUTATION.
YOU DIDN'T CREATE SPIDER-WOMAN.
BUT I BELIEVE YOU PLANTED THE SEEDS FOR HER.
YOU CAN PROVE THE LINK BETWEEN THIS RADIATION AND HER POWERS.
YOU WILL HELP ME DO THIS, NORMAN.
YOU WILL HELP ME CATCH SPIDER-WOMAN.
AND AFTER YOU DO, I WILL CLEAR HARRY OSBORN'S NAME...
...AND GIVE YOU YOUR FAMILY BACK.

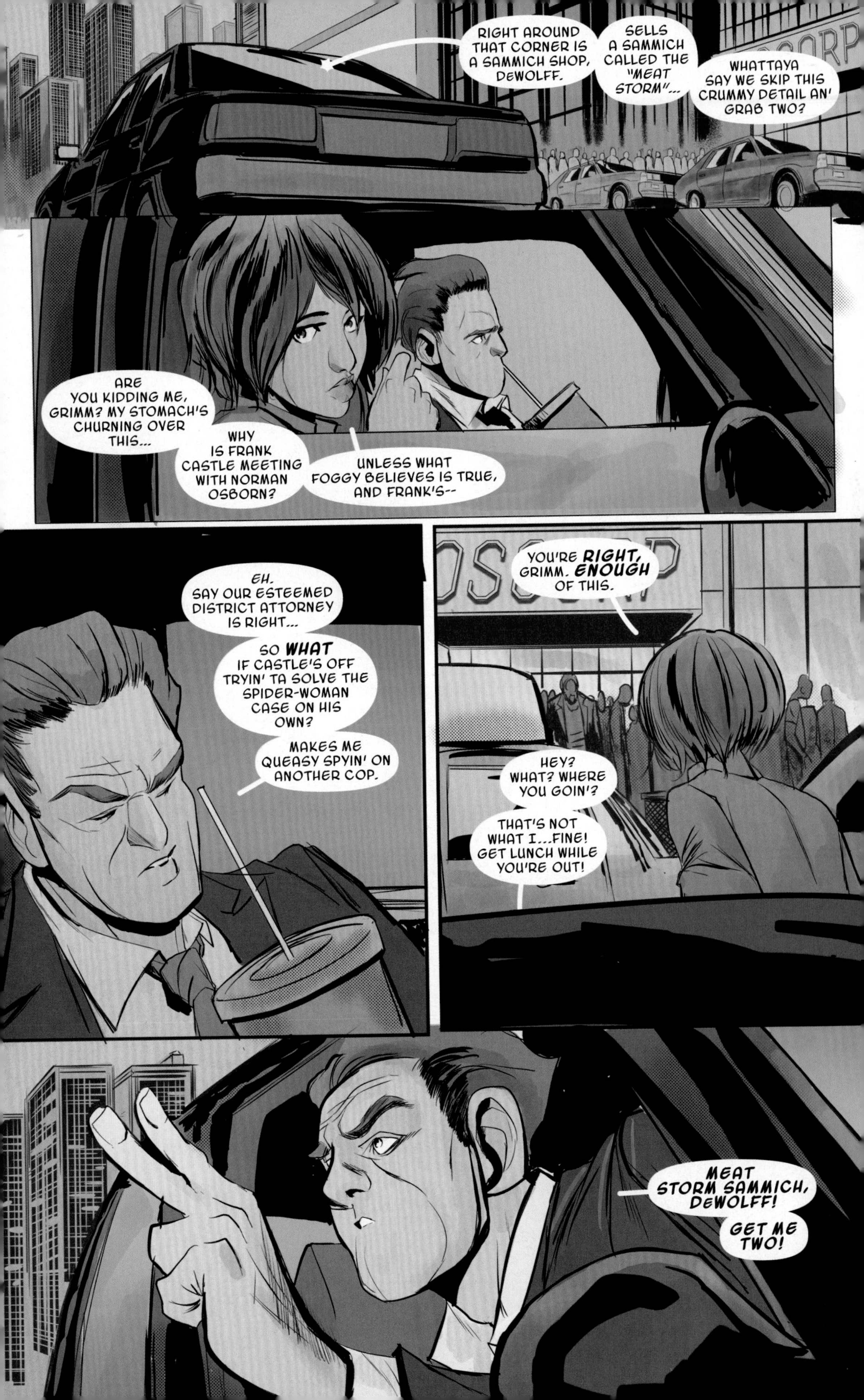
RIGHT AROUND THAT CORNER IS A SAMMICH SHOP, DeWOLFF.
SELLS A SAMMICH CALLED THE "MEAT STORM"...
WHATTAYA SAY WE SKIP THIS CRUMMY DETAIL AN' GRAB TWO?
ARE YOU KIDDING ME, GRIMM? MY STOMACH'S CHURNING OVER THIS...
WHY IS FRANK CASTLE MEETING WITH NORMAN OSBORN?
UNLESS WHAT FOGGY BELIEVES IS TRUE, AND FRANK'S--
EH. SAY OUR ESTEEMED DISTRICT ATTORNEY IS RIGHT...
SO WHAT IF CASTLE'S OFF TRYIN' TA SOLVE THE SPIDER-WOMAN CASE ON HIS OWN?
MAKES ME QUEASY SPYIN' ON ANOTHER COP.
YOU'RE RIGHT, GRIMM. ENOUGH OF THIS.
HEY? WHAT? WHERE YOU GOIN'?
THAT'S NOT WHAT I...FINE! GET LUNCH WHILE YOU'RE OUT!
MEAT STORM SAMMICH, DeWOLFF!
GET ME TWO!

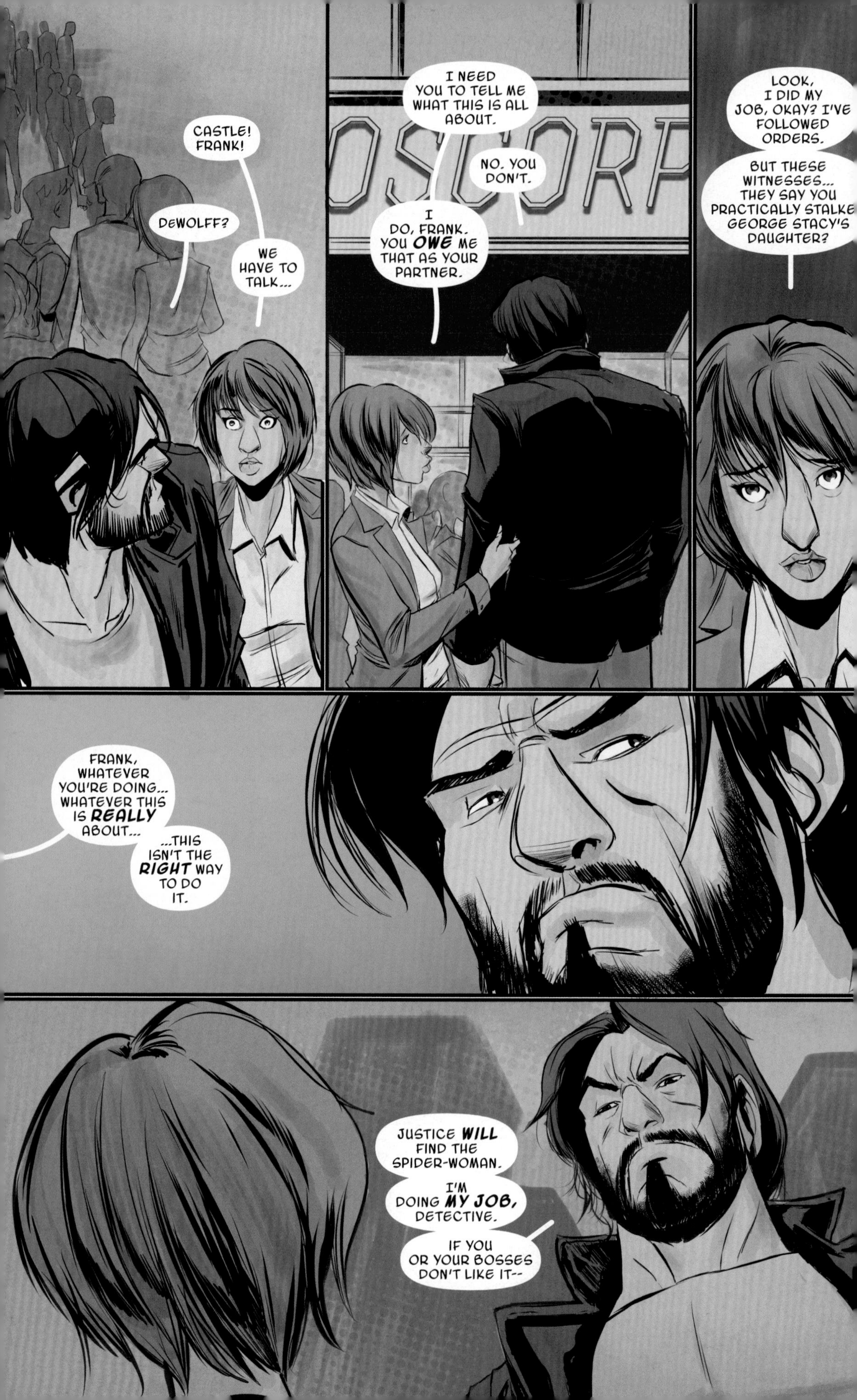

CASTLE! FRANK!
DEWOLFF?
WE HAVE TO TALK...
I NEED YOU TO TELL ME WHAT THIS IS ALL ABOUT.
OSCORP
NO. YOU DON'T.
I DO, FRANK. YOU OWE ME THAT AS YOUR PARTNER.
LOOK, I DID MY JOB, OKAY? I'VE FOLLOWED ORDERS.
BUT THESE WITNESSES... THEY SAY YOU PRACTICALLY STALKE GEORGE STACY'S DAUGHTER?
FRANK, WHATEVER YOU'RE DOING... WHATEVER THIS IS REALLY ABOUT...
...THIS ISN'T THE RIGHT WAY TO DO IT.
JUSTICE WILL FIND THE SPIDER-WOMAN.
I'M DOING MY JOB, DETECTIVE.
IF YOU OR YOUR BOSSES DON'T LIKE IT--

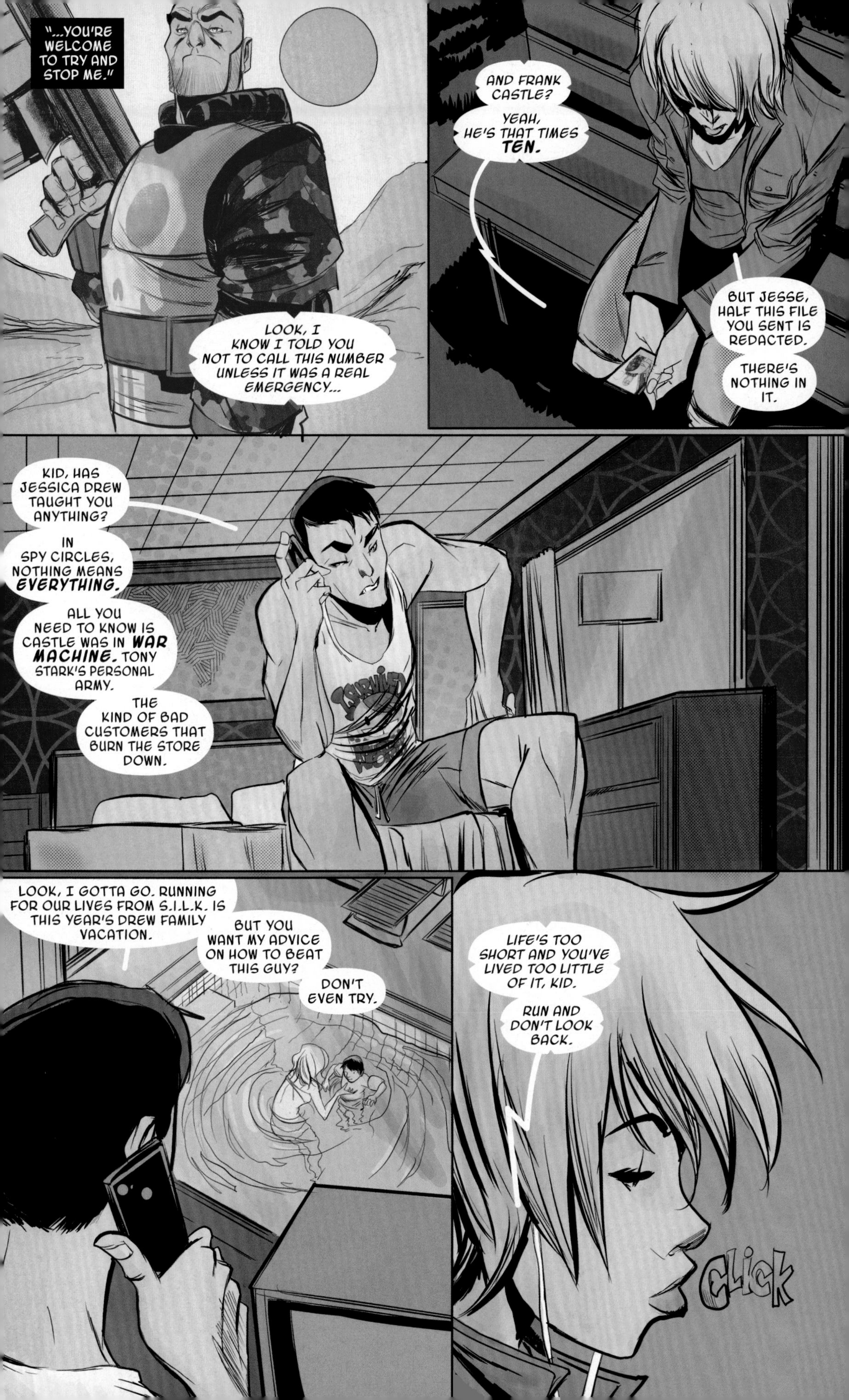
"...YOU'RE WELCOME TO TRY AND STOP ME."
LOOK, I KNOW I TOLD YOU NOT TO CALL THIS NUMBER UNLESS IT WAS A REAL EMERGENCY...
AND FRANK CASTLE?
YEAH, HE'S THAT TIMES TEN.
BUT JESSE, HALF THIS FILE YOU SENT IS REDACTED.
THERE'S NOTHING IN IT.
KID, HAS JESSICA DREW TAUGHT YOU ANYTHING?
IN SPY CIRCLES, NOTHING MEANS EVERYTHING.
ALL YOU NEED TO KNOW IS CASTLE WAS IN WAR MACHINE. TONY STARK'S PERSONAL ARMY.
THE KIND OF BAD CUSTOMERS THAT BURN THE STORE DOWN.
LOOK, I GOTTA GO. RUNNING FOR OUR LIVES FROM S.I.L.K. IS THIS YEAR'S DREW FAMILY VACATION.
BUT YOU WANT MY ADVICE ON HOW TO BEAT THIS GUY?
DON'T EVEN TRY.
LIFE'S TOO SHORT AND YOU'VE LIVED TOO LITTLE OF IT, KID.
RUN AND DON'T LOOK BACK.
CLICK

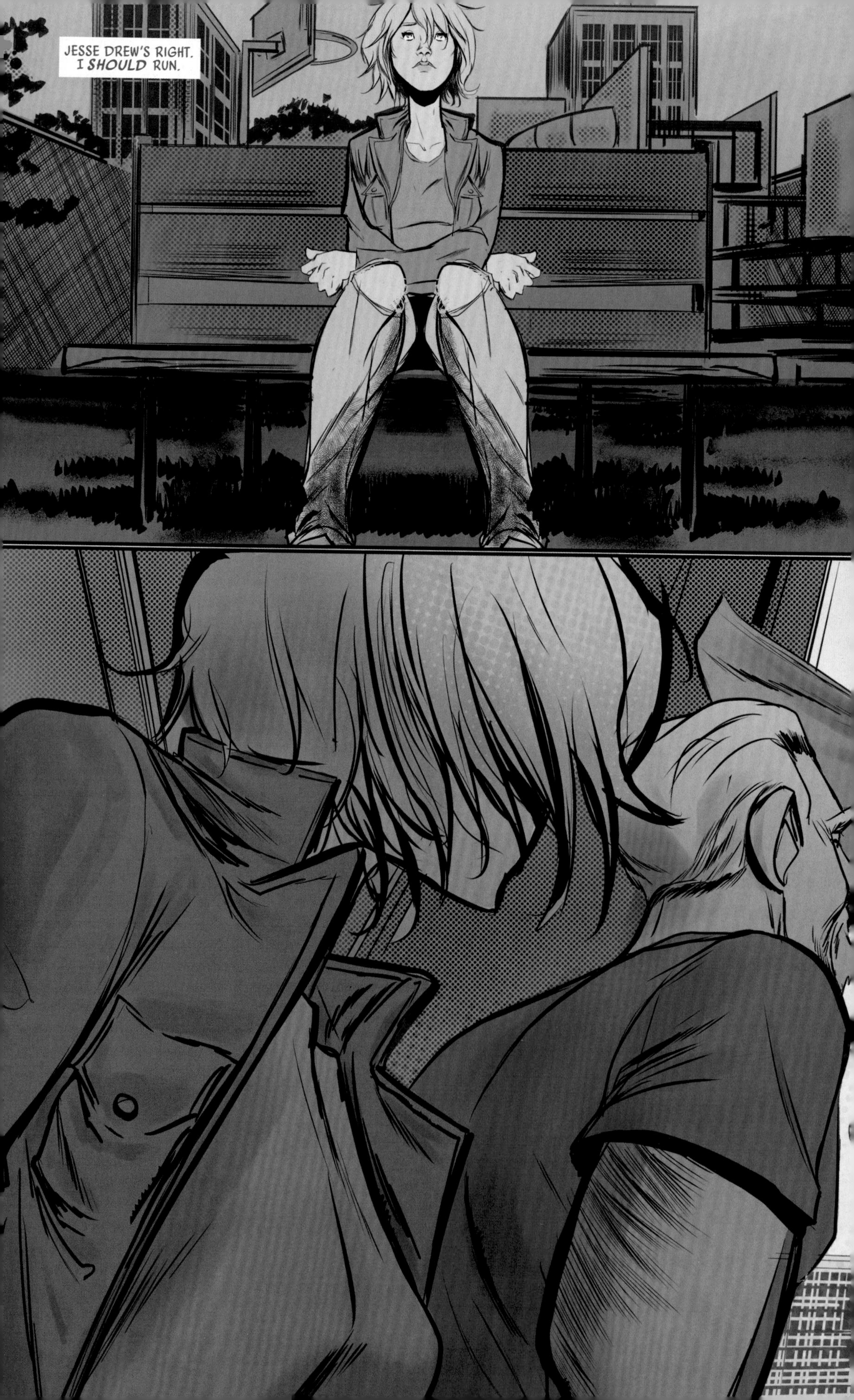
JESSE DREW'S RIGHT. I SHOULD RUN.

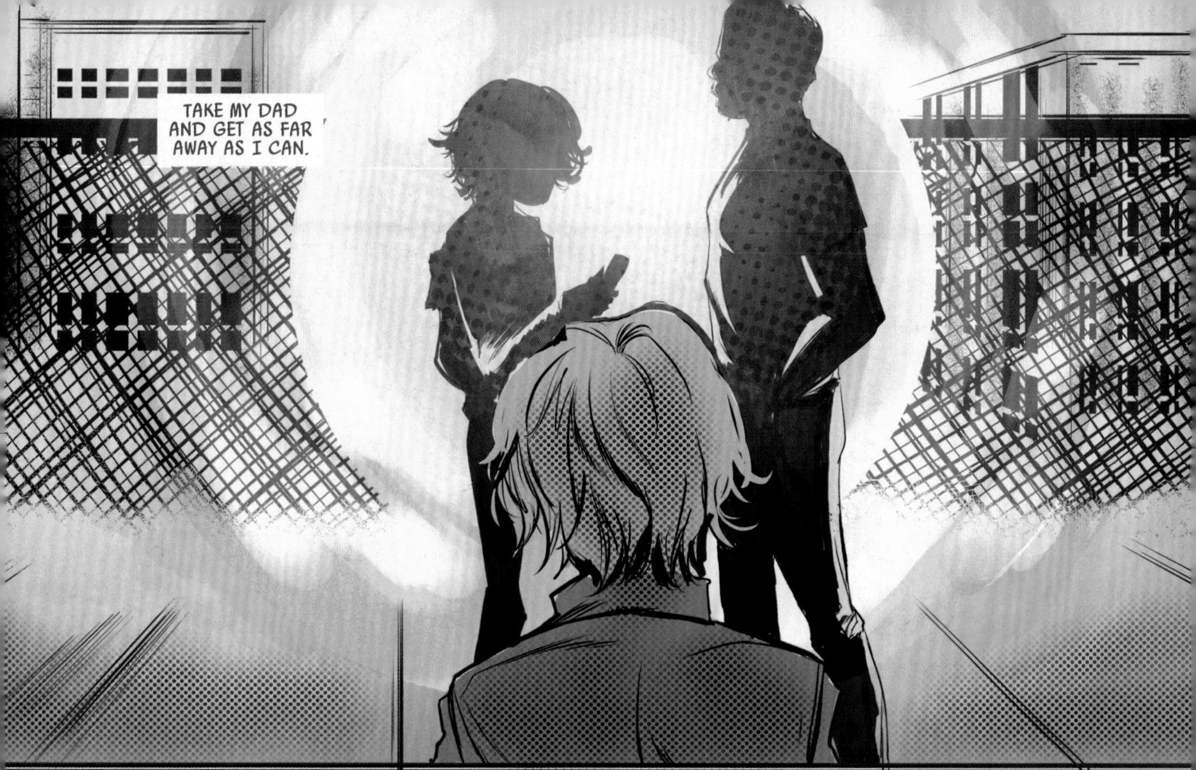
TAKE MY DAD AND GET AS FAR AWAY AS I CAN.

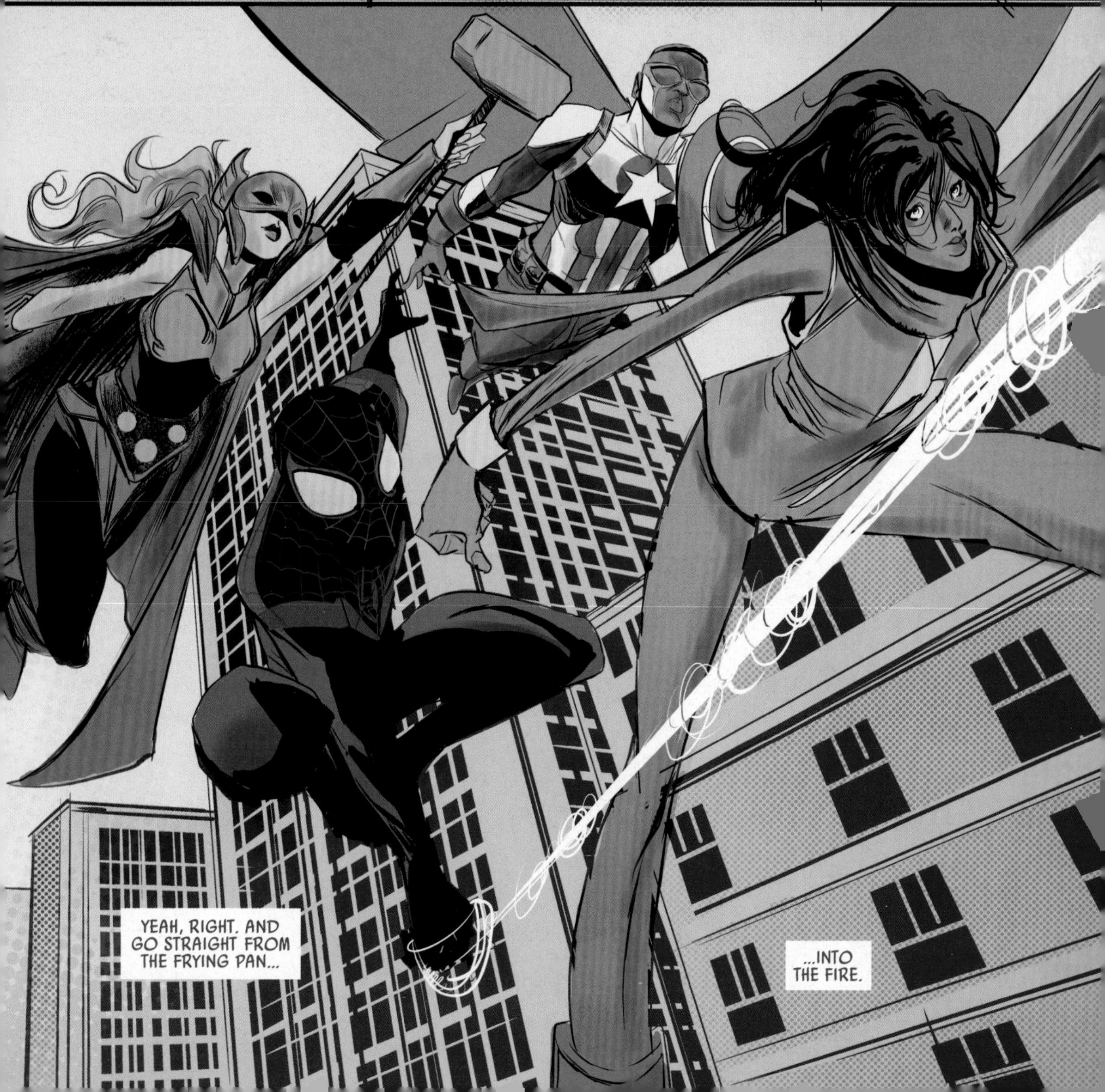
YEAH, RIGHT. AND GO STRAIGHT FROM THE FRYING PAN...
...INTO THE FIRE.

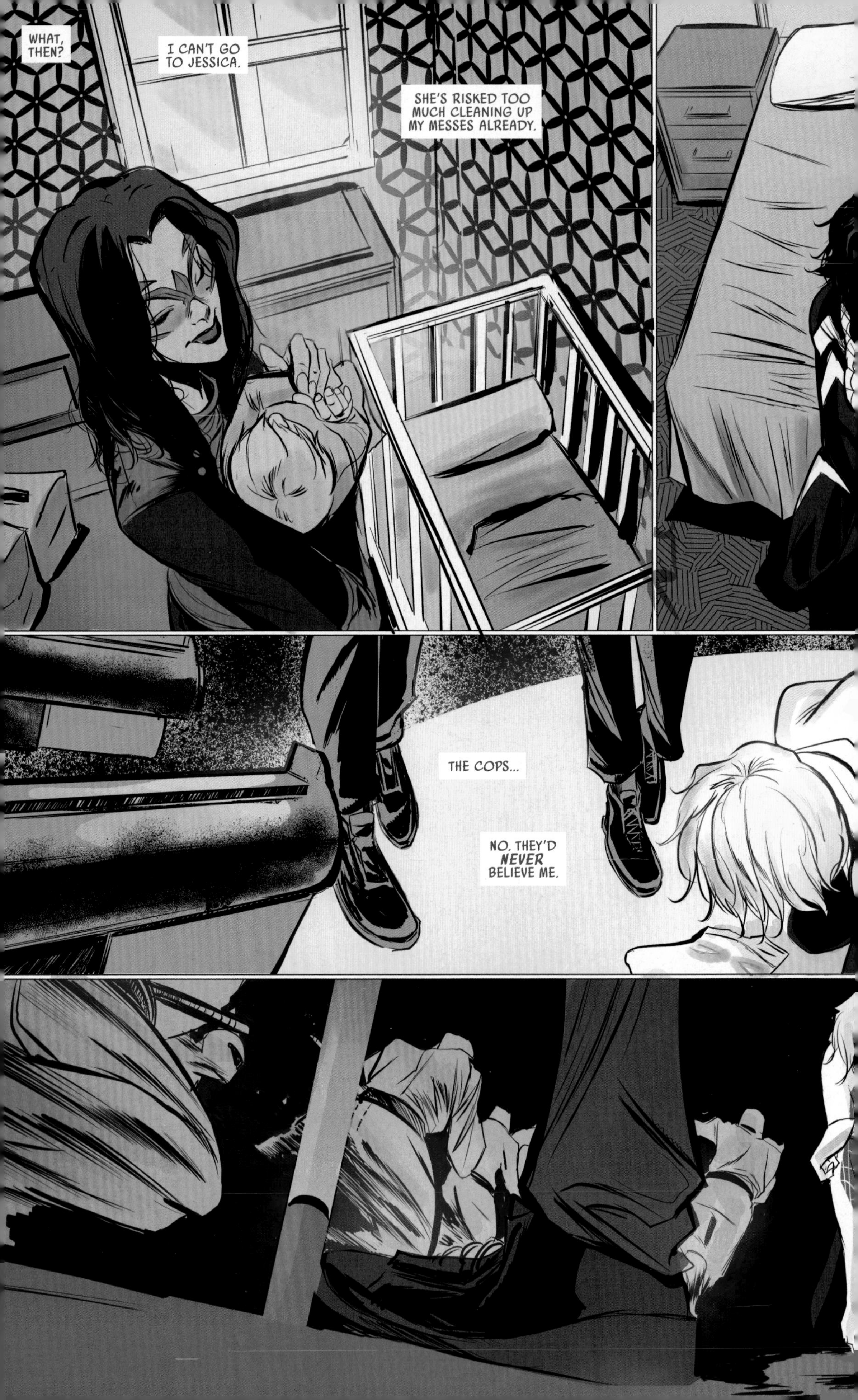
WHAT, THEN?
I CAN'T GO TO JESSICA.
SHE'S RISKED TOO MUCH CLEANING UP MY MESSES ALREADY.
THE COPS...
NO. THEY'D *NEVER* BELIEVE ME.

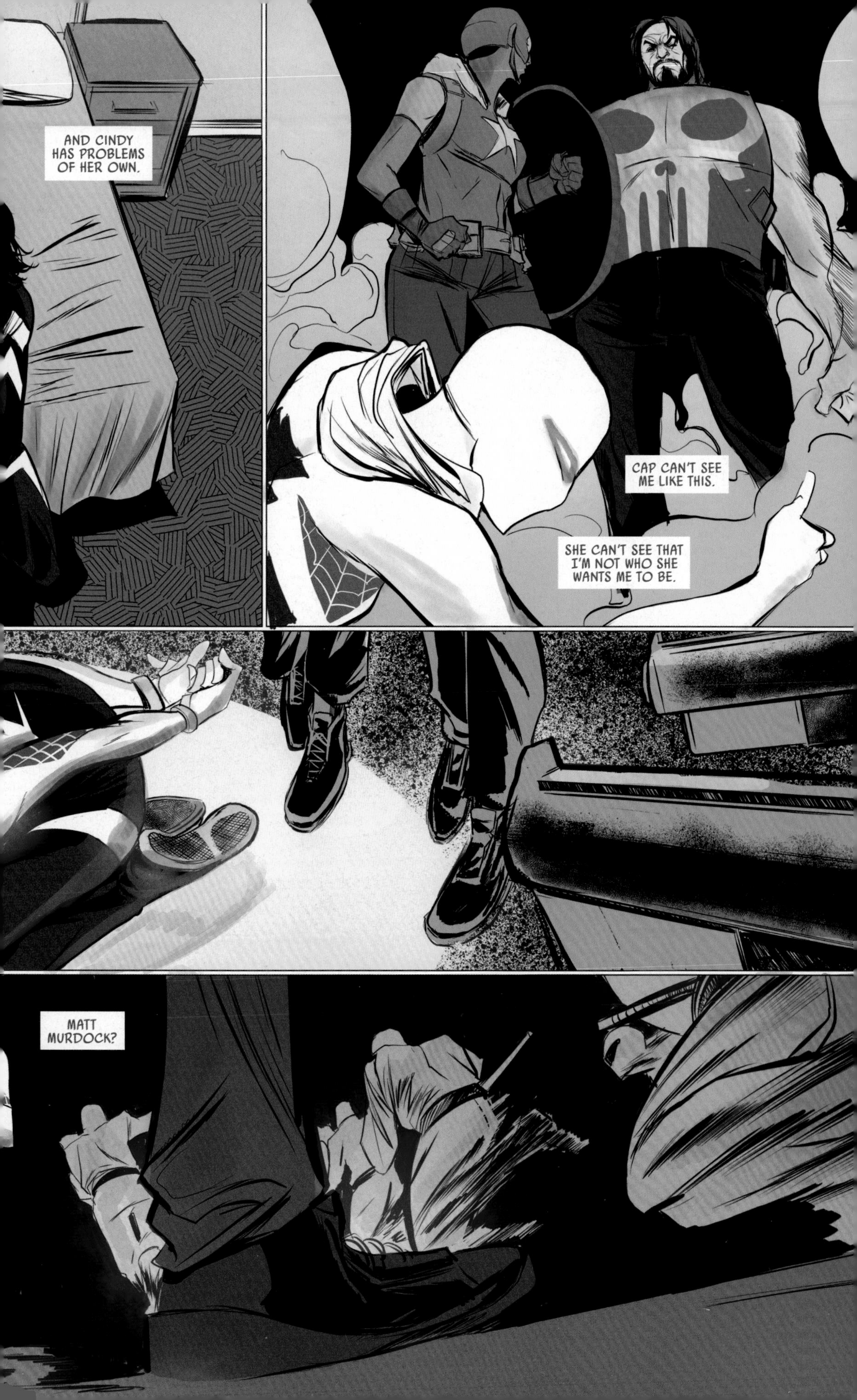

AND CINDY HAS PROBLEMS OF HER OWN.
CAP CAN'T SEE ME LIKE THIS.
SHE CAN'T SEE THAT I'M NOT WHO SHE WANTS ME TO BE.
MATT MURDOCK?

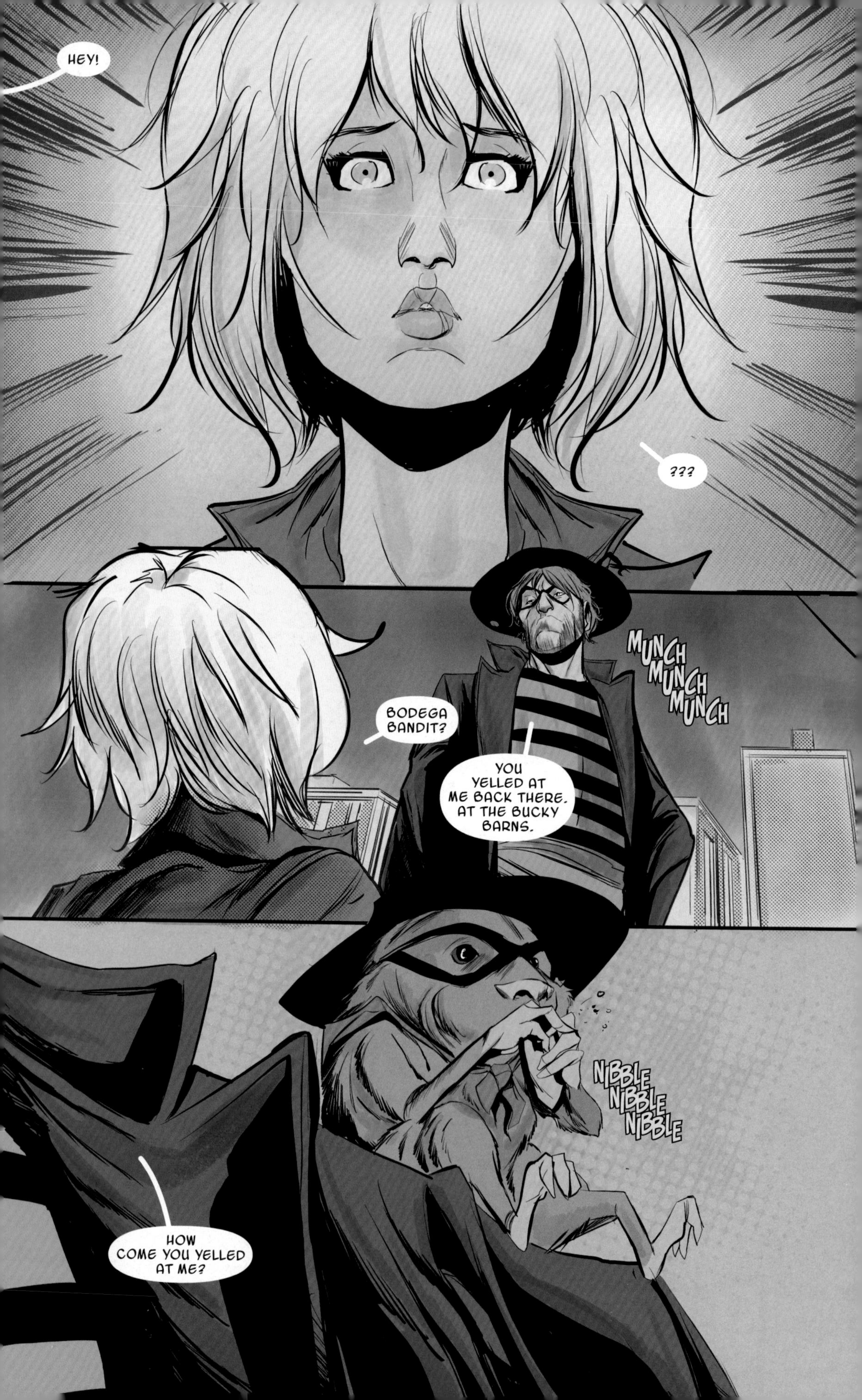
HEY!
???
BODEGA BANDIT?
YOU YELLED AT ME BACK THERE. AT THE BUCKY BARNS.
MUNCH MUNCH MUNCH
NIBBLE NIBBLE NIBBLE
HOW COME YOU YELLED AT ME?

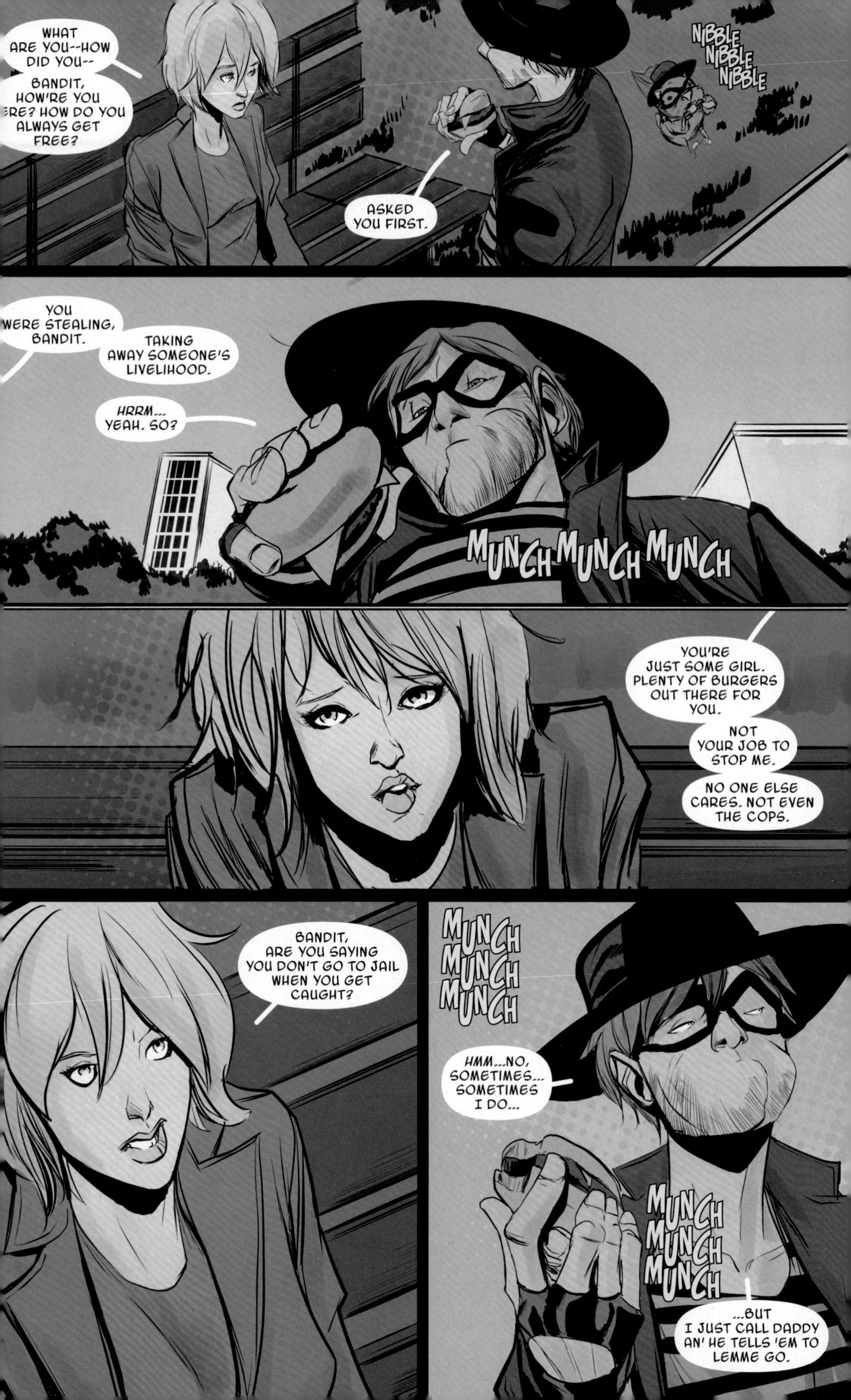
WHAT ARE YOU--HOW DID YOU--
BANDIT, HOW'RE YOU ERE? HOW DO YOU ALWAYS GET FREE?
NIBBLE NIBBLE NIBBLE
ASKED YOU FIRST.
YOU WERE STEALING, BANDIT.
TAKING AWAY SOMEONE'S LIVELIHOOD.
HRRM... YEAH. SO?
MUNCH MUNCH MUNCH
YOU'RE JUST SOME GIRL. PLENTY OF BURGERS OUT THERE FOR YOU.
NOT YOUR JOB TO STOP ME.
NO ONE ELSE CARES. NOT EVEN THE COPS.
BANDIT, ARE YOU SAYING YOU DON'T GO TO JAIL WHEN YOU GET CAUGHT?
MUNCH MUNCH MUNCH
HMM...NO, SOMETIMES... SOMETIMES I DO...
MUNCH MUNCH MUNCH
...BUT I JUST CALL DADDY AN' HE TELLS 'EM TO LEMME GO.

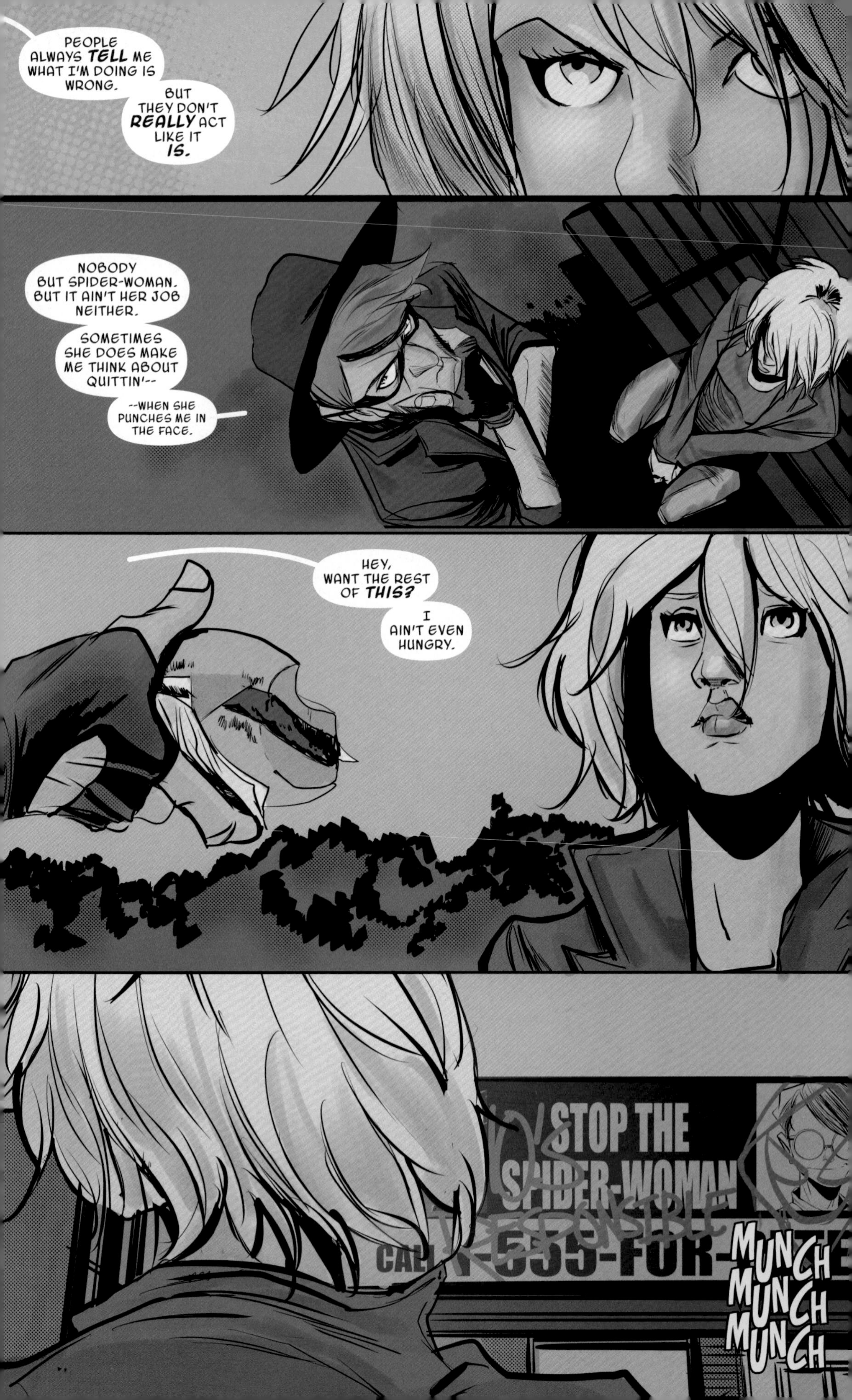
PEOPLE ALWAYS TELL ME WHAT I'M DOING IS WRONG.
BUT THEY DON'T REALLY ACT LIKE IT IS.
NOBODY BUT SPIDER-WOMAN. BUT IT AIN'T HER JOB NEITHER.
SOMETIMES SHE DOES MAKE ME THINK ABOUT QUITTIN'--
--WHEN SHE PUNCHES ME IN THE FACE.
HEY, WANT THE REST OF THIS?
I AIN'T EVEN HUNGRY.
STOP THE SPIDER-WOMAN
RESPONSIBLE
CALL
-555-FOR-
MUNCH MUNCH MUNCH

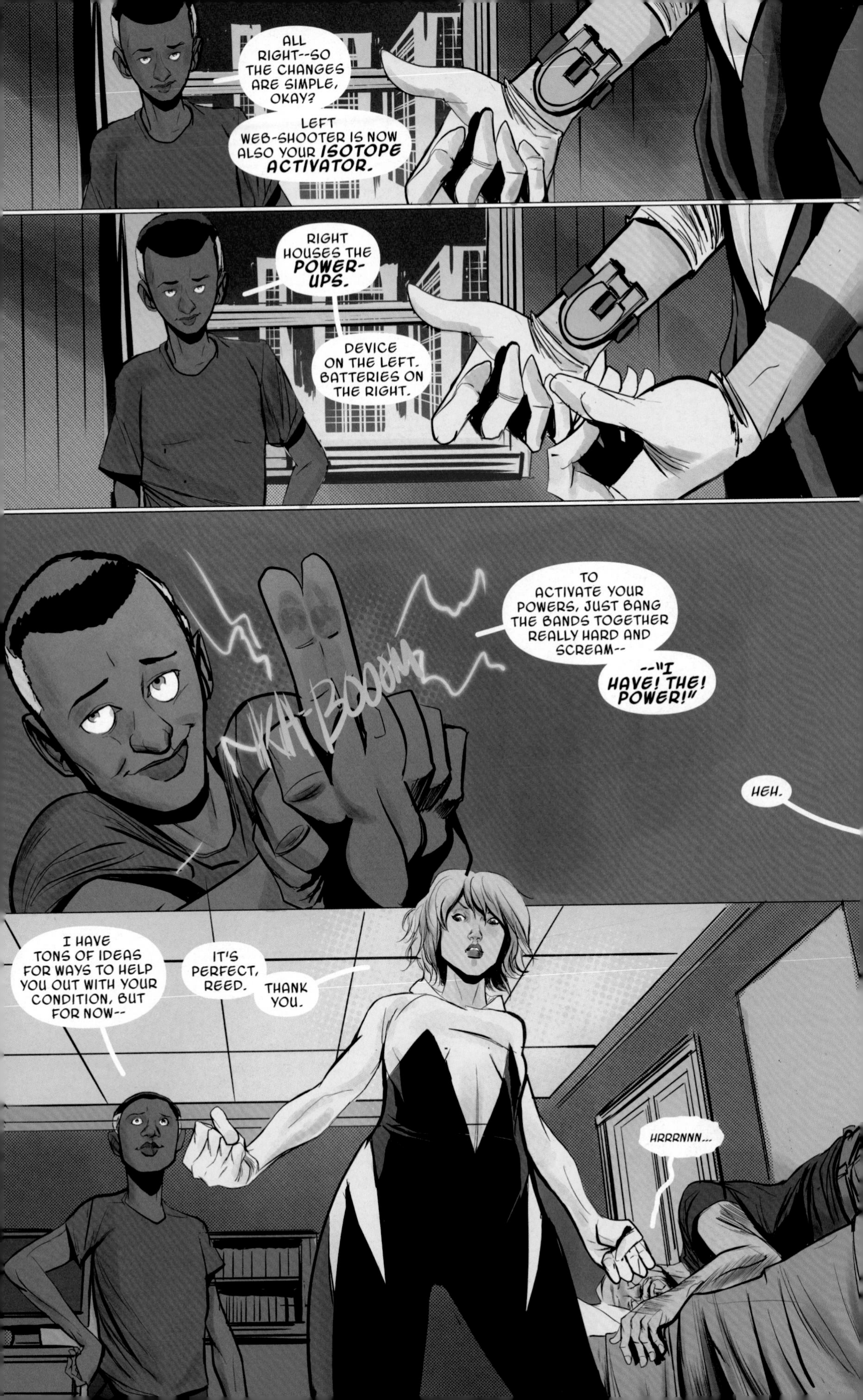

ALL RIGHT--SO THE CHANGES ARE SIMPLE, OKAY?
LEFT WEB-SHOOTER IS NOW ALSO YOUR ISOTOPE ACTIVATOR.
RIGHT HOUSES THE POWER-UPS.
DEVICE ON THE LEFT. BATTERIES ON THE RIGHT.
TO ACTIVATE YOUR POWERS, JUST BANG THE BANDS TOGETHER REALLY HARD AND SCREAM--
--"I HAVE! THE! POWER!"
NKA-BOOOM
HEH.
I HAVE TONS OF IDEAS FOR WAYS TO HELP YOU OUT WITH YOUR CONDITION, BUT FOR NOW--
IT'S PERFECT, REED.
THANK YOU.
HRRRNNN...

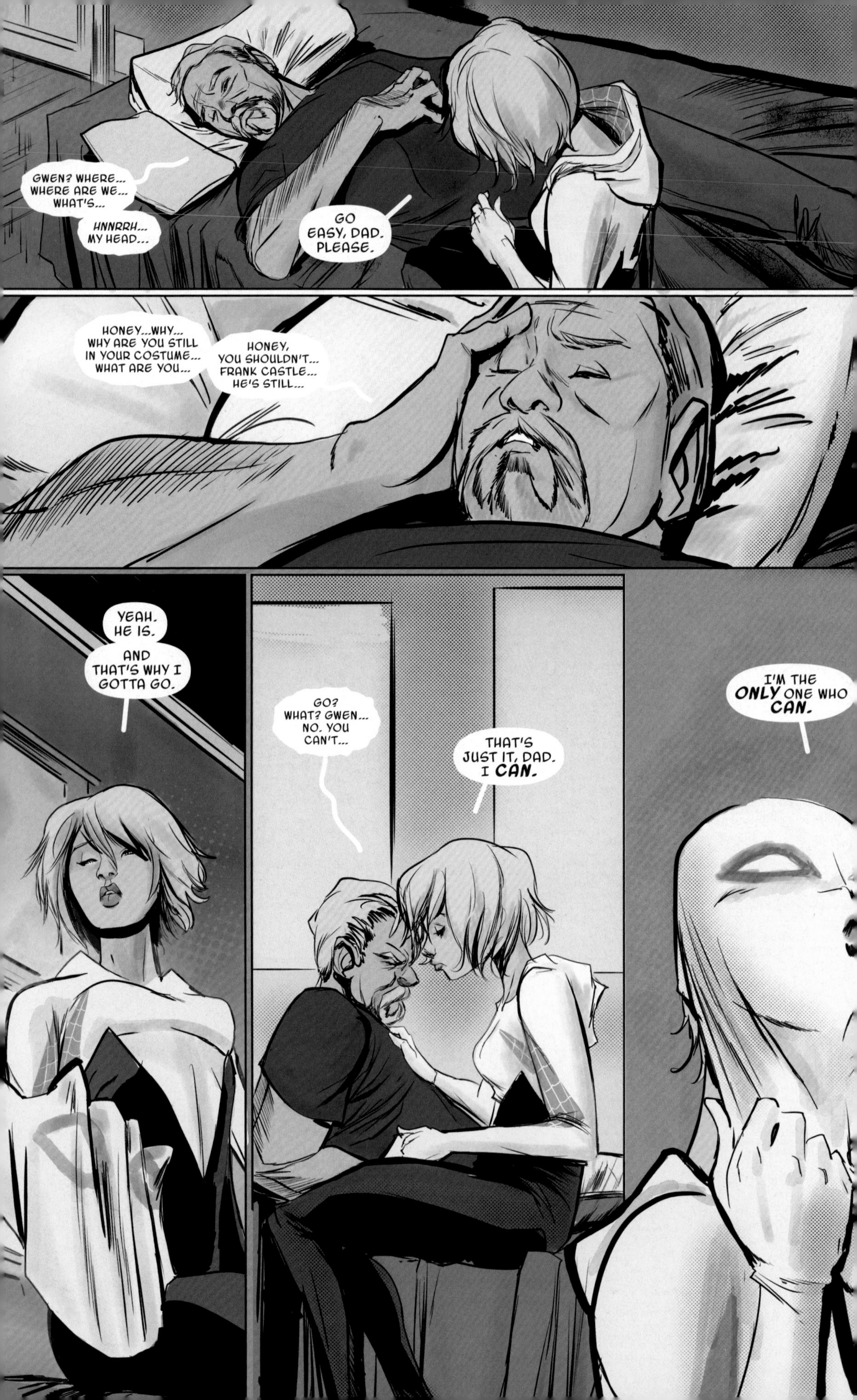
GWEN? WHERE... WHERE ARE WE... WHAT'S...
HNNRRH... MY HEAD...
GO EASY, DAD. PLEASE.
HONEY...WHY... WHY ARE YOU STILL IN YOUR COSTUME... WHAT ARE YOU...
HONEY, YOU SHOULDN'T... FRANK CASTLE... HE'S STILL...
YEAH. HE IS.
AND THAT'S WHY I GOTTA GO.
GO? WHAT? GWEN... NO. YOU CAN'T...
THAT'S JUST IT, DAD. I CAN.
I'M THE ONLY ONE WHO CAN.

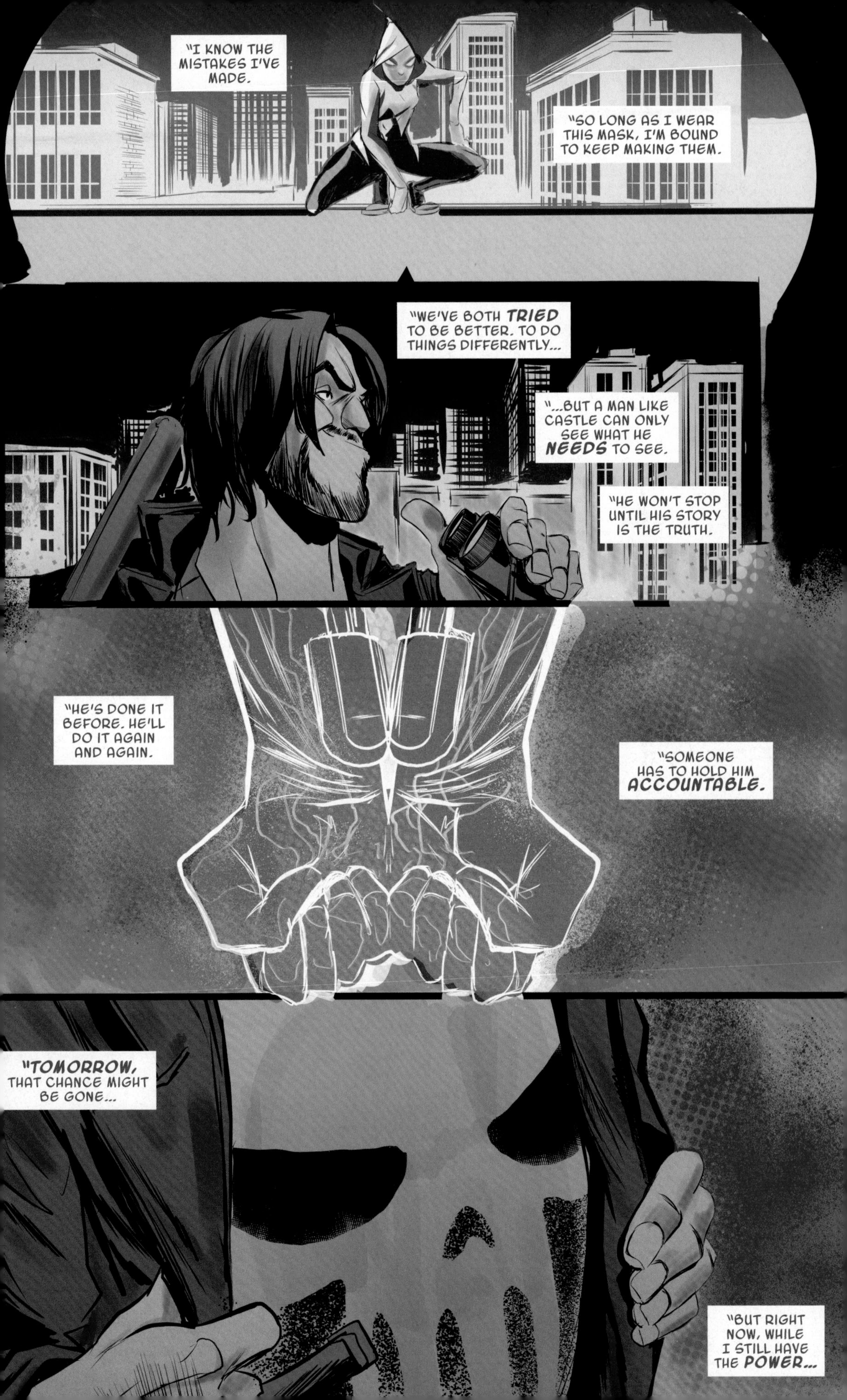
"I KNOW THE MISTAKES I'VE MADE.
"SO LONG AS I WEAR THIS MASK, I'M BOUND TO KEEP MAKING THEM.
"WE'VE BOTH TRIED TO BE BETTER. TO DO THINGS DIFFERENTLY...
"...BUT A MAN LIKE CASTLE CAN ONLY SEE WHAT HE NEEDS TO SEE.
"HE WON'T STOP UNTIL HIS STORY IS THE TRUTH.
"HE'S DONE IT BEFORE. HE'LL DO IT AGAIN AND AGAIN.
"SOMEONE HAS TO HOLD HIM ACCOUNTABLE.
"TOMORROW, THAT CHANCE MIGHT BE GONE...
"BUT RIGHT NOW, WHILE I STILL HAVE THE POWER...

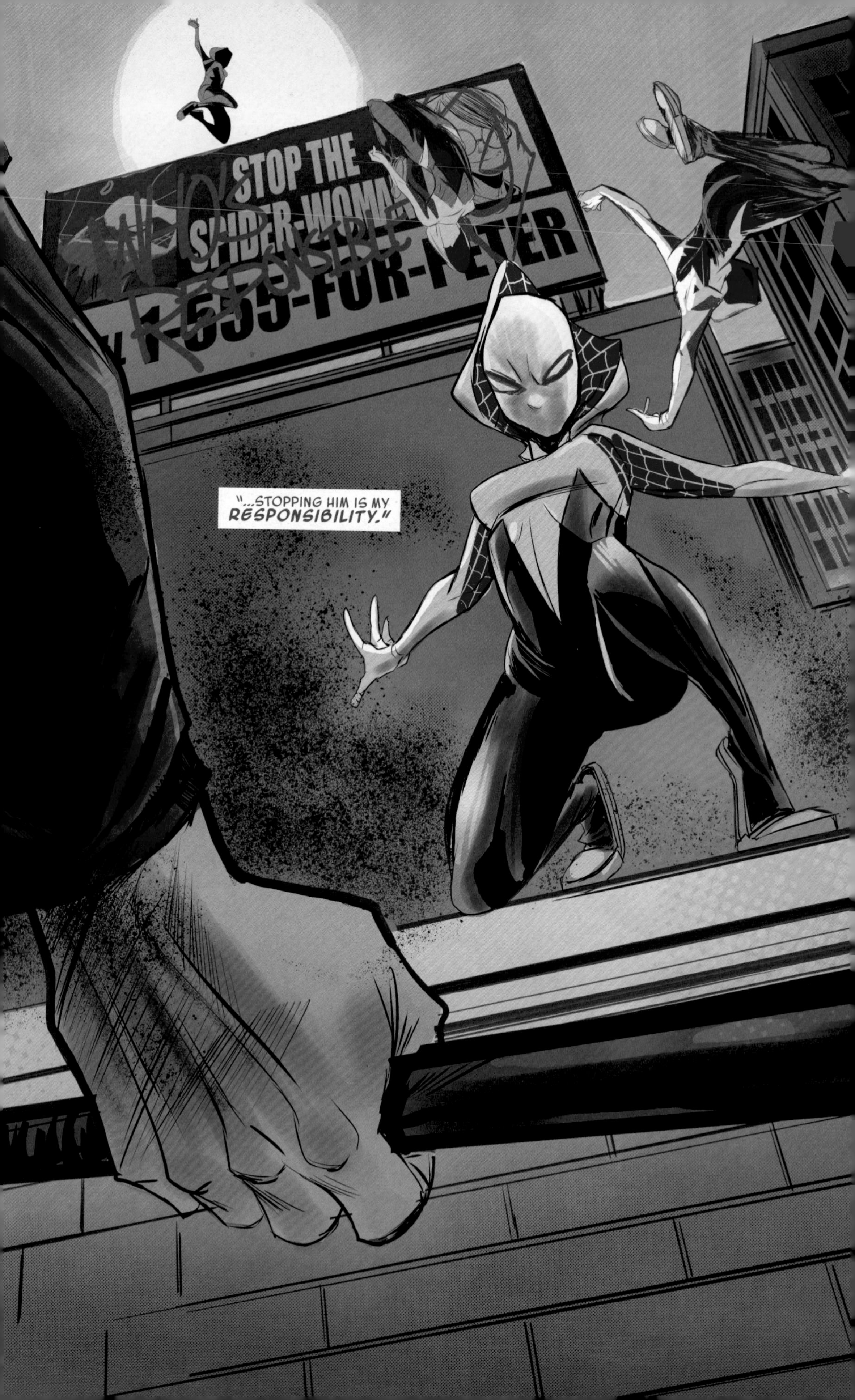
STOP THE
WHO'S RESPONSIBLE
"...STOPPING HIM IS MY RESPONSIBILITY."

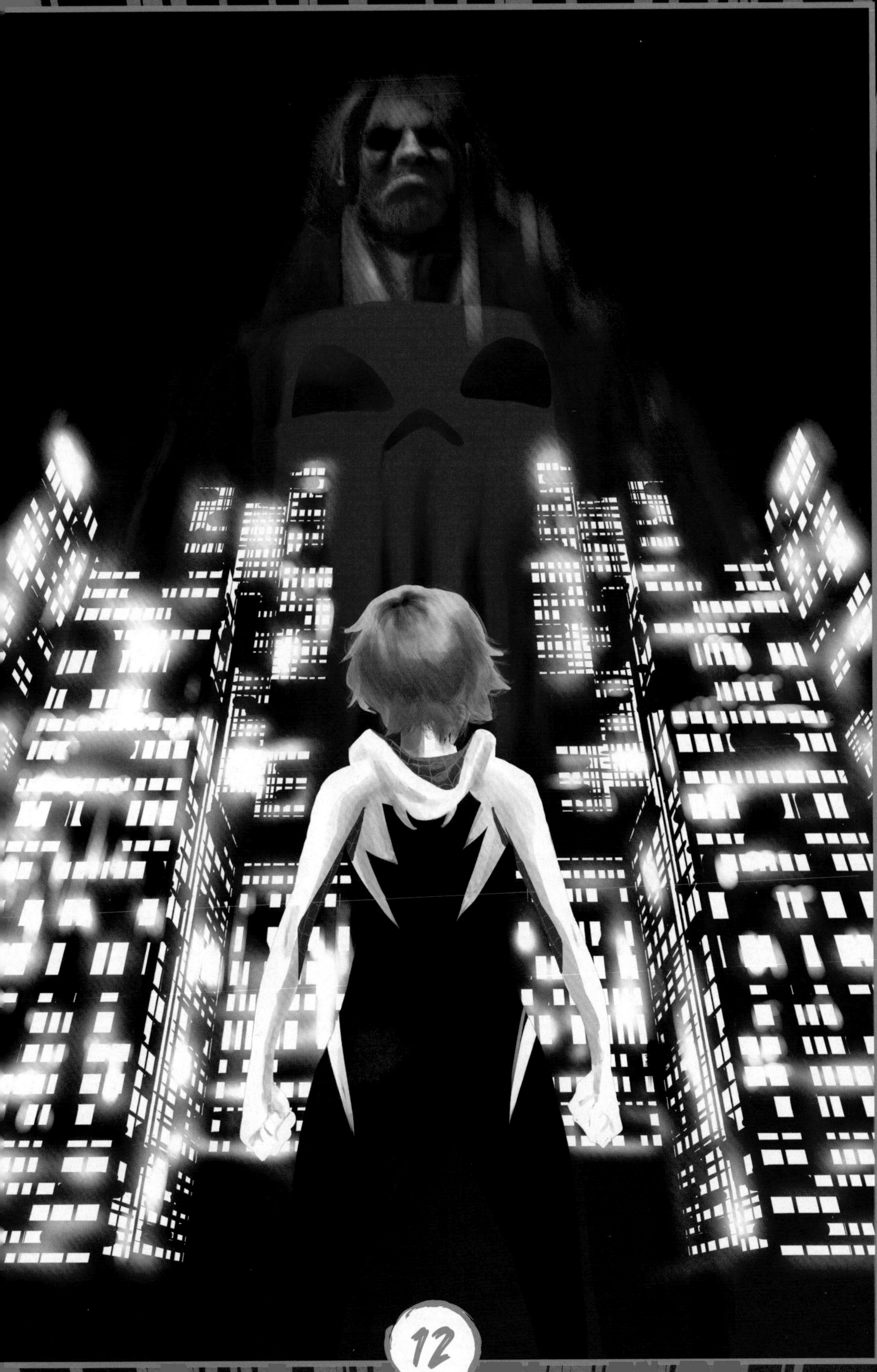

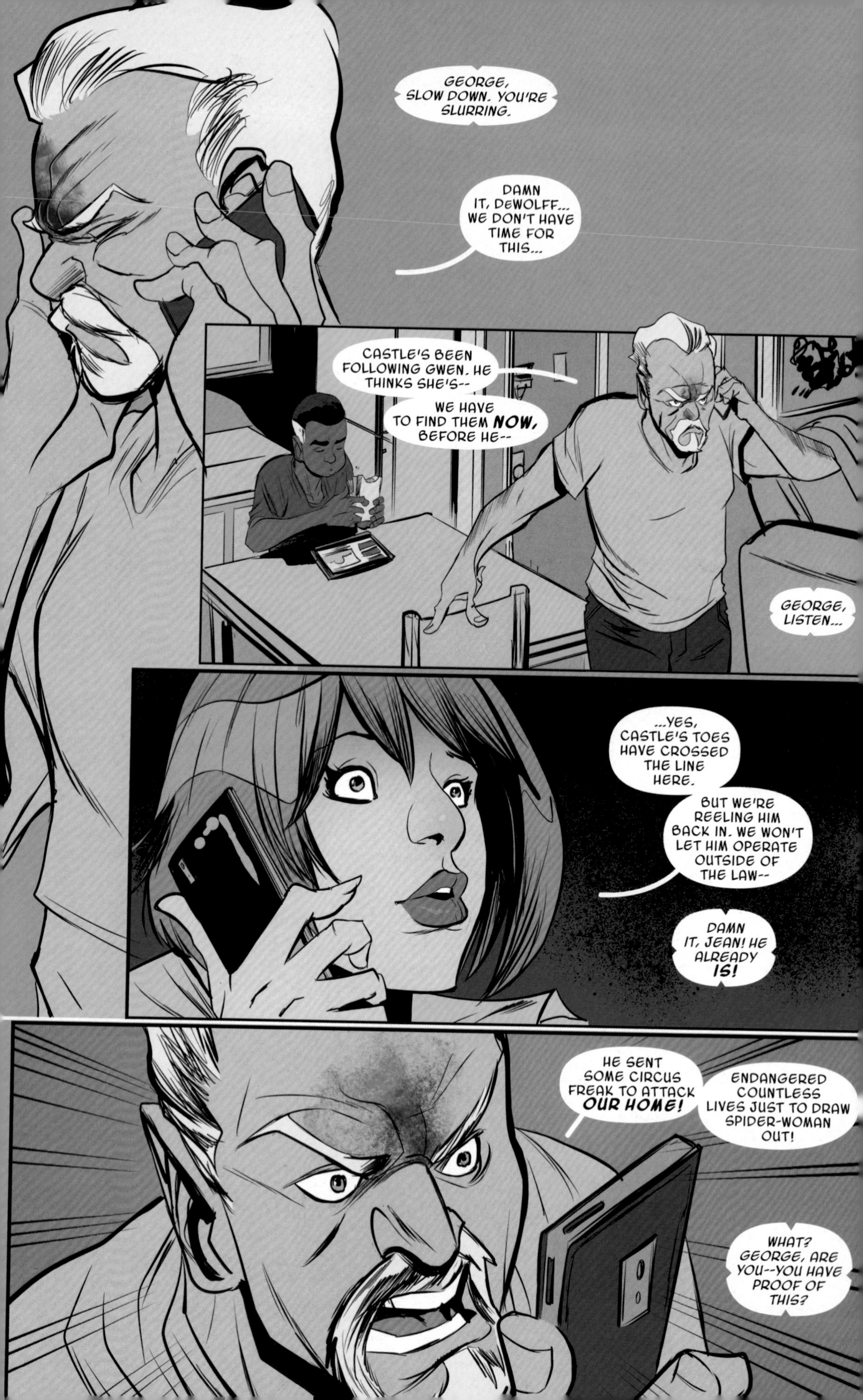
GEORGE, SLOW DOWN. YOU'RE SLURRING.
DAMN IT, DEWOLFF... WE DON'T HAVE TIME FOR THIS...
CASTLE'S BEEN FOLLOWING GWEN. HE THINKS SHE'S--
WE HAVE TO FIND THEM **NOW,** BEFORE HE--
GEORGE, LISTEN...
...YES, CASTLE'S TOES HAVE CROSSED THE LINE HERE.
BUT WE'RE REELING HIM BACK IN. WE WON'T LET HIM OPERATE OUTSIDE OF THE LAW--
DAMN IT, JEAN! HE ALREADY **IS!**
HE SENT SOME CIRCUS FREAK TO ATTACK **OUR HOME!**
ENDANGERED COUNTLESS LIVES JUST TO DRAW SPIDER-WOMAN OUT!
WHAT? GEORGE, ARE YOU--YOU HAVE PROOF OF THIS?

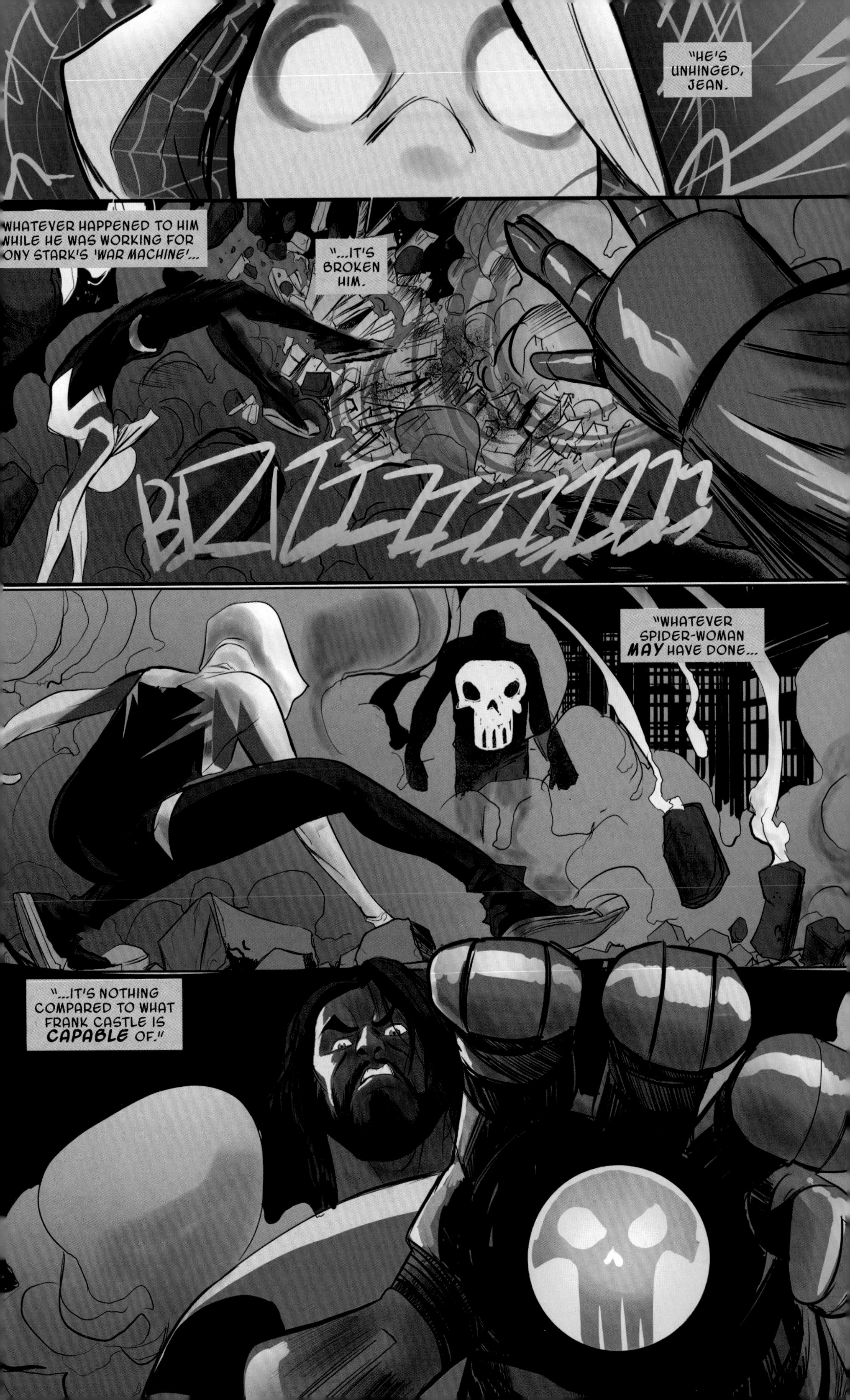
"HE'S UNHINGED, JEAN.
WHATEVER HAPPENED TO HIM WHILE HE WAS WORKING FOR ONY STARK'S 'WAR MACHINE'...
"...IT'S BROKEN HIM.
"WHATEVER SPIDER-WOMAN MAY HAVE DONE...
"...IT'S NOTHING COMPARED TO WHAT FRANK CASTLE IS CAPABLE OF."

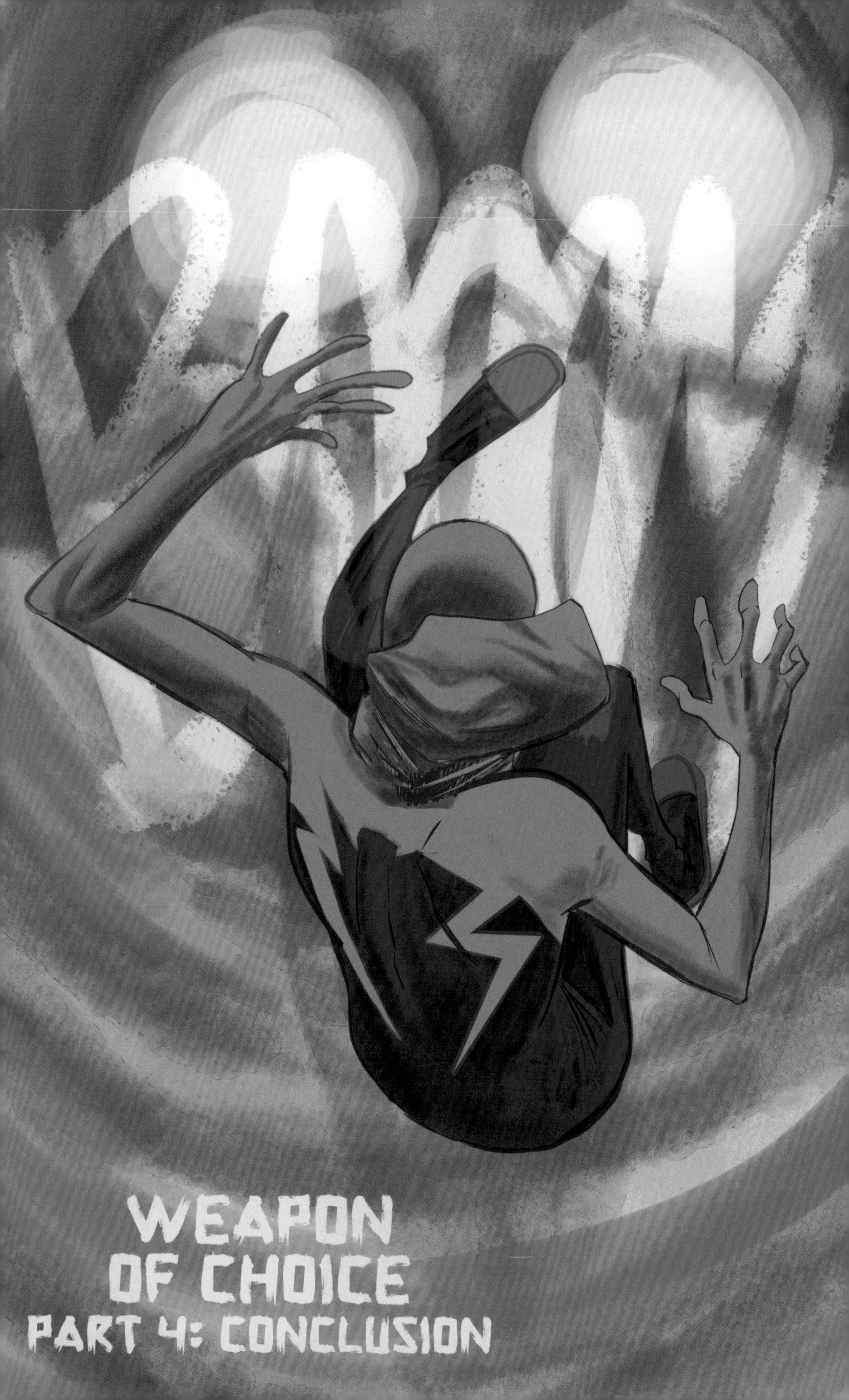
WEAPON
OF CHOICE
PART 4: CONCLUSION

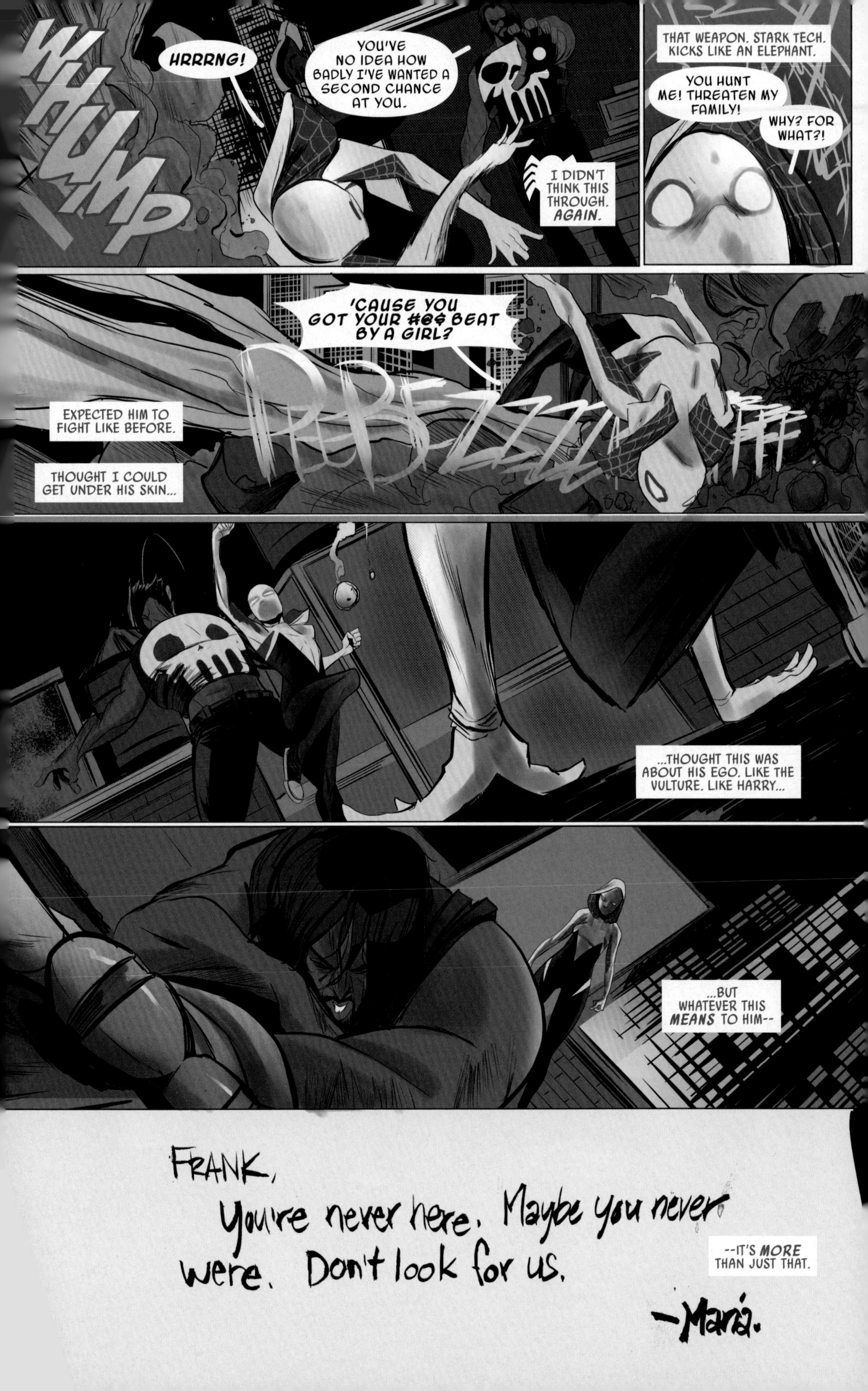
WHUMP
HRRRNG!
YOU'VE NO IDEA HOW BADLY I'VE WANTED A SECOND CHANCE AT YOU.
I DIDN'T THINK THIS THROUGH. AGAIN.
THAT WEAPON. STARK TECH. KICKS LIKE AN ELEPHANT.
YOU HUNT ME! THREATEN MY FAMILY!
WHY? FOR WHAT?!
'CAUSE YOU GOT YOUR #@$ BEAT BY A GIRL?
EXPECTED HIM TO FIGHT LIKE BEFORE.
THOUGHT I COULD GET UNDER HIS SKIN...
...THOUGHT THIS WAS ABOUT HIS EGO. LIKE THE VULTURE. LIKE HARRY...
...BUT WHATEVER THIS MEANS TO HIM--
FRANK,
You're never here. Maybe you never were. Don't look for us.
—María.
--IT'S MORE THAN JUST THAT.

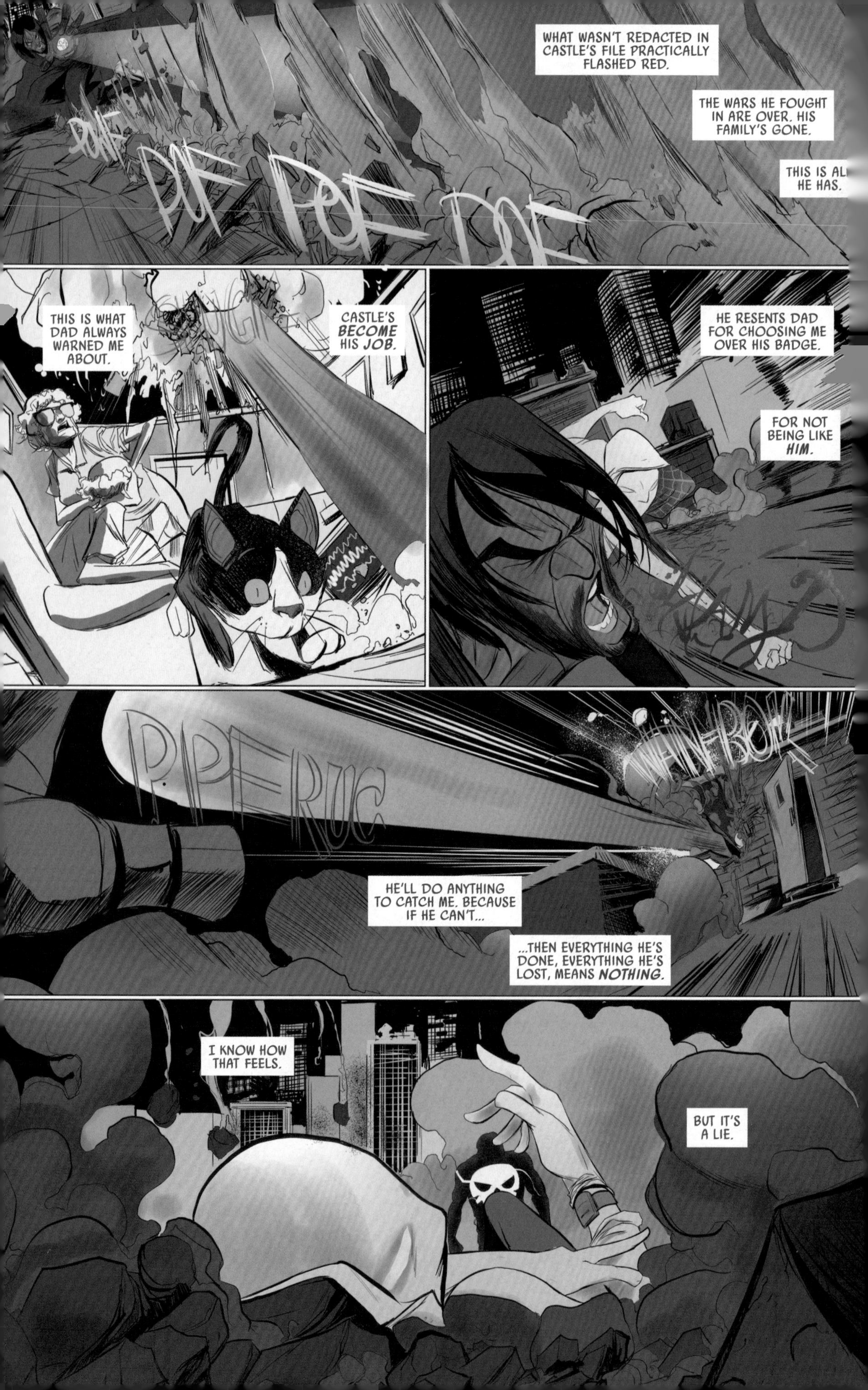
WHAT WASN'T REDACTED IN CASTLE'S FILE PRACTICALLY FLASHED RED.
THE WARS HE FOUGHT IN ARE OVER. HIS FAMILY'S GONE.
THIS IS AL HE HAS.
THIS IS WHAT DAD ALWAYS WARNED ME ABOUT.
CASTLE'S ***BECOME*** HIS ***JOB.***
HE RESENTS DAD FOR CHOOSING ME OVER HIS BADGE.
FOR NOT BEING LIKE ***HIM.***
HE'LL DO ANYTHING TO CATCH ME. BECAUSE IF HE CAN'T...
...THEN EVERYTHING HE'S DONE, EVERYTHING HE'S LOST, MEANS ***NOTHING.***
I KNOW HOW THAT FEELS.
BUT IT'S A LIE.

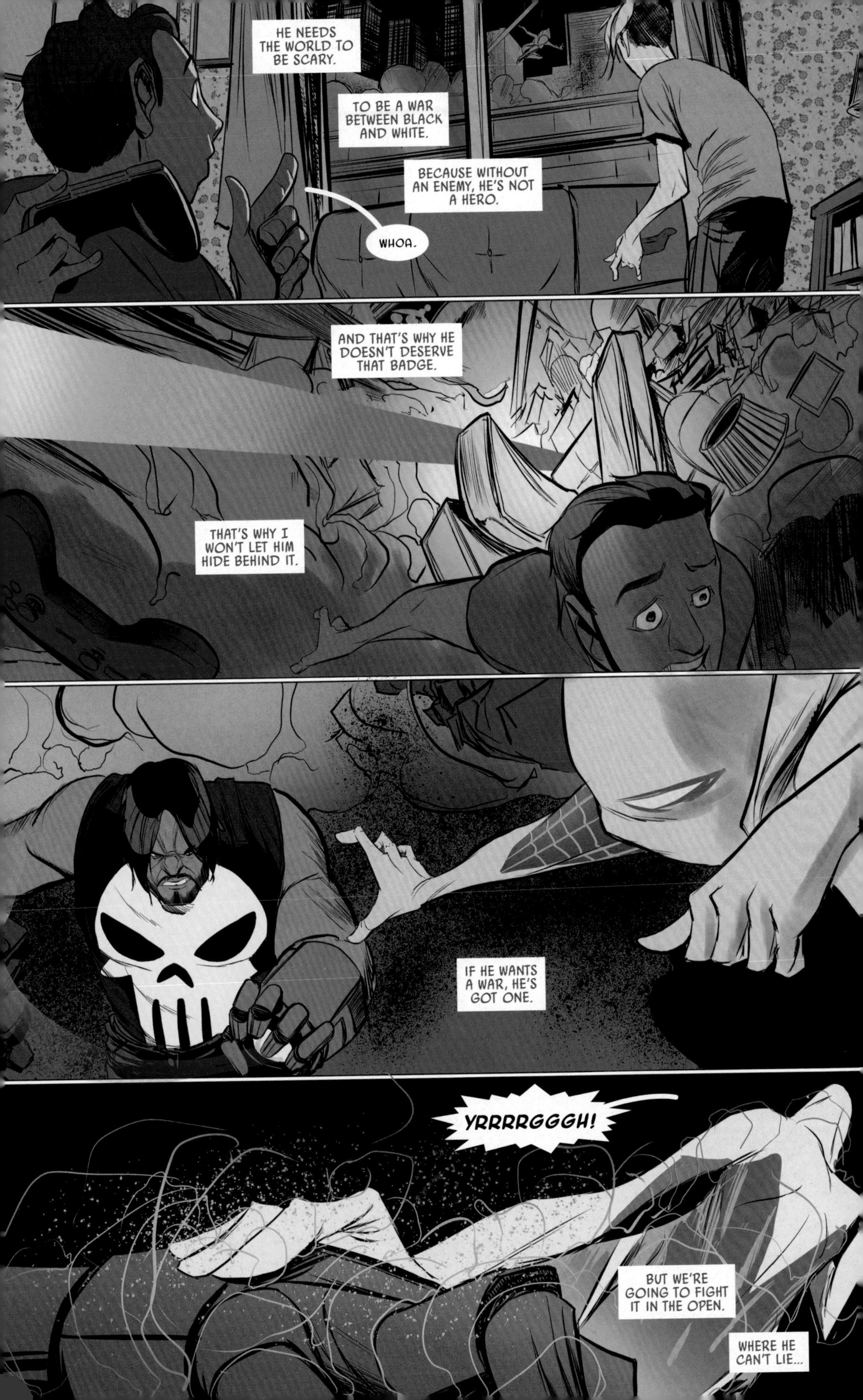
HE NEEDS THE WORLD TO BE SCARY.
TO BE A WAR BETWEEN BLACK AND WHITE.
BECAUSE WITHOUT AN ENEMY, HE'S NOT A HERO.
WHOA.
AND THAT'S WHY HE DOESN'T DESERVE THAT BADGE.
THAT'S WHY I WON'T LET HIM HIDE BEHIND IT.
IF HE WANTS A WAR, HE'S GOT ONE.
YRRRRGGGH!
BUT WE'RE GOING TO FIGHT IT IN THE OPEN.
WHERE HE CAN'T LIE...

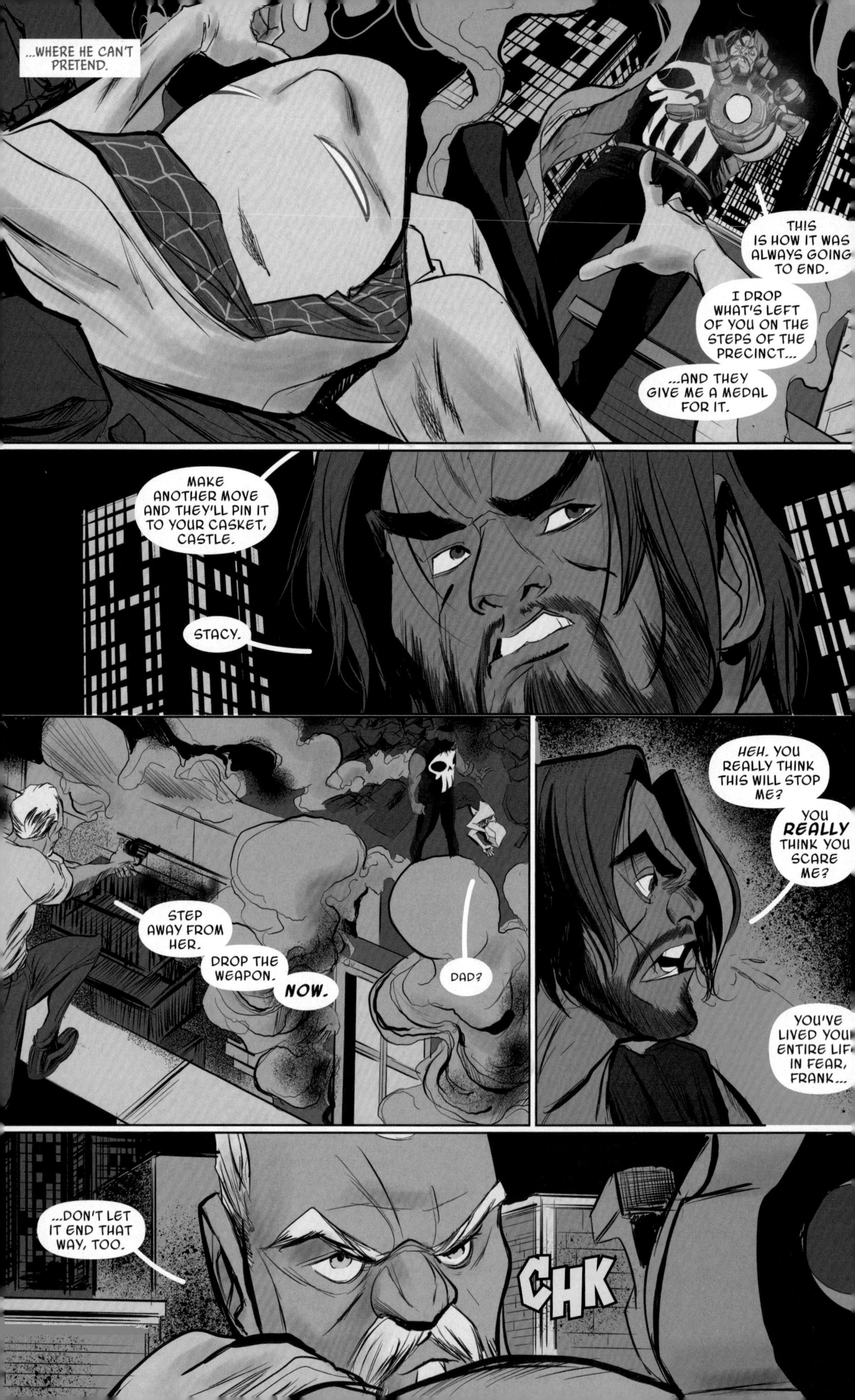
...WHERE HE CAN'T PRETEND.
THIS IS HOW IT WAS ALWAYS GOING TO END.
I DROP WHAT'S LEFT OF YOU ON THE STEPS OF THE PRECINCT...
...AND THEY GIVE ME A MEDAL FOR IT.
MAKE ANOTHER MOVE AND THEY'LL PIN IT TO YOUR CASKET, CASTLE.
STACY.
STEP AWAY FROM HER.
DROP THE WEAPON.
NOW.
DAD?
HEH. YOU REALLY THINK THIS WILL STOP ME?
YOU REALLY THINK YOU SCARE ME?
YOU'VE LIVED YOUR ENTIRE LIFE IN FEAR, FRANK...
...DON'T LET IT END THAT WAY, TOO.
CHK

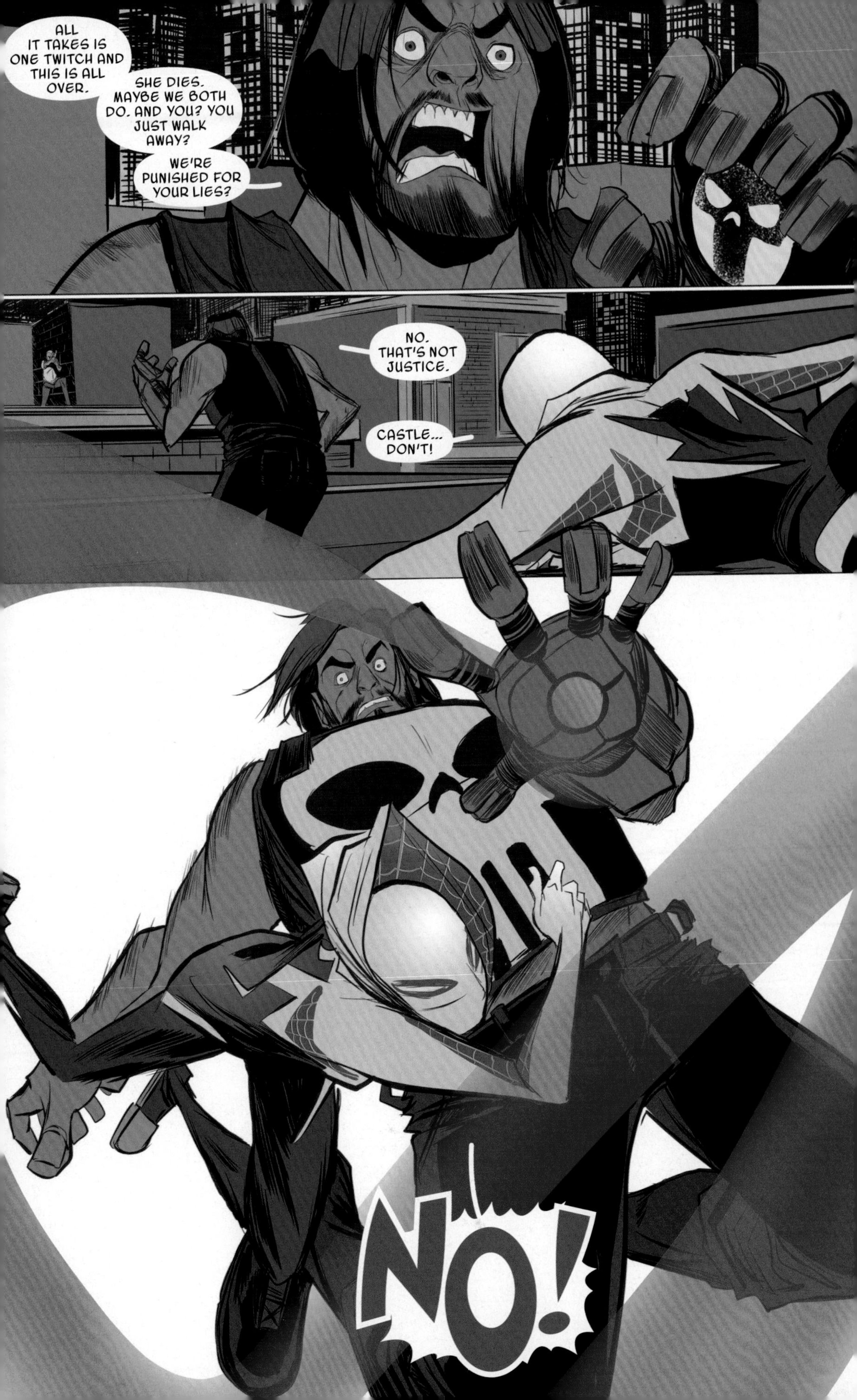
ALL IT TAKES IS ONE TWITCH AND THIS IS ALL OVER.
SHE DIES. MAYBE WE BOTH DO. AND YOU? YOU JUST WALK AWAY?
WE'RE PUNISHED FOR YOUR LIES?
NO. THAT'S NOT JUSTICE.
CASTLE... DON'T!
NO!

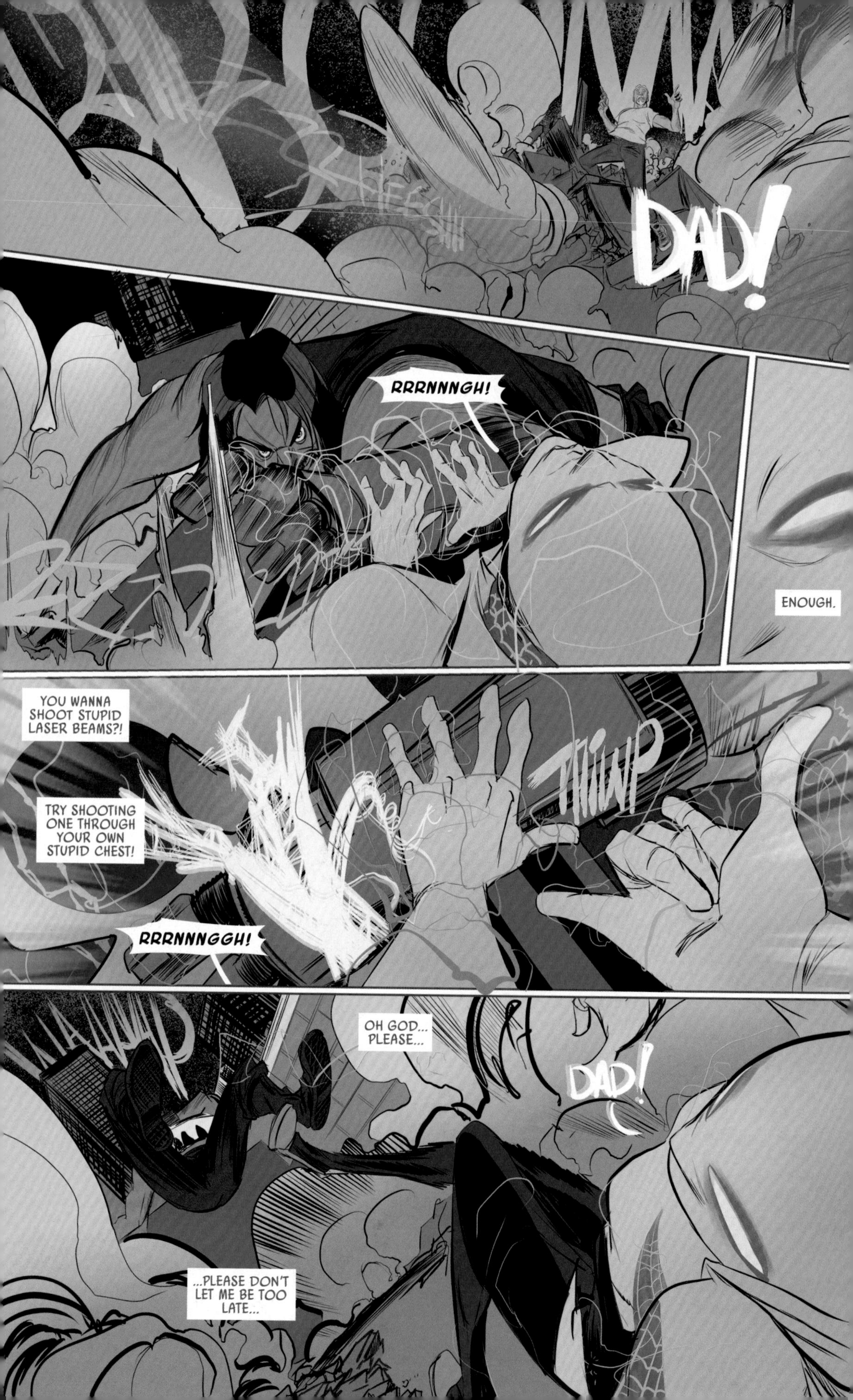

DAD!
RRRNNNGH!
ENOUGH.
YOU WANNA SHOOT STUPID LASER BEAMS?!
TRY SHOOTING ONE THROUGH YOUR OWN STUPID CHEST!
RRRNNNGGH!
OH GOD... PLEASE...
DAD!
...PLEASE DON'T LET ME BE TOO LATE...

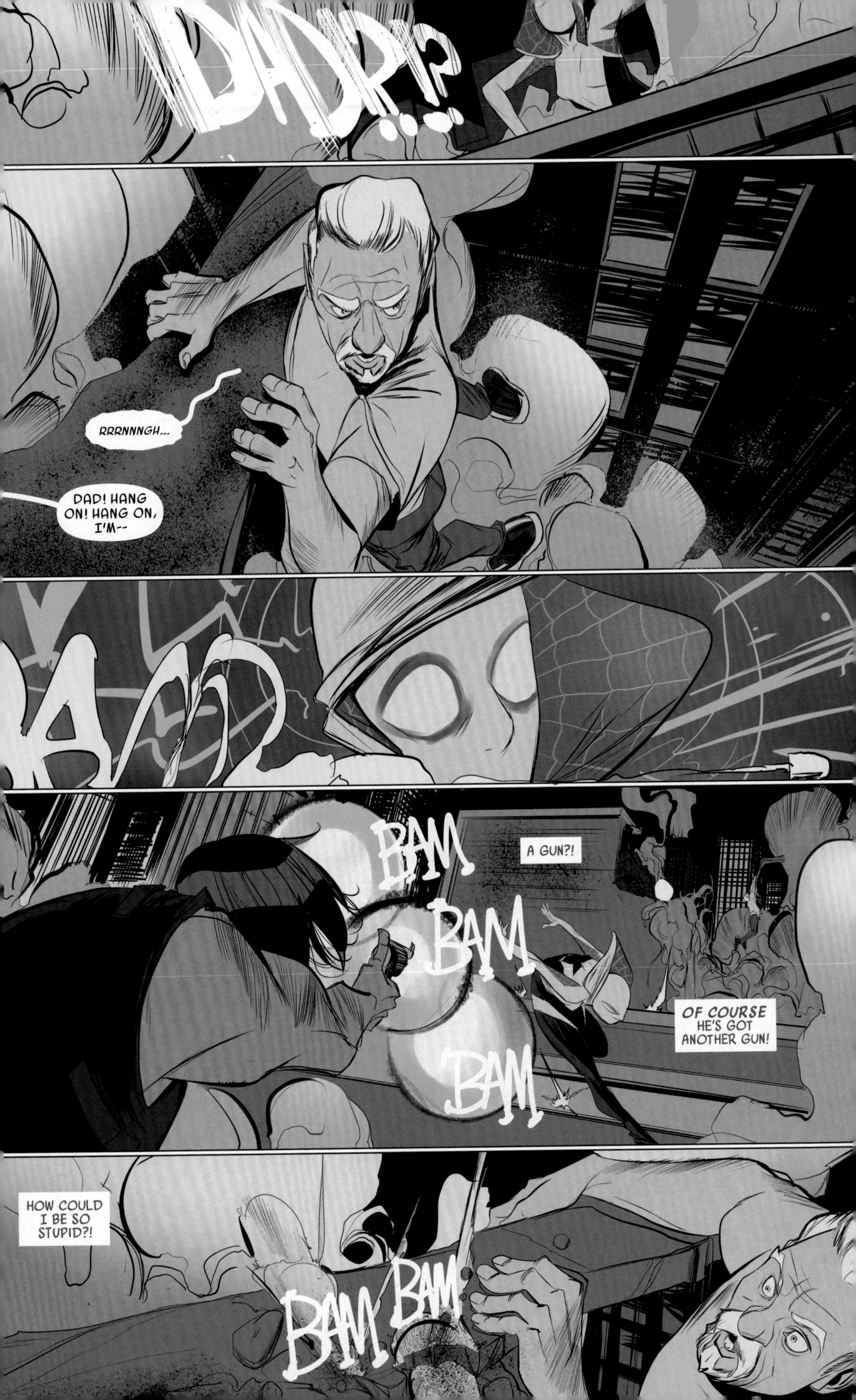
DAD?!
RRRNNNGH...
DAD! HANG ON! HANG ON, I'M--
BAM
A GUN?!
BAM
OF COURSE HE'S GOT ANOTHER GUN!
BAM
HOW COULD I BE SO STUPID?!
BAM BAM

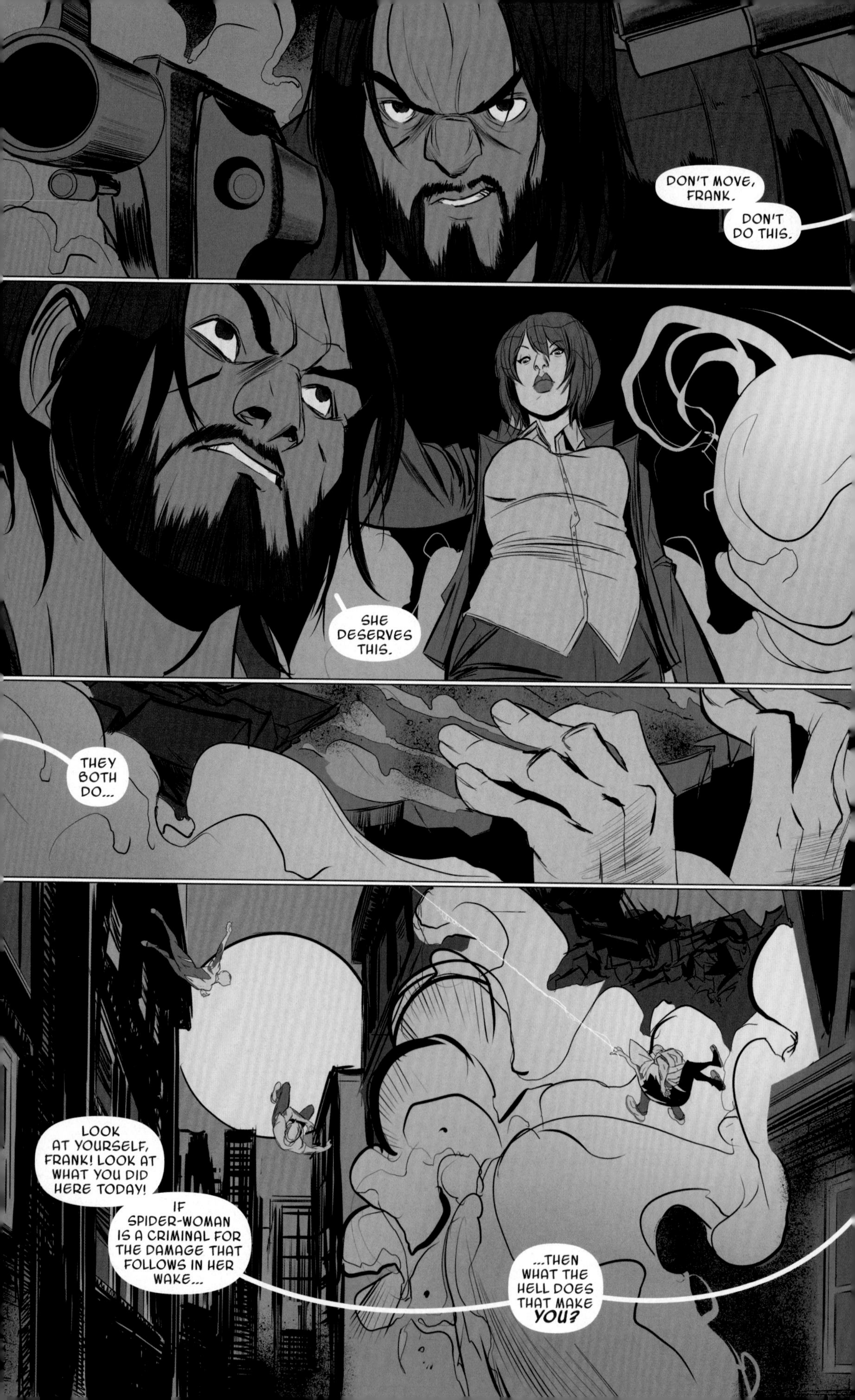
DON'T MOVE, FRANK.
DON'T DO THIS.
SHE DESERVES THIS.
THEY BOTH DO...
LOOK AT YOURSELF, FRANK! LOOK AT WHAT YOU DID HERE TODAY!
IF SPIDER-WOMAN IS A CRIMINAL FOR THE DAMAGE THAT FOLLOWS IN HER WAKE...
...THEN WHAT THE HELL DOES THAT MAKE *YOU?*

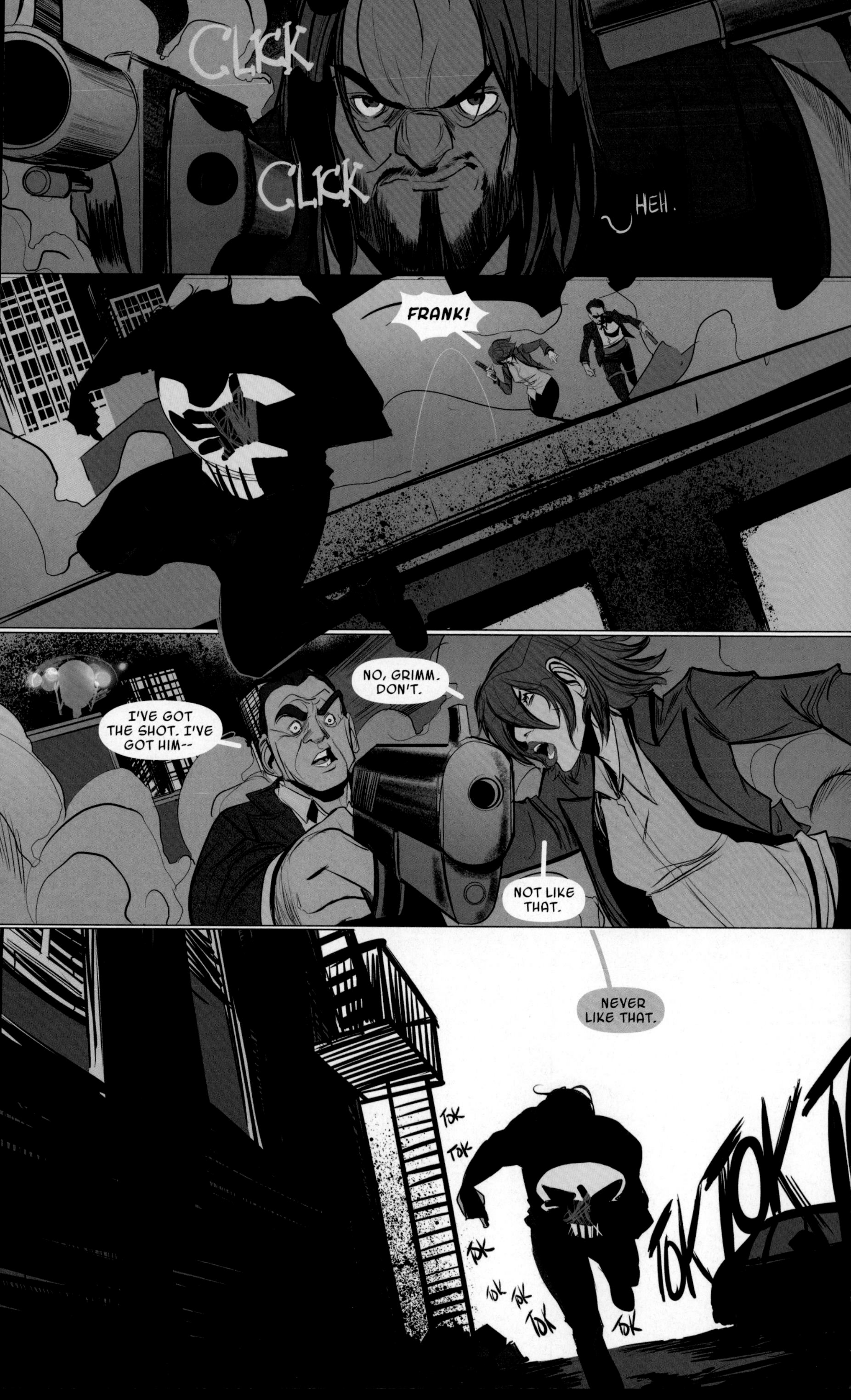
CLICK
CLICK
HEH.
FRANK!
NO, GRIMM. DON'T.
I'VE GOT THE SHOT. I'VE GOT HIM--
NOT LIKE THAT.
NEVER LIKE THAT.
TOK
TOK
TOK
TOK TOK
TOK
TOK
TOK TOK T

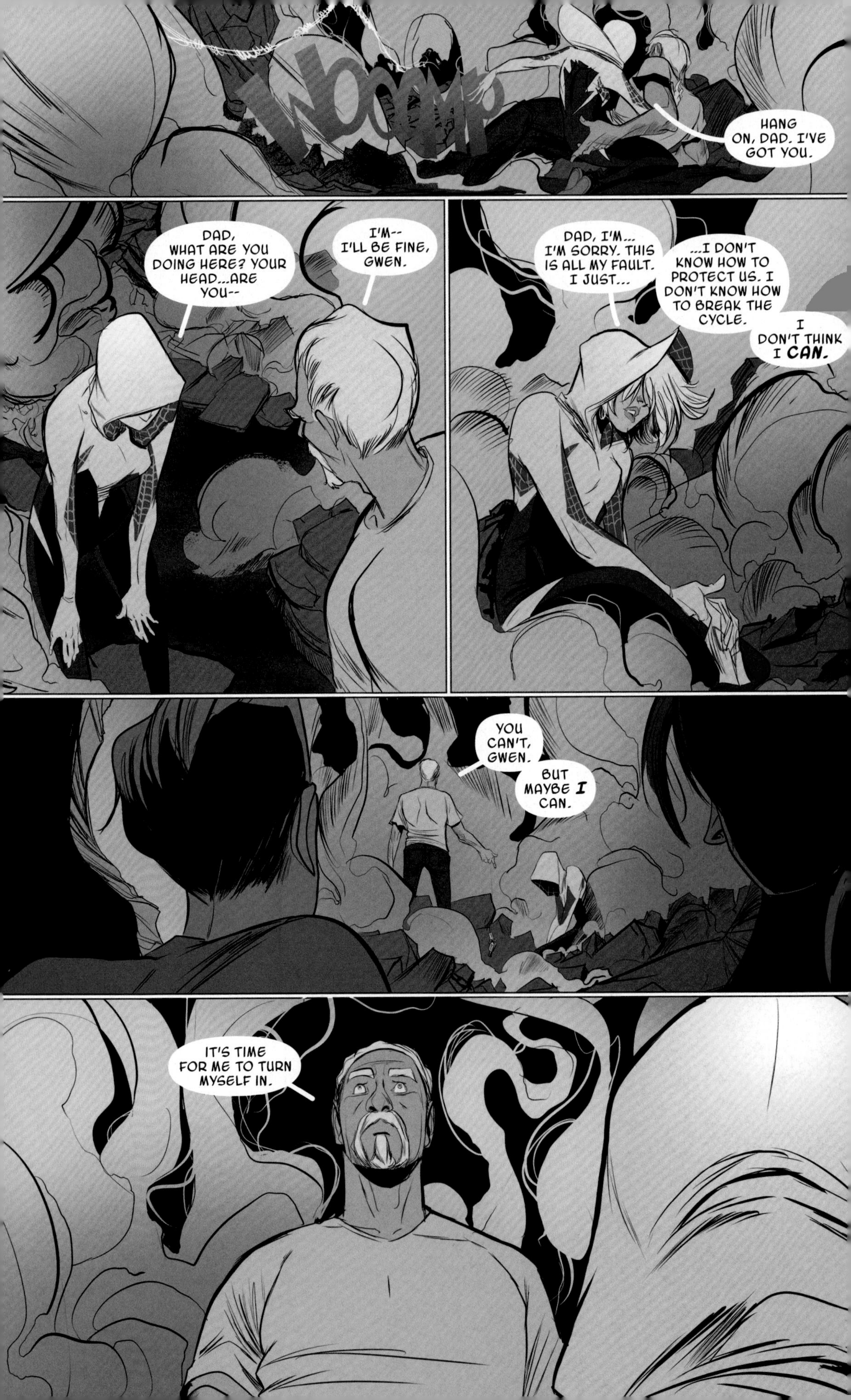
WOOMP
HANG ON, DAD. I'VE GOT YOU.
DAD, WHAT ARE YOU DOING HERE? YOUR HEAD...ARE YOU--
I'M-- I'LL BE FINE, GWEN.
DAD, I'M... I'M SORRY. THIS IS ALL MY FAULT. I JUST...
...I DON'T KNOW HOW TO PROTECT US. I DON'T KNOW HOW TO BREAK THE CYCLE.
I DON'T THINK I **CAN.**
YOU CAN'T, GWEN.
BUT MAYBE ***I*** CAN.
IT'S TIME FOR ME TO TURN MYSELF IN.

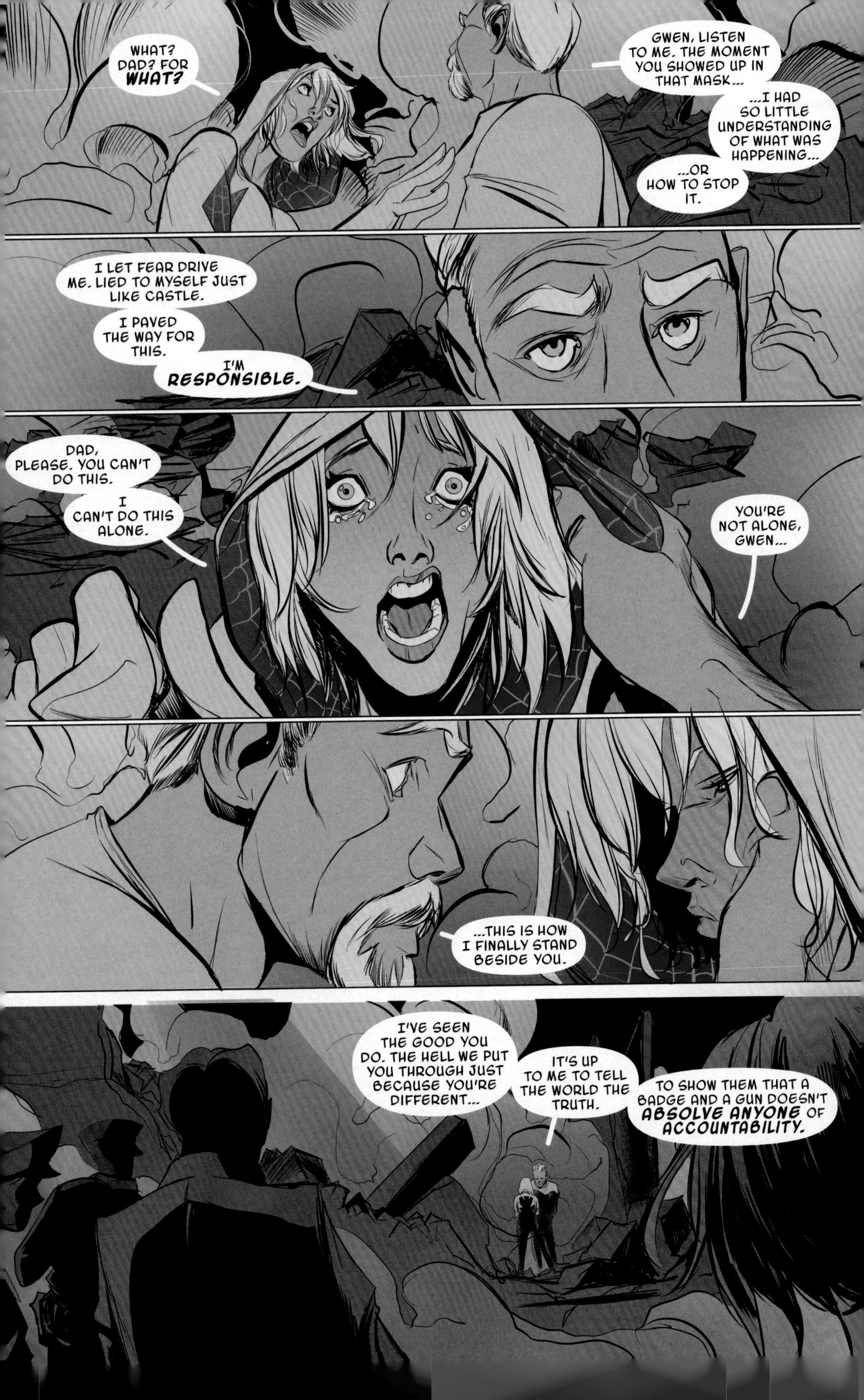
WHAT? DAD? FOR WHAT?
GWEN, LISTEN TO ME. THE MOMENT YOU SHOWED UP IN THAT MASK...
...I HAD SO LITTLE UNDERSTANDING OF WHAT WAS HAPPENING...
...OR HOW TO STOP IT.
I LET FEAR DRIVE ME. LIED TO MYSELF JUST LIKE CASTLE.
I PAVED THE WAY FOR THIS.
I'M RESPONSIBLE.
DAD, PLEASE. YOU CAN'T DO THIS.
I CAN'T DO THIS ALONE.
YOU'RE NOT ALONE, GWEN...
...THIS IS HOW I FINALLY STAND BESIDE YOU.
I'VE SEEN THE GOOD YOU DO. THE HELL WE PUT YOU THROUGH JUST BECAUSE YOU'RE DIFFERENT...
IT'S UP TO ME TO TELL THE WORLD THE TRUTH.
TO SHOW THEM THAT A BADGE AND A GUN DOESN'T ABSOLVE ANYONE OF ACCOUNTABILITY.

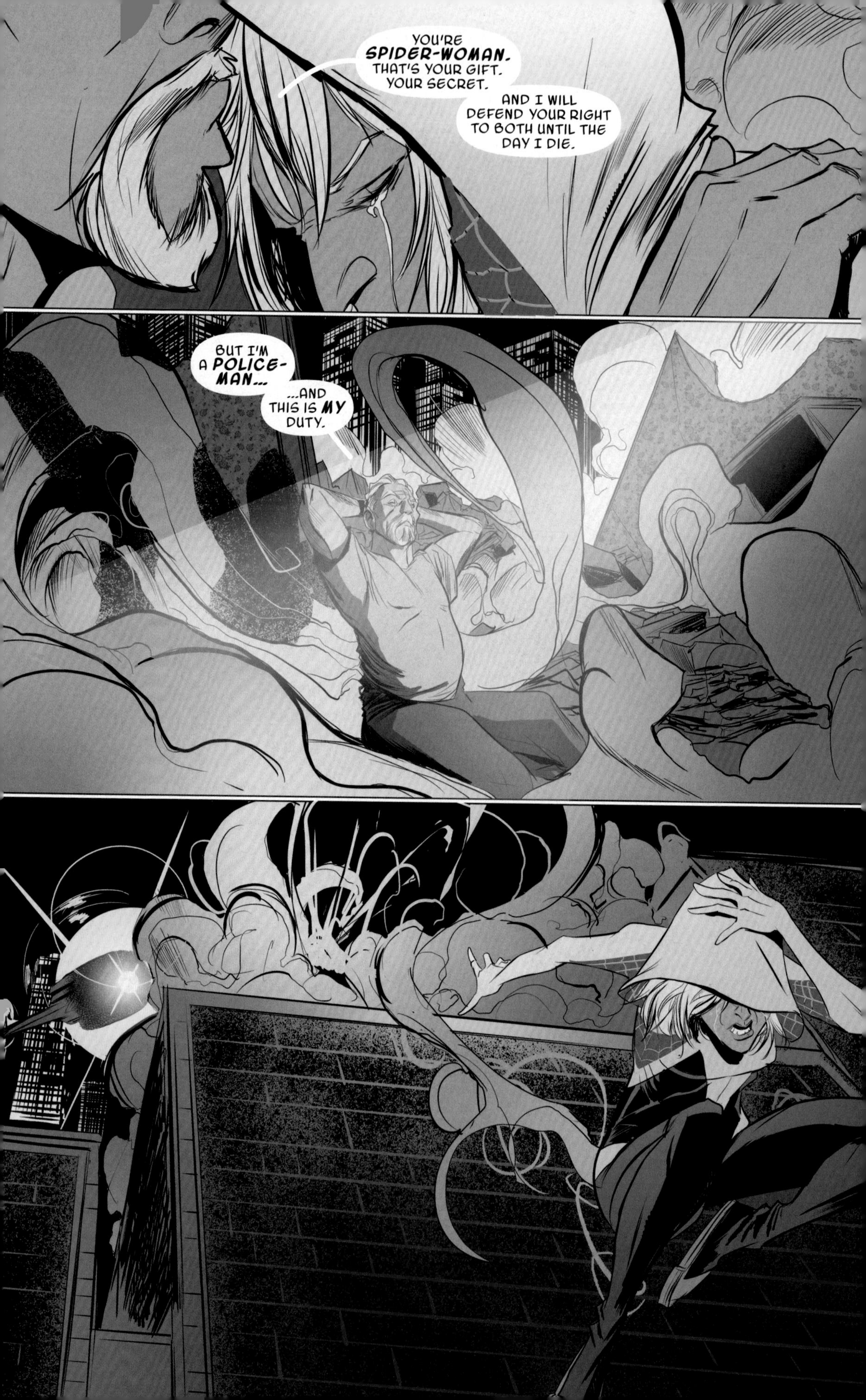
YOU'RE SPIDER-WOMAN. THAT'S YOUR GIFT. YOUR SECRET.
AND I WILL DEFEND YOUR RIGHT TO BOTH UNTIL THE DAY I DIE.
BUT I'M A POLICE-MAN...
...AND THIS IS MY DUTY.

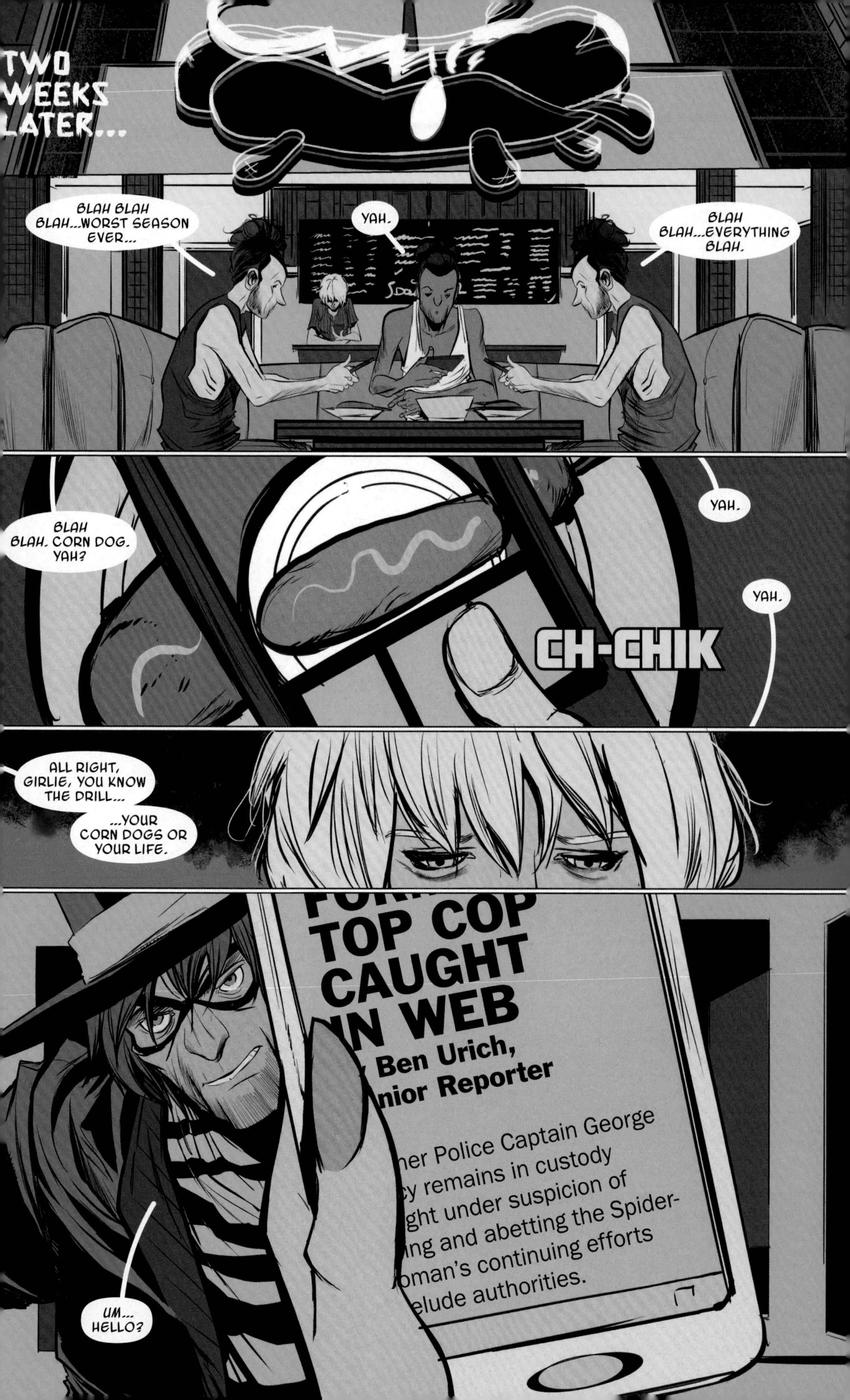
TWO WEEKS LATER...
BLAH BLAH BLAH...WORST SEASON EVER...
YAH.
BLAH BLAH...EVERYTHING BLAH.
BLAH BLAH. CORN DOG. YAH?
YAH.
YAH.
CH-CHIK
ALL RIGHT, GIRLIE, YOU KNOW THE DRILL...
...YOUR CORN DOGS OR YOUR LIFE.
TOP COP CAUGHT IN WEB
Ben Urich,
nior Reporter
her Police Captain George
cy remains in custody
ght under suspicion of
ing and abetting the Spider-
oman's continuing efforts
elude authorities.
UM... HELLO?

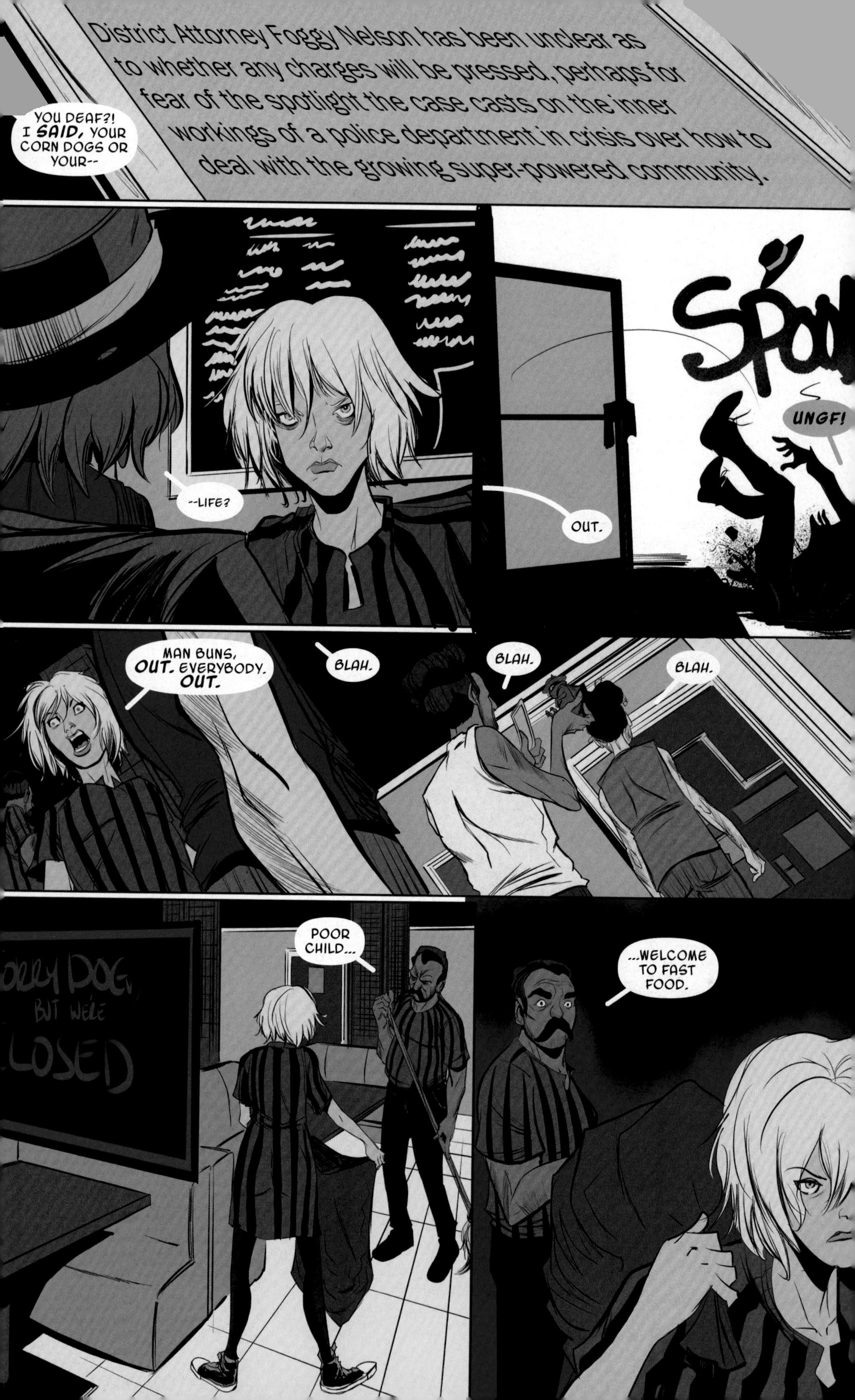
District Attorney Foggy Nelson has been unclear as to whether any charges will be pressed, perhaps for fear of the spotlight the case casts on the inner workings of a police department in crisis over how to deal with the growing super-powered community.
YOU DEAF?! I SAID, YOUR CORN DOGS OR YOUR--
--LIFE?
OUT.
UNGF!
MAN BUNS, OUT. EVERYBODY. OUT.
BLAH.
BLAH.
BLAH.
POOR CHILD...
...WELCOME TO FAST FOOD.

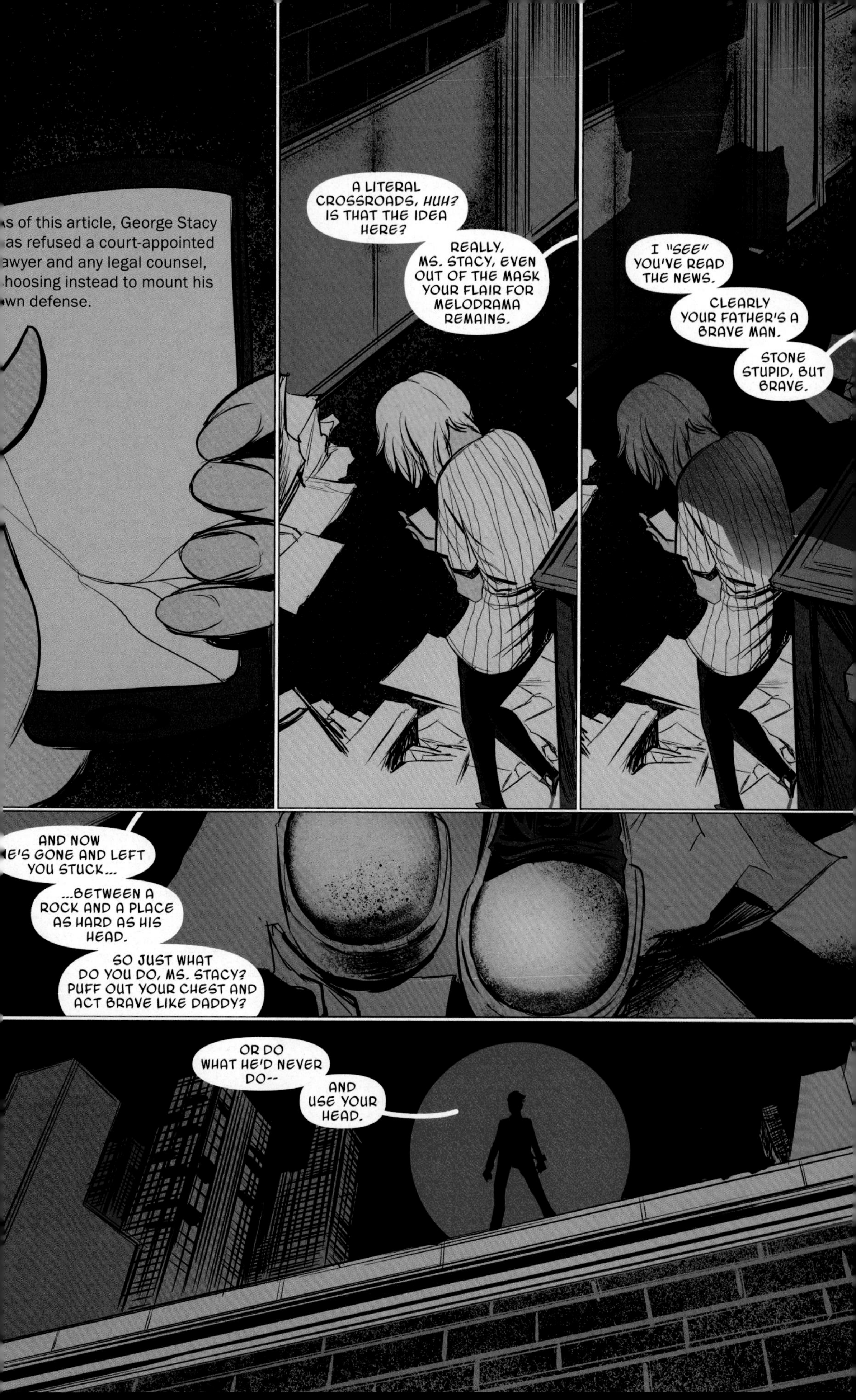

ₛs of this article, George Stacy ₐas refused a court-appointed ₐwyer and any legal counsel, ₕhoosing instead to mount his ₒwn defense.
A LITERAL CROSSROADS, HUH? IS THAT THE IDEA HERE?
REALLY, MS. STACY, EVEN OUT OF THE MASK YOUR FLAIR FOR MELODRAMA REMAINS.
I "SEE" YOU'VE READ THE NEWS.
CLEARLY YOUR FATHER'S A BRAVE MAN.
STONE STUPID, BUT BRAVE.
AND NOW HE'S GONE AND LEFT YOU STUCK...
...BETWEEN A ROCK AND A PLACE AS HARD AS HIS HEAD.
SO JUST WHAT DO YOU DO, MS. STACY? PUFF OUT YOUR CHEST AND ACT BRAVE LIKE DADDY?
OR DO WHAT HE'D NEVER DO--
AND USE YOUR HEAD.

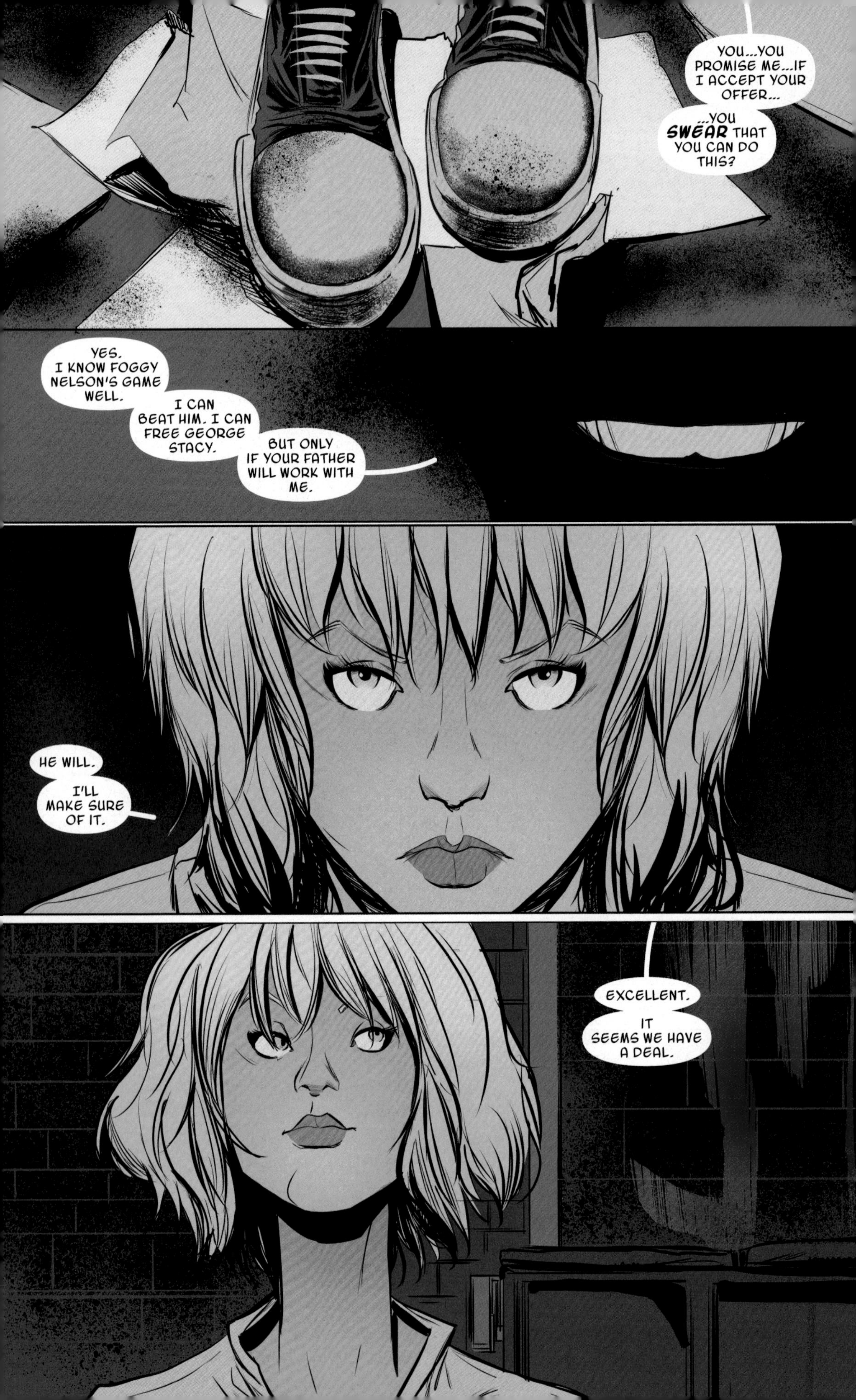

YOU...YOU PROMISE ME...IF I ACCEPT YOUR OFFER...
...YOU SWEAR THAT YOU CAN DO THIS?
YES. I KNOW FOGGY NELSON'S GAME WELL.
I CAN BEAT HIM. I CAN FREE GEORGE STACY.
BUT ONLY IF YOUR FATHER WILL WORK WITH ME.
HE WILL.
I'LL MAKE SURE OF IT.
EXCELLENT.
IT SEEMS WE HAVE A DEAL.

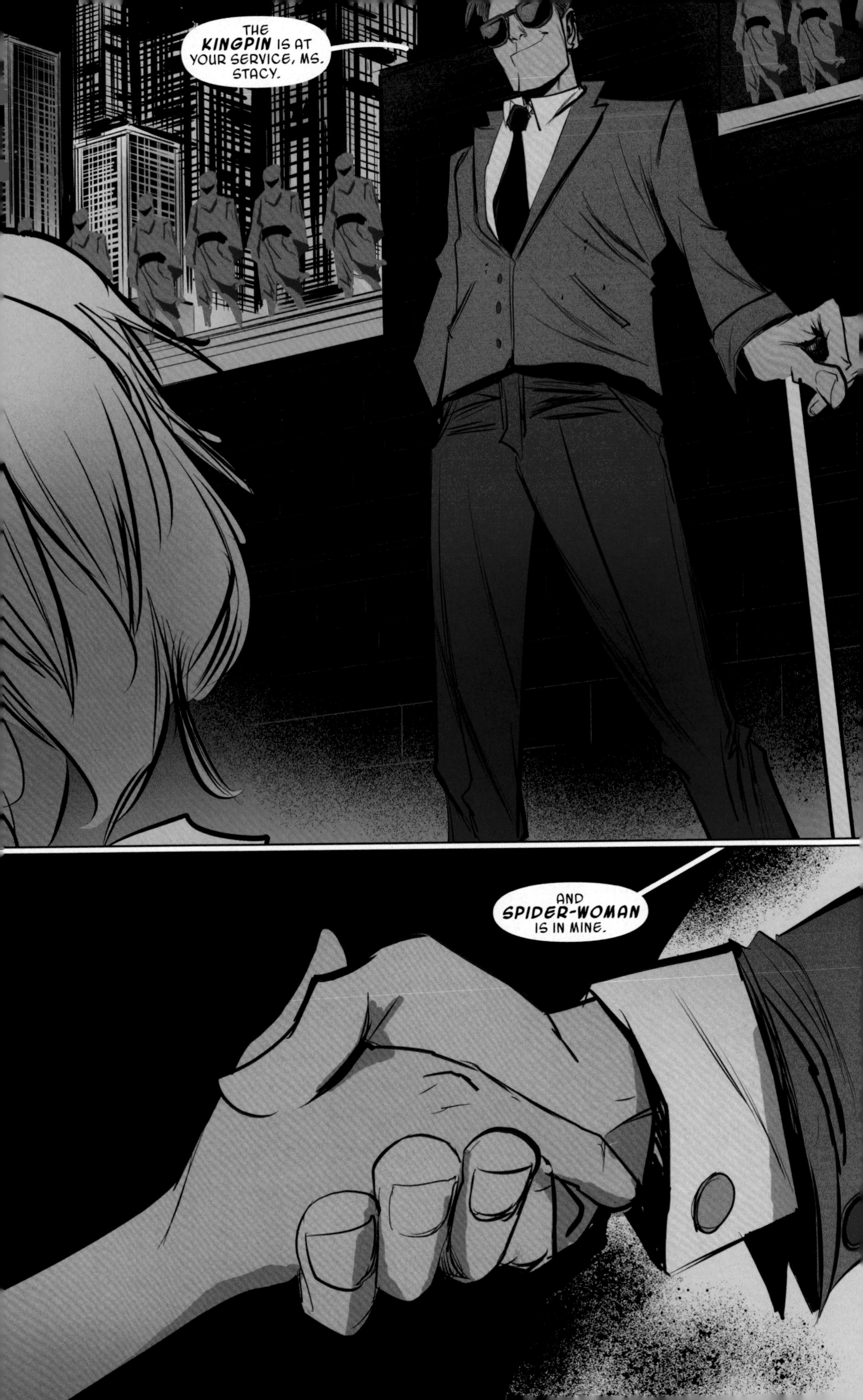
THE KINGPIN IS AT YOUR SERVICE, MS. STACY.
AND SPIDER-WOMAN IS IN MINE.

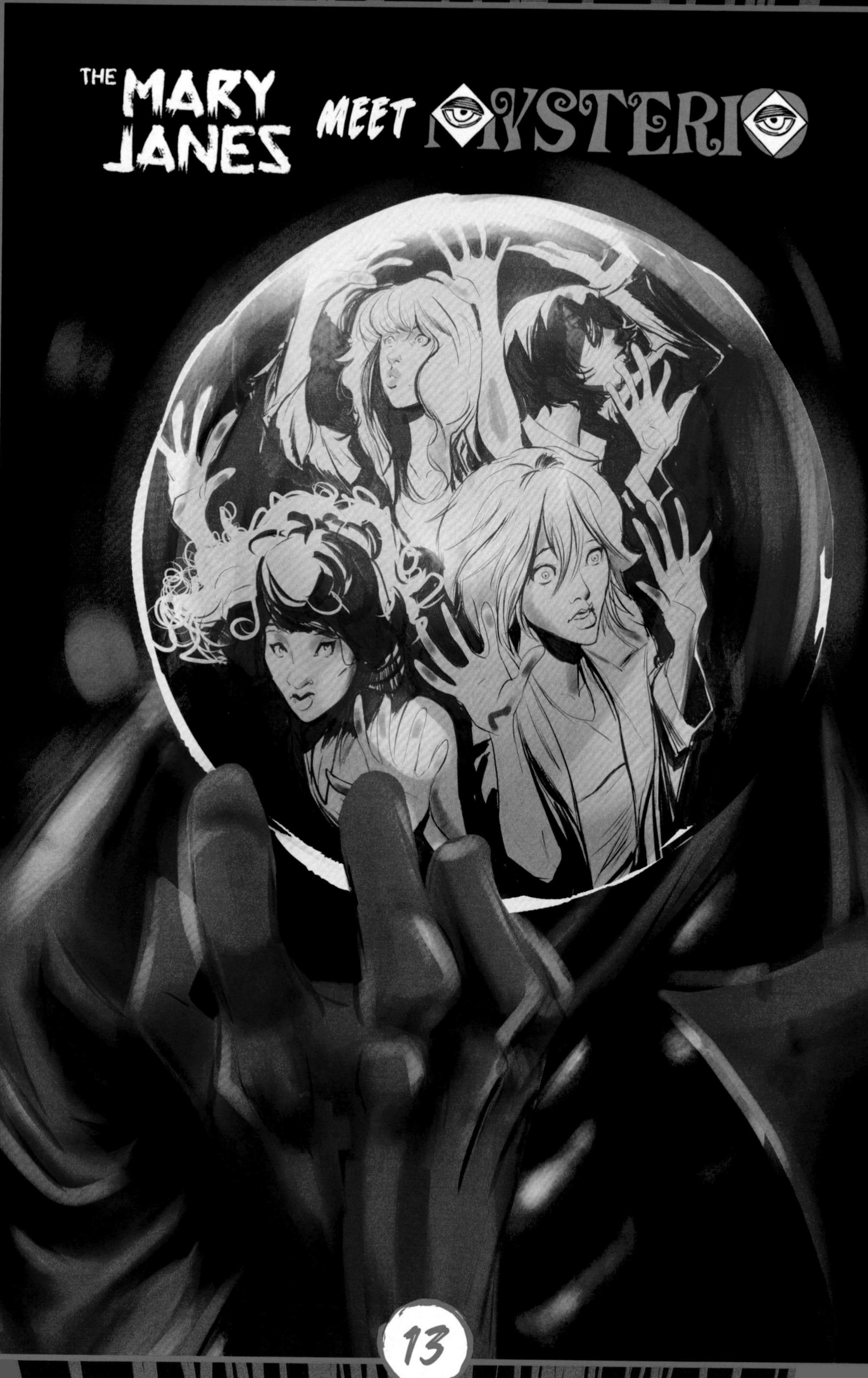
THE MARY JANES
MEET MYSTERIO

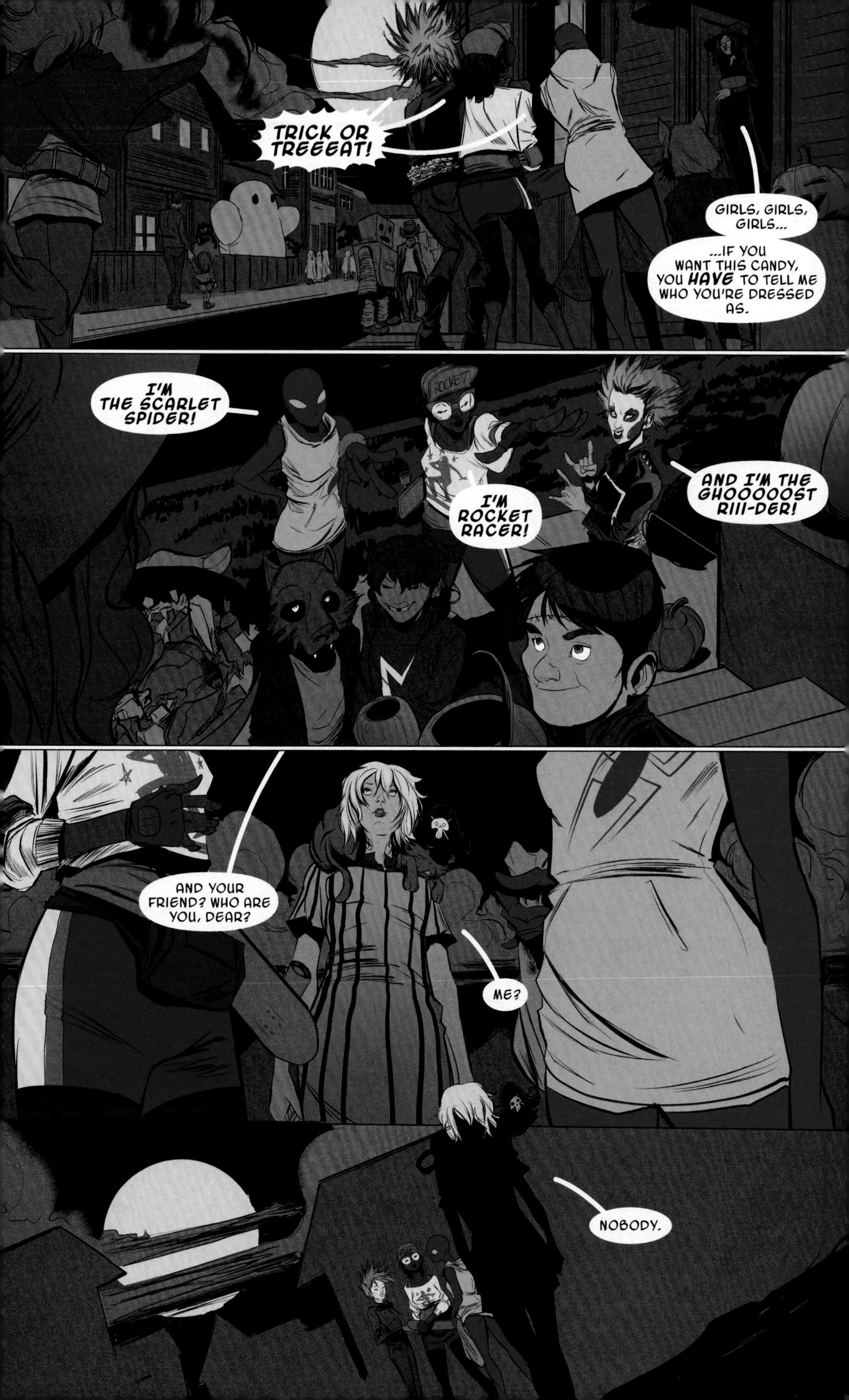
TRICK OR TREEEAT!
GIRLS, GIRLS, GIRLS...
...IF YOU WANT THIS CANDY, YOU HAVE TO TELL ME WHO YOU'RE DRESSED AS.
I'M THE SCARLET SPIDER!
I'M ROCKET RACER!
AND I'M THE GHOOOOOST RIII-DER!
AND YOUR FRIEND? WHO ARE YOU, DEAR?
ME?
NOBODY.

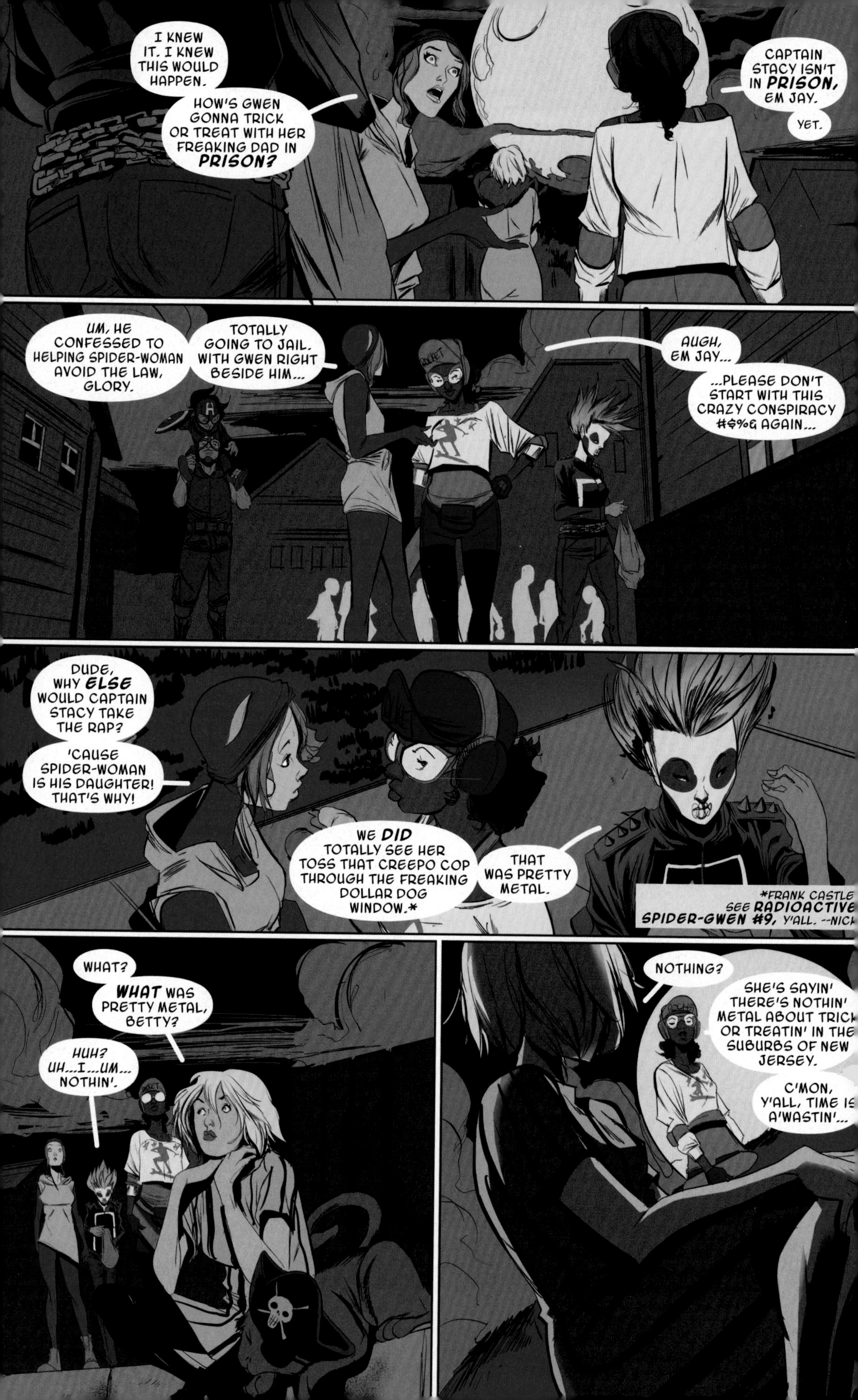
I KNEW IT. I KNEW THIS WOULD HAPPEN.
HOW'S GWEN GONNA TRICK OR TREAT WITH HER FREAKING DAD IN PRISON?
CAPTAIN STACY ISN'T IN PRISON, EM JAY.
YET.
UM, HE CONFESSED TO HELPING SPIDER-WOMAN AVOID THE LAW, GLORY.
TOTALLY GOING TO JAIL. WITH GWEN RIGHT BESIDE HIM...
AUGH, EM JAY...
...PLEASE DON'T START WITH THIS CRAZY CONSPIRACY #$%& AGAIN...
ROCKET
DUDE, WHY ELSE WOULD CAPTAIN STACY TAKE THE RAP?
'CAUSE SPIDER-WOMAN IS HIS DAUGHTER! THAT'S WHY!
WE DID TOTALLY SEE HER TOSS THAT CREEPO COP THROUGH THE FREAKING DOLLAR DOG WINDOW.*
THAT WAS PRETTY METAL.
*FRANK CASTLE SEE RADIOACTIVE SPIDER-GWEN #9, Y'ALL. --NICK
WHAT?
WHAT WAS PRETTY METAL, BETTY?
HUH? UH...I...UM... NOTHIN'.
NOTHING?
SHE'S SAYIN' THERE'S NOTHIN' METAL ABOUT TRICK OR TREATIN' IN THE SUBURBS OF NEW JERSEY.
C'MON, Y'ALL, TIME IS A'WASTIN'...

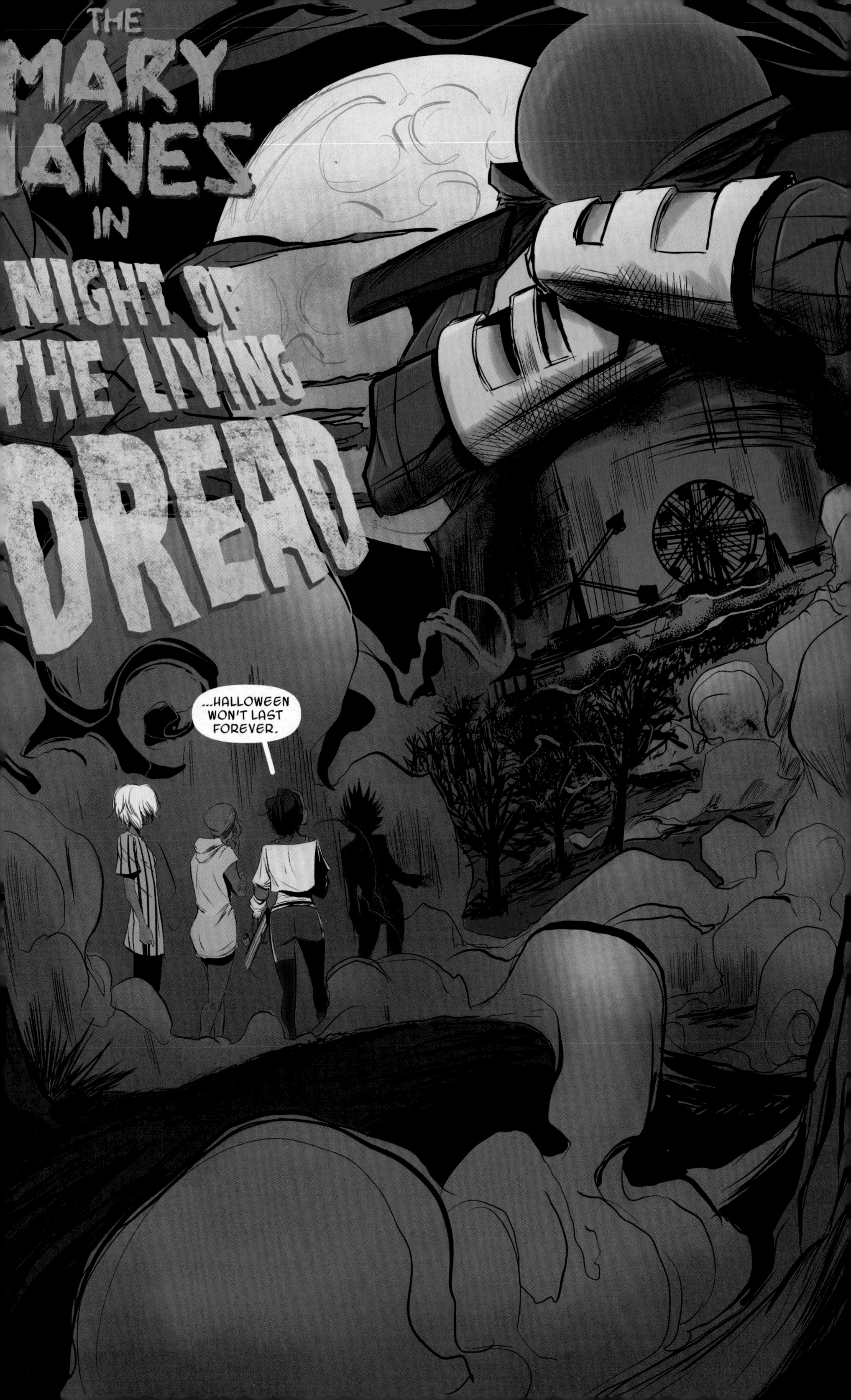
THE MARY JANES IN
NIGHT OF THE LIVING DREAD
...HALLOWEEN WON'T LAST FOREVER.

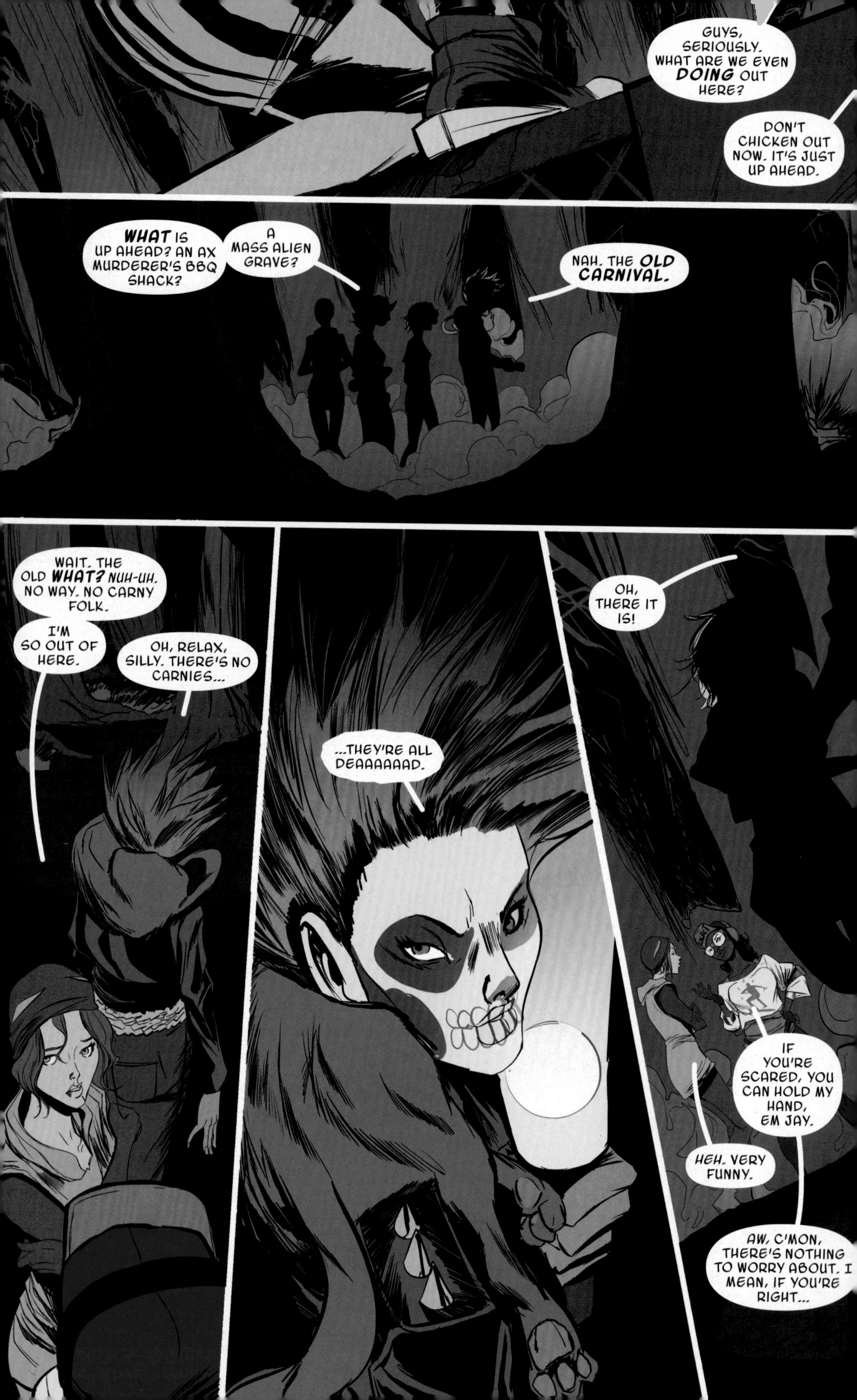
GUYS, SERIOUSLY. WHAT ARE WE EVEN DOING OUT HERE?
DON'T CHICKEN OUT NOW. IT'S JUST UP AHEAD.
WHAT IS UP AHEAD? AN AX MURDERER'S BBQ SHACK?
A MASS ALIEN GRAVE?
NAH. THE OLD CARNIVAL.
WAIT. THE OLD WHAT? NUH-UH. NO WAY. NO CARNY FOLK.
I'M SO OUT OF HERE.
OH, RELAX, SILLY. THERE'S NO CARNIES...
...THEY'RE ALL DEAAAAAAD.
OH, THERE IT IS!
IF YOU'RE SCARED, YOU CAN HOLD MY HAND, EM JAY.
HEH. VERY FUNNY.
AW, C'MON, THERE'S NOTHING TO WORRY ABOUT. I MEAN, IF YOU'RE RIGHT...

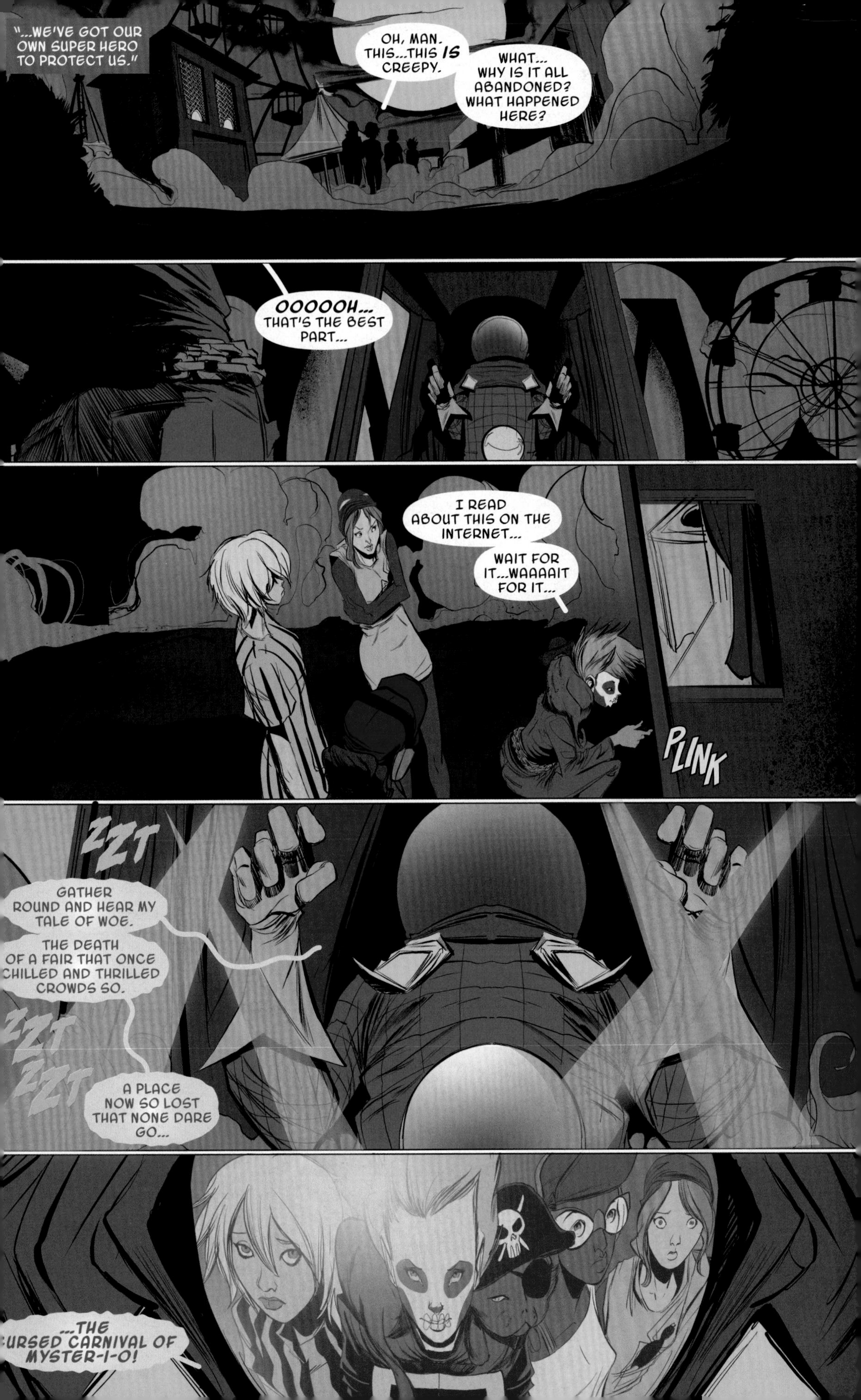
"...WE'VE GOT OUR OWN SUPER HERO TO PROTECT US."
OH, MAN. THIS...THIS IS CREEPY.
WHAT... WHY IS IT ALL ABANDONED? WHAT HAPPENED HERE?
OOOOOH... THAT'S THE BEST PART...
I READ ABOUT THIS ON THE INTERNET...
WAIT FOR IT...WAAAAIT FOR IT...
PLINK
ZZT
GATHER ROUND AND HEAR MY TALE OF WOE.
THE DEATH OF A FAIR THAT ONCE CHILLED AND THRILLED CROWDS SO.
ZZT ZZT
A PLACE NOW SO LOST THAT NONE DARE GO...
...THE CURSED CARNIVAL OF MYSTER-I-O!

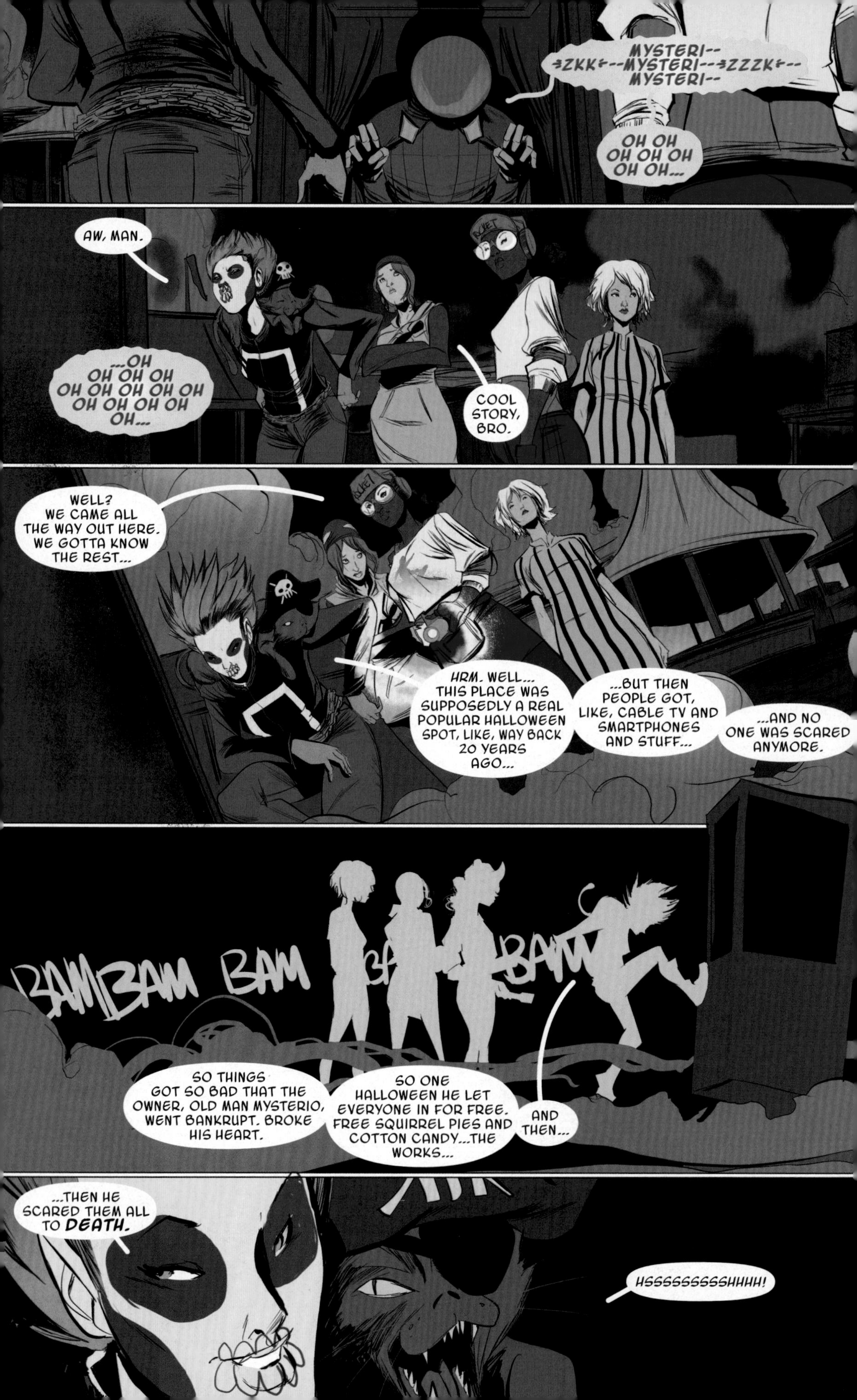

MYSTERI-- ZKK --MYSTERI-- ZZZK -- MYSTERI--
OH OH OH OH OH OH OH...
AW, MAN.
...OH OH OH OH OH OH OH OH OH OH OH OH OH OH...
COOL STORY, BRO.
WELL? WE CAME ALL THE WAY OUT HERE. WE GOTTA KNOW THE REST...
HRM. WELL... THIS PLACE WAS SUPPOSEDLY A REAL POPULAR HALLOWEEN SPOT, LIKE, WAY BACK 20 YEARS AGO...
...BUT THEN PEOPLE GOT, LIKE, CABLE TV AND SMARTPHONES AND STUFF...
...AND NO ONE WAS SCARED ANYMORE.
BAM BAM BAM BAM
SO THINGS GOT SO BAD THAT THE OWNER, OLD MAN MYSTERIO, WENT BANKRUPT. BROKE HIS HEART.
SO ONE HALLOWEEN HE LET EVERYONE IN FOR FREE. FREE SQUIRREL PIES AND COTTON CANDY...THE WORKS...
AND THEN...
...THEN HE SCARED THEM ALL TO DEATH.
HSSSSSSSSSHHHH!

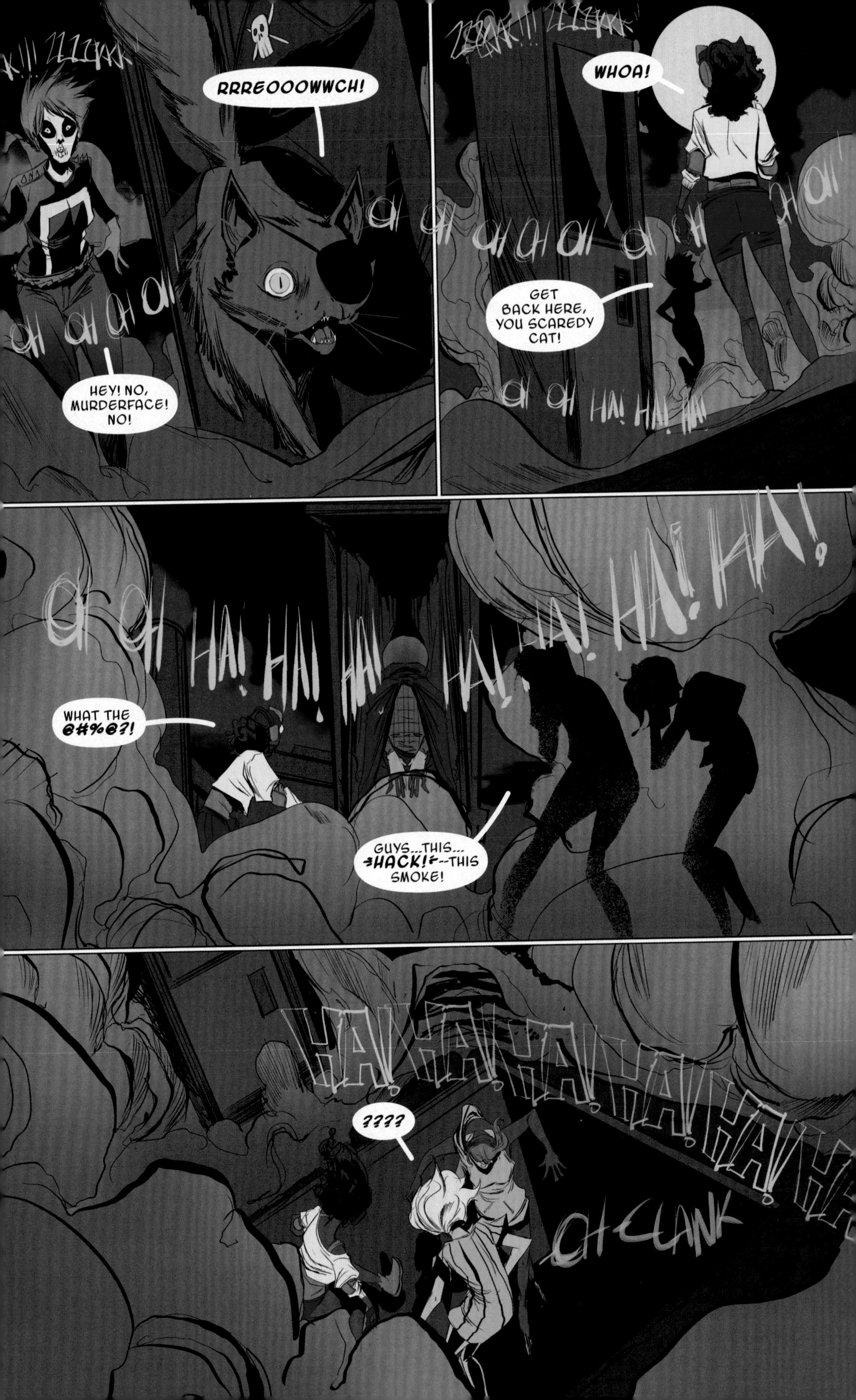
RRREOOOWWCH!
HEY! NO, MURDERFACE! NO!
WHOA!
GET BACK HERE, YOU SCAREDY CAT!
WHAT THE @#%@?!
GUYS...THIS... HACK! --THIS SMOKE!
????
CH CLANK

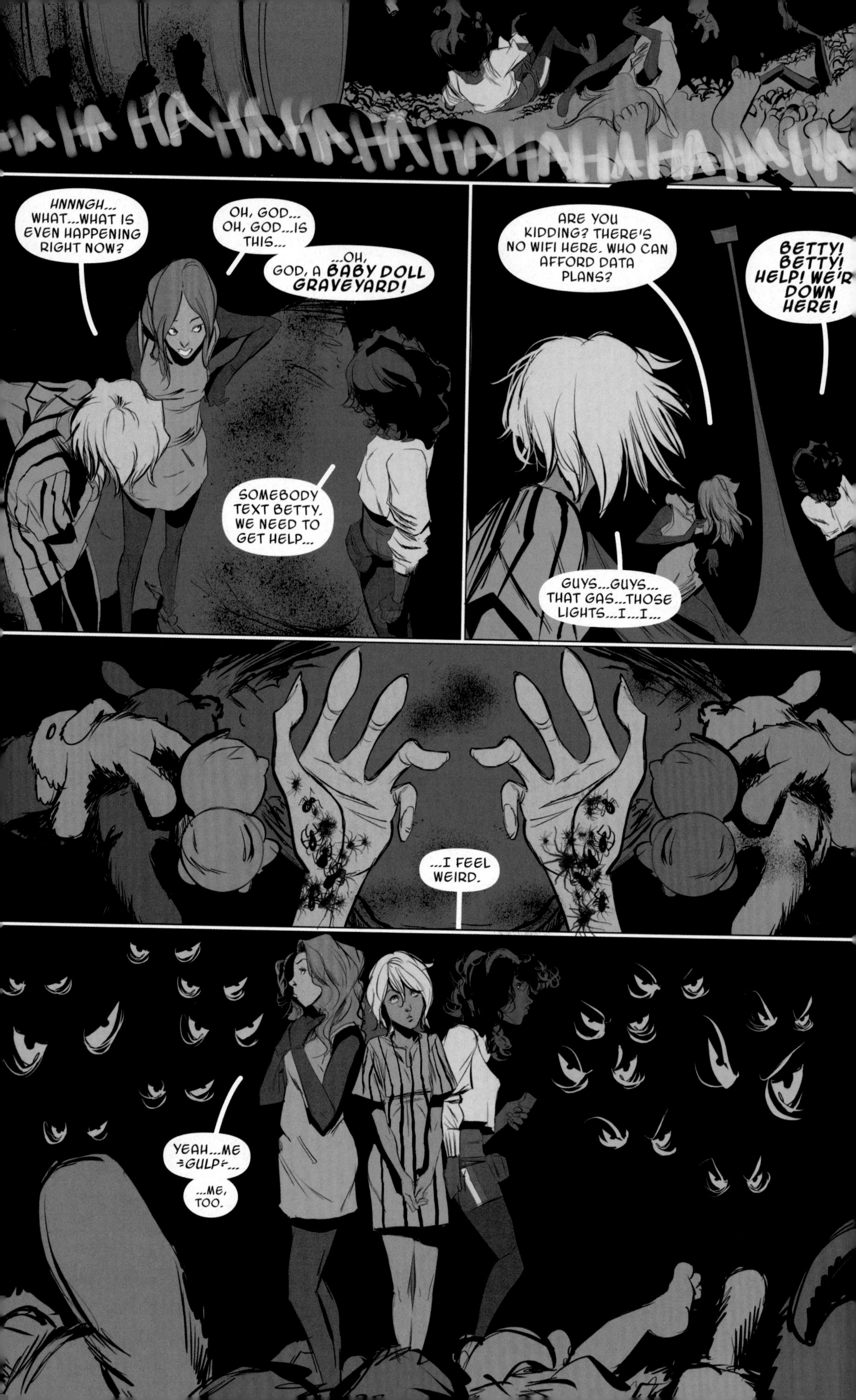
HAHAHAHAHAHAHAHAHAHAHAHAHA
HNNNGH... WHAT...WHAT IS EVEN HAPPENING RIGHT NOW?
OH, GOD... OH, GOD...IS THIS...
...OH, GOD, A BABY DOLL GRAVEYARD!
SOMEBODY TEXT BETTY. WE NEED TO GET HELP...
ARE YOU KIDDING? THERE'S NO WIFI HERE. WHO CAN AFFORD DATA PLANS?
BETTY! BETTY! HELP! WE'R DOWN HERE!
GUYS...GUYS... THAT GAS...THOSE LIGHTS...I...I...
...I FEEL WEIRD.
YEAH...ME =GULP=...
...ME, TOO.

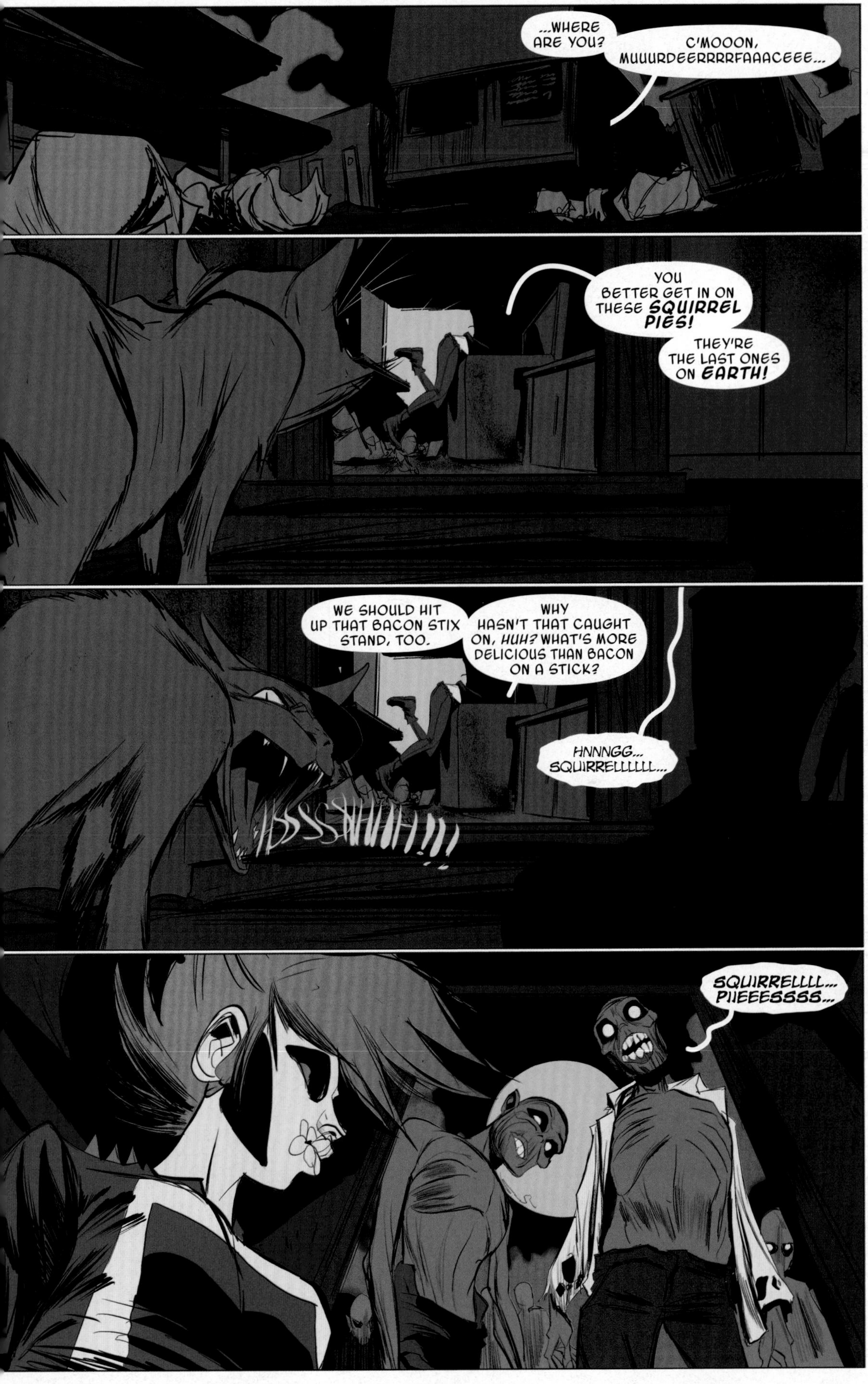
...WHERE ARE YOU?
C'MOOON, MUUURDEERRRRFAAACEEE...
YOU BETTER GET IN ON THESE SQUIRREL PIES!
THEY'RE THE LAST ONES ON EARTH!
WE SHOULD HIT UP THAT BACON STIX STAND, TOO.
WHY HASN'T THAT CAUGHT ON, HUH? WHAT'S MORE DELICIOUS THAN BACON ON A STICK?
HNNNGG... SQUIRRELLLLLLL...
HSSSSWHHH!!!
SQUIRRELLLL... PIIEEESSSS...

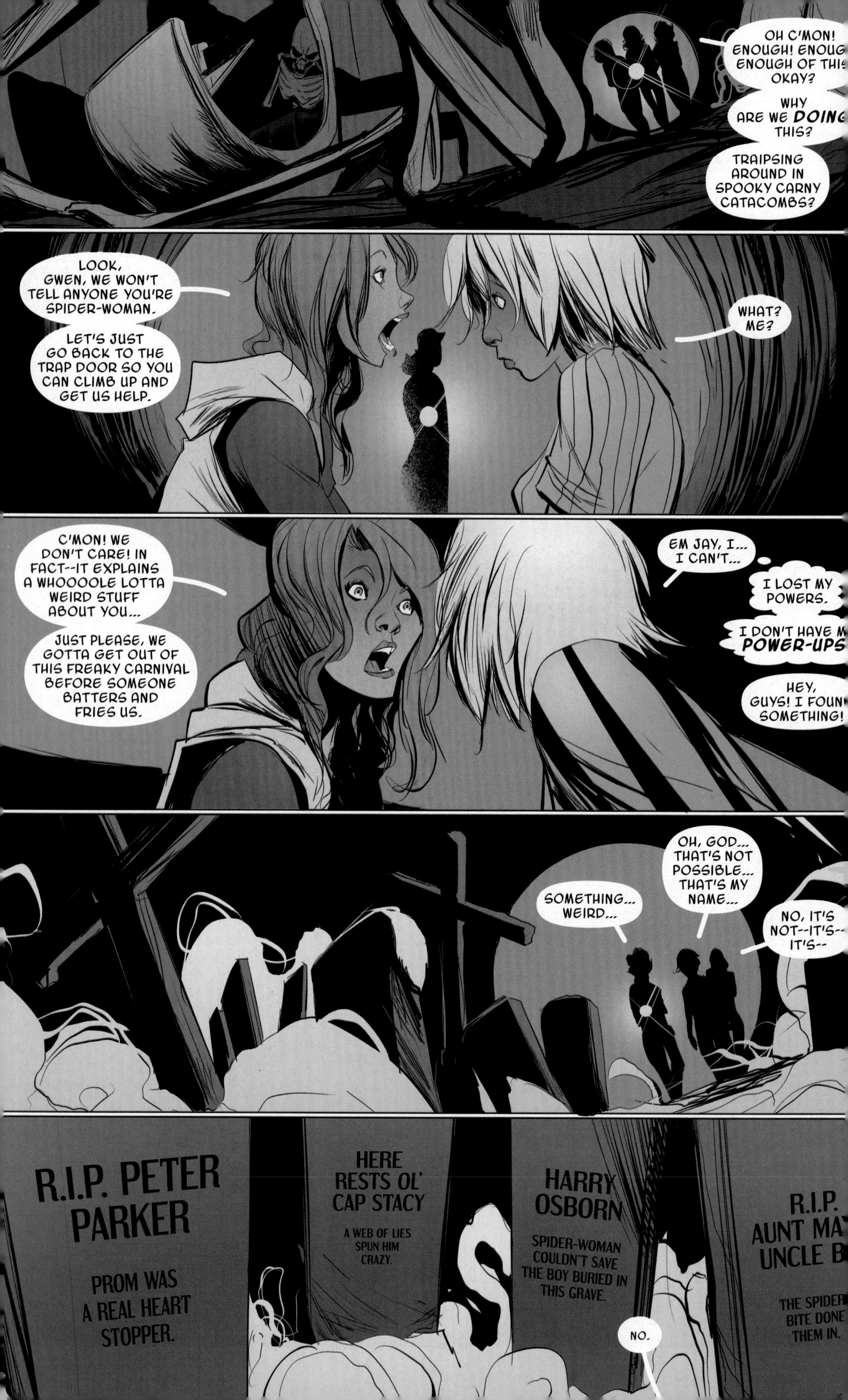
OH C'MON! ENOUGH! ENOUG ENOUGH OF THIS OKAY?
WHY ARE WE DOING THIS?
TRAIPSING AROUND IN SPOOKY CARNY CATACOMBS?
LOOK, GWEN, WE WON'T TELL ANYONE YOU'RE SPIDER-WOMAN.
LET'S JUST GO BACK TO THE TRAP DOOR SO YOU CAN CLIMB UP AND GET US HELP.
WHAT? ME?
C'MON! WE DON'T CARE! IN FACT--IT EXPLAINS A WHOOOOLE LOTTA WEIRD STUFF ABOUT YOU...
JUST PLEASE, WE GOTTA GET OUT OF THIS FREAKY CARNIVAL BEFORE SOMEONE BATTERS AND FRIES US.
EM JAY, I... I CAN'T...
I LOST MY POWERS.
I DON'T HAVE M POWER-UPS
HEY, GUYS! I FOUN SOMETHING!
SOMETHING... WEIRD...
OH, GOD... THAT'S NOT POSSIBLE... THAT'S MY NAME...
NO, IT'S NOT--IT'S-- IT'S--
R.I.P. PETER PARKER
PROM WAS A REAL HEART STOPPER.
HERE RESTS OL' CAP STACY
A WEB OF LIES SPUN HIM CRAZY.
HARRY OSBORN
SPIDER-WOMAN COULDN'T SAVE THE BOY BURIED IN THIS GRAVE.
R.I.P. AUNT MA UNCLE B
THE SPIDER BITE DONE THEM IN.
NO.

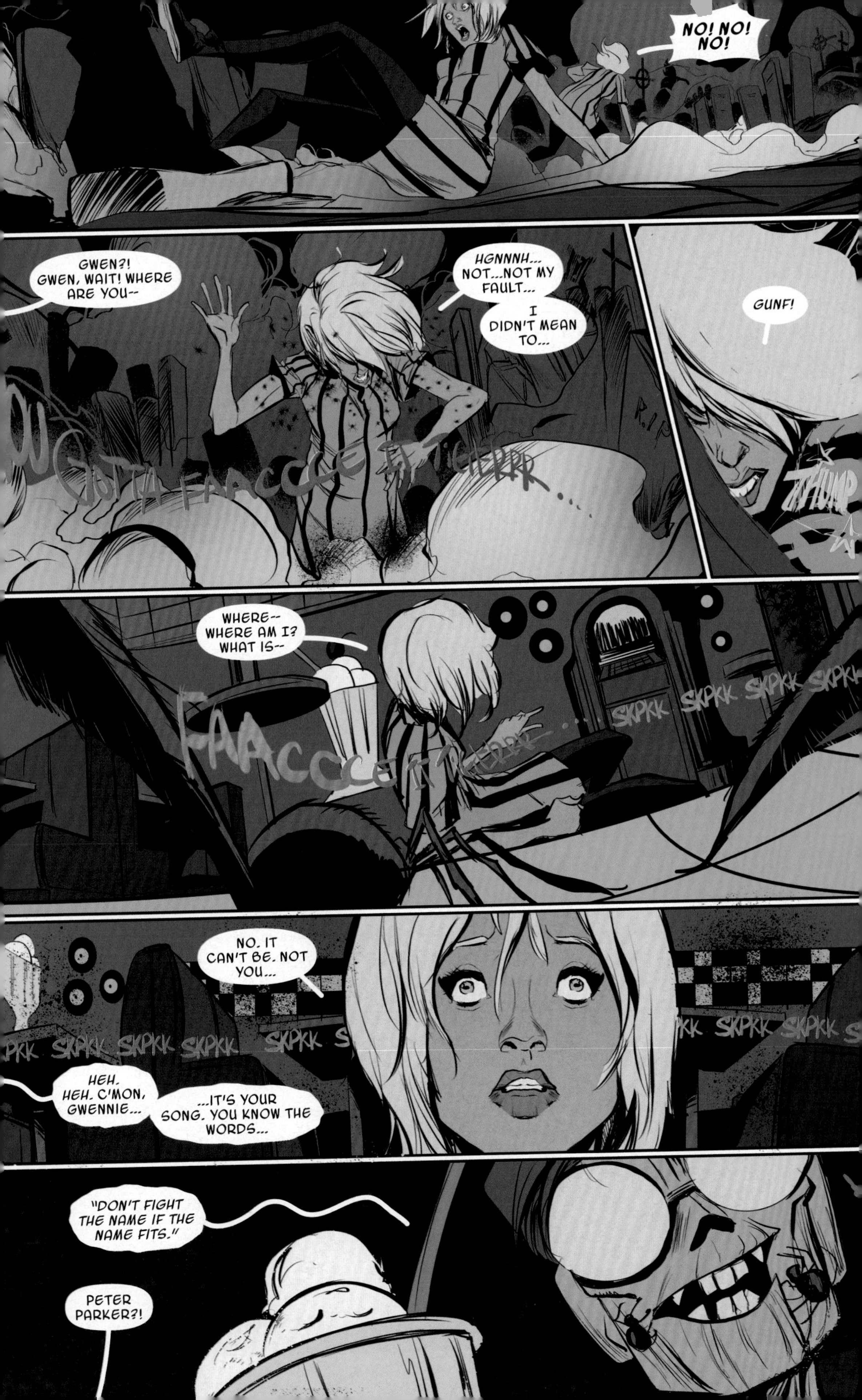
NO! NO! NO!
GWEN?! GWEN, WAIT! WHERE ARE YOU--
HGNNNH... NOT...NOT MY FAULT...
I DIDN'T MEAN TO...
GOTTA FAACCCE IT TIGERRR...
GUNF!
THUMP
WHERE-- WHERE AM I? WHAT IS--
FAACCCE IT TIGERRR...
SKPKK SKPKK SKPKK SKPKK
NO. IT CAN'T BE. NOT YOU...
SKPKK SKPKK SKPKK SKPKK
HEH. HEH. C'MON, GWENNIE...
...IT'S YOUR SONG. YOU KNOW THE WORDS...
"DON'T FIGHT THE NAME IF THE NAME FITS."
PETER PARKER?!

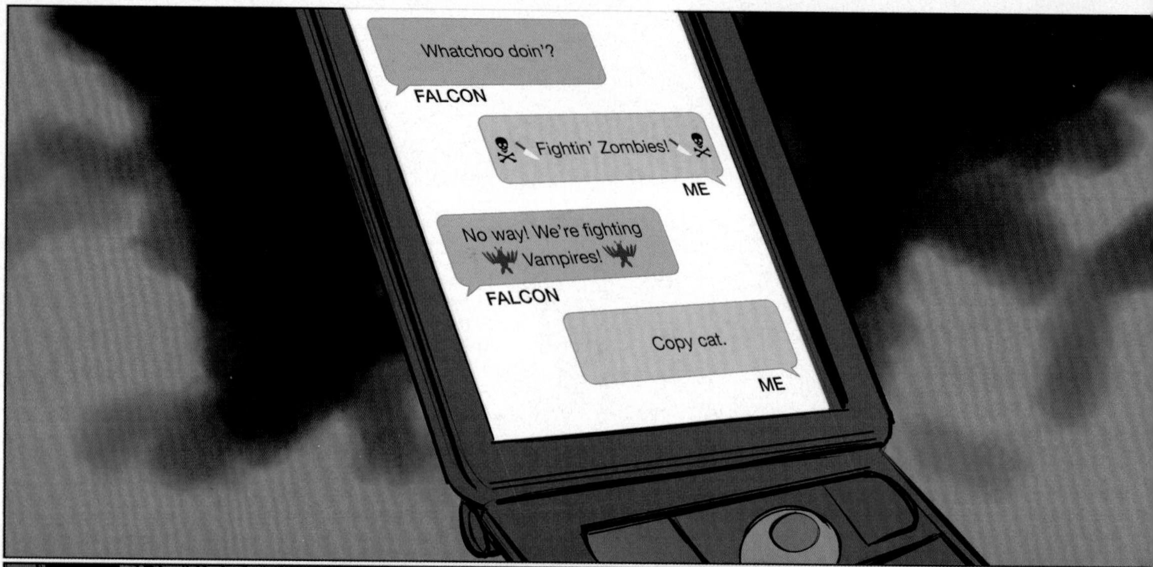
Whatchoo doin'?
FALCON
Fightin' Zombies!
ME
No way! We're fighting Vampires!
FALCON
Copy cat.
ME

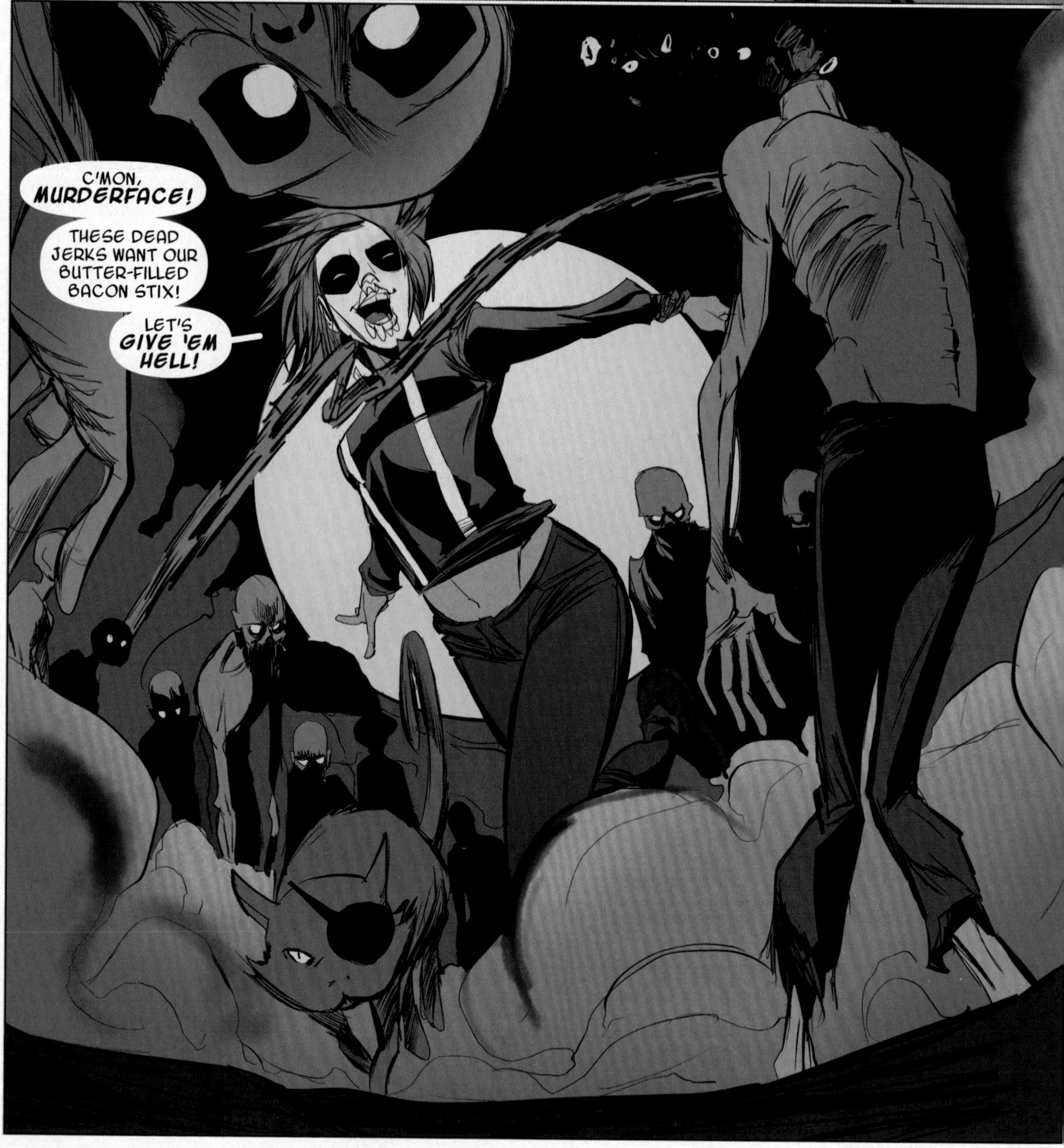
C'MON, MURDERFACE!
THESE DEAD JERKS WANT OUR BUTTER-FILLED BACON STIX!
LET'S GIVE 'EM HELL!

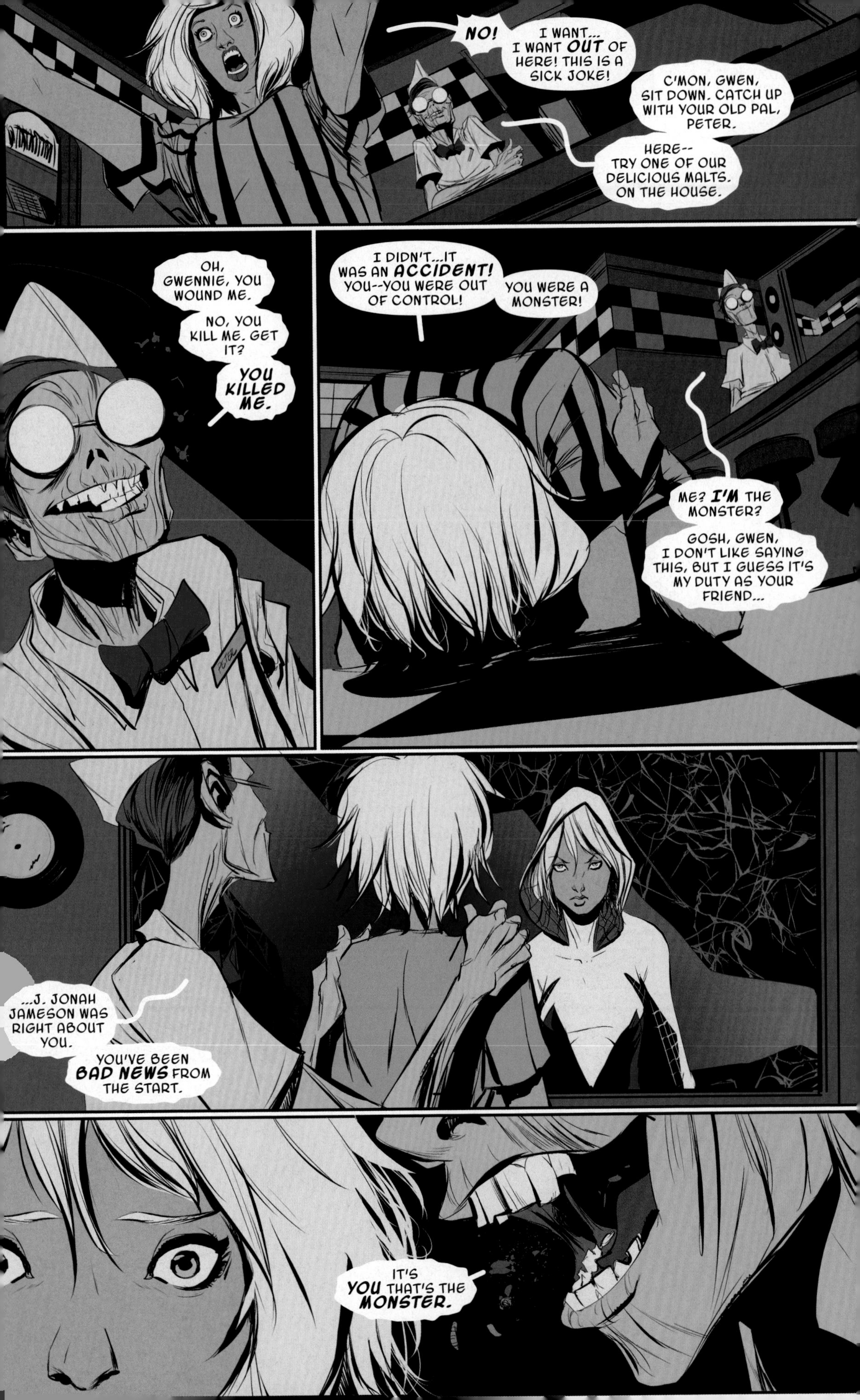
NO!
I WANT... I WANT OUT OF HERE! THIS IS A SICK JOKE!
C'MON, GWEN, SIT DOWN. CATCH UP WITH YOUR OLD PAL, PETER.
HERE-- TRY ONE OF OUR DELICIOUS MALTS. ON THE HOUSE.
OH, GWENNIE, YOU WOUND ME.
NO, YOU KILL ME. GET IT?
YOU KILLED ME.
I DIDN'T...IT WAS AN ACCIDENT! YOU--YOU WERE OUT OF CONTROL!
YOU WERE A MONSTER!
ME? I'M THE MONSTER?
GOSH, GWEN, I DON'T LIKE SAYING THIS, BUT I GUESS IT'S MY DUTY AS YOUR FRIEND...
...J. JONAH JAMESON WAS RIGHT ABOUT YOU.
YOU'VE BEEN BAD NEWS FROM THE START.
IT'S YOU THAT'S THE MONSTER.

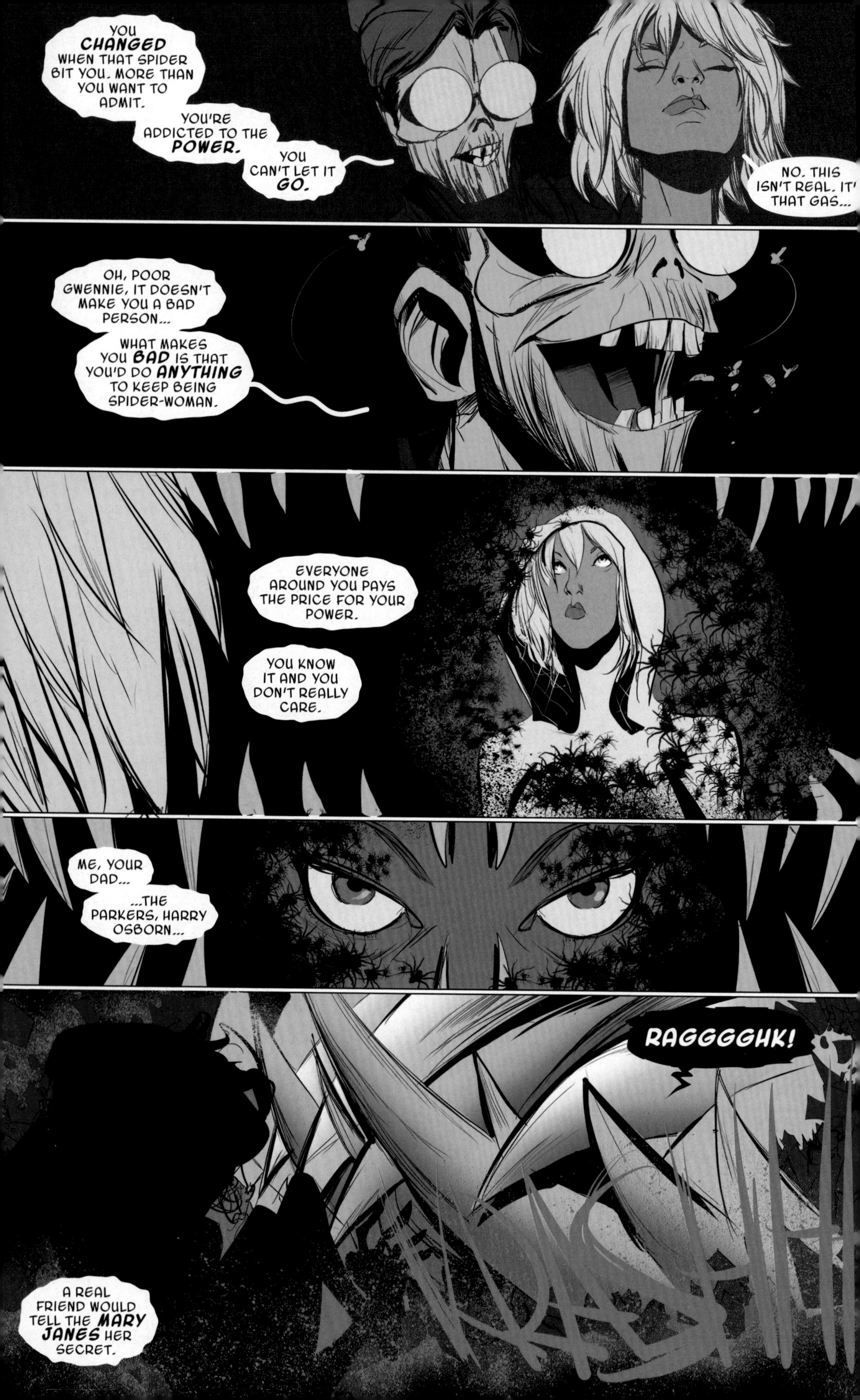
YOU CHANGED WHEN THAT SPIDER BIT YOU. MORE THAN YOU WANT TO ADMIT.
YOU'RE ADDICTED TO THE POWER.
YOU CAN'T LET IT GO.
NO. THIS ISN'T REAL. IT' THAT GAS...
OH, POOR GWENNIE, IT DOESN'T MAKE YOU A BAD PERSON...
WHAT MAKES YOU BAD IS THAT YOU'D DO ANYTHING TO KEEP BEING SPIDER-WOMAN.
EVERYONE AROUND YOU PAYS THE PRICE FOR YOUR POWER.
YOU KNOW IT AND YOU DON'T REALLY CARE.
ME, YOUR DAD...
...THE PARKERS, HARRY OSBORN...
RAGGGGHK!
A REAL FRIEND WOULD TELL THE MARY JANES HER SECRET.

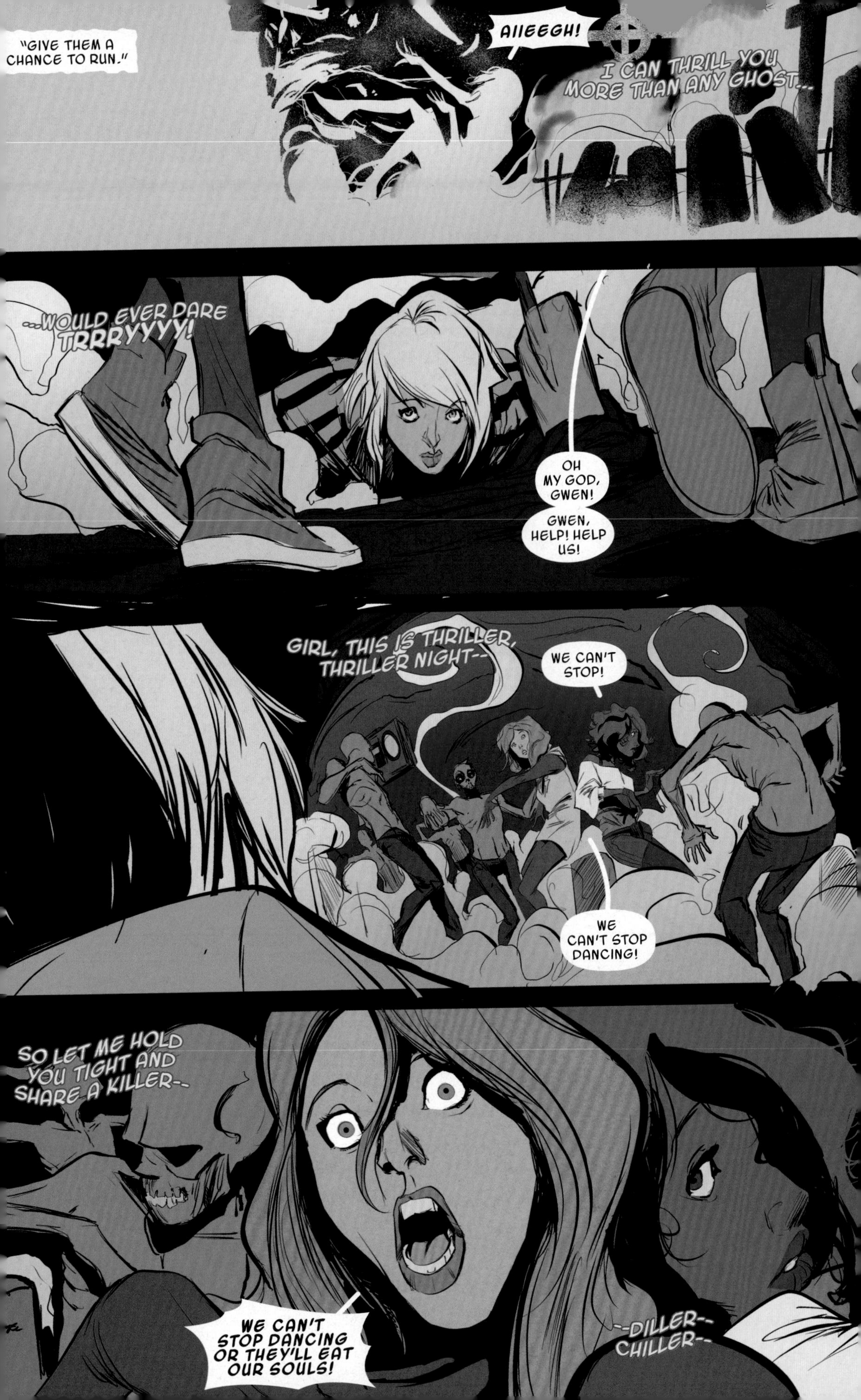
"GIVE THEM A CHANCE TO RUN."
AIIEEGH!
I CAN THRILL YOU MORE THAN ANY GHOST...
...WOULD EVER DARE TRRRYYYY!
OH MY GOD, GWEN!
GWEN, HELP! HELP US!
GIRL, THIS IS THRILLER, THRILLER NIGHT--
WE CAN'T STOP!
WE CAN'T STOP DANCING!
SO LET ME HOLD YOU TIGHT AND SHARE A KILLER--
WE CAN'T STOP DANCING OR THEY'LL EAT OUR SOULS!
--DILLER--
CHILLER--

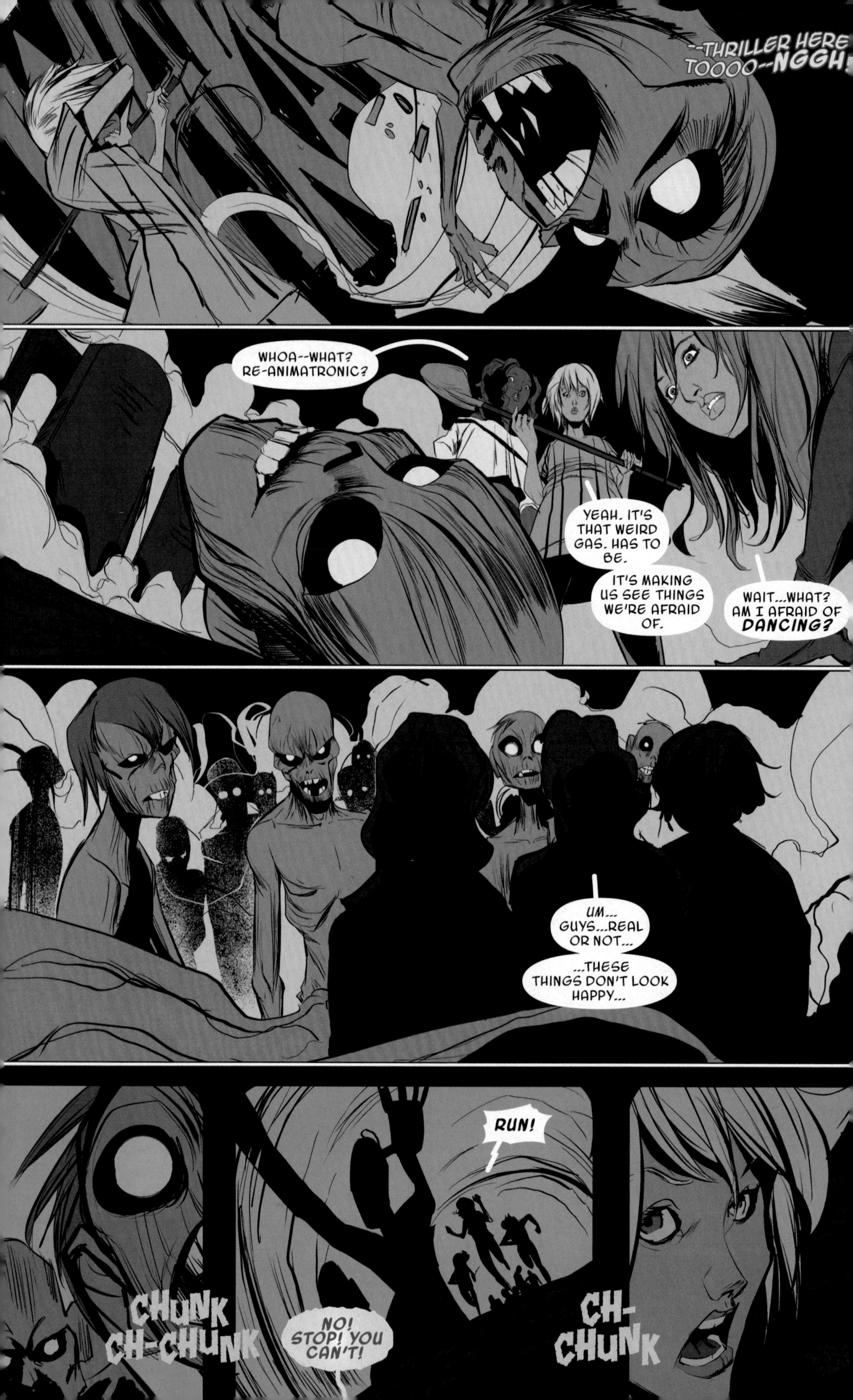
--THRILLER HERE TOOOO--NGGH!
WHOA--WHAT? RE-ANIMATRONIC?
YEAH. IT'S THAT WEIRD GAS. HAS TO BE.
IT'S MAKING US SEE THINGS WE'RE AFRAID OF.
WAIT...WHAT? AM I AFRAID OF DANCING?
UM... GUYS...REAL OR NOT...
...THESE THINGS DON'T LOOK HAPPY...
RUN!
CHUNK CH-CHUNK
NO! STOP! YOU CAN'T!
CH-CHUNK

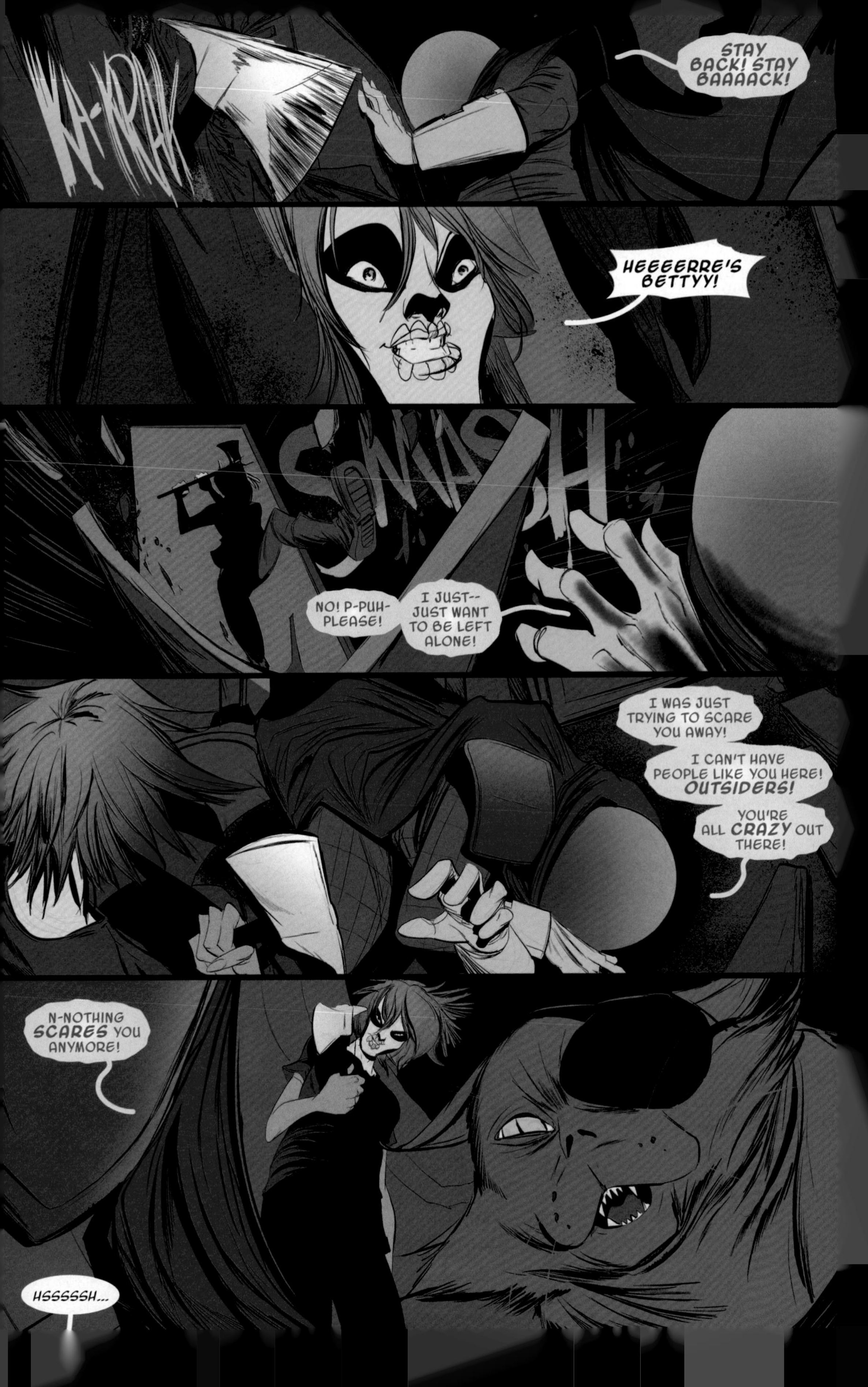
KA-KRAK
STAY BACK! STAY BAAAACK!
HEEEERRE'S BETTYY!
SMASH
NO! P-PUH-PLEASE!
I JUST-- JUST WANT TO BE LEFT ALONE!
I WAS JUST TRYING TO SCARE YOU AWAY!
I CAN'T HAVE PEOPLE LIKE YOU HERE! OUTSIDERS!
YOU'RE ALL CRAZY OUT THERE!
N-NOTHING SCARES YOU ANYMORE!
HSSSSSH...

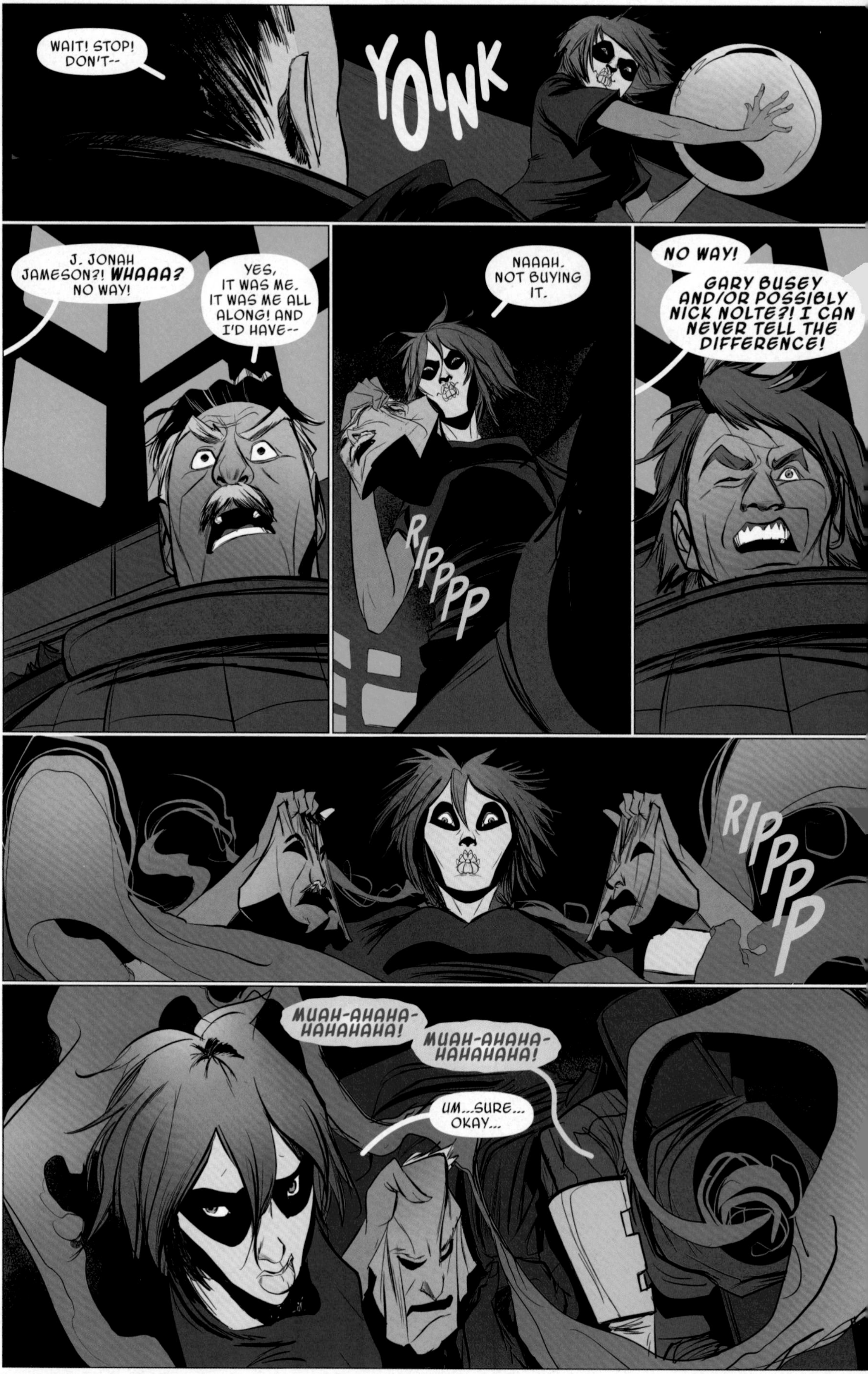
WAIT! STOP! DON'T--
YOINK
J. JONAH JAMESON?! WHAAA? NO WAY!
YES, IT WAS ME. IT WAS ME ALL ALONG! AND I'D HAVE--
NAAAH. NOT BUYING IT.
RIPPPP
NO WAY!
GARY BUSEY AND/OR POSSIBLY NICK NOLTE?! I CAN NEVER TELL THE DIFFERENCE!
RIPPPP
MUAH-AHAHA-HAHAHAHA!
MUAH-AHAHA-HAHAHAHA!
UM...SURE... OKAY...

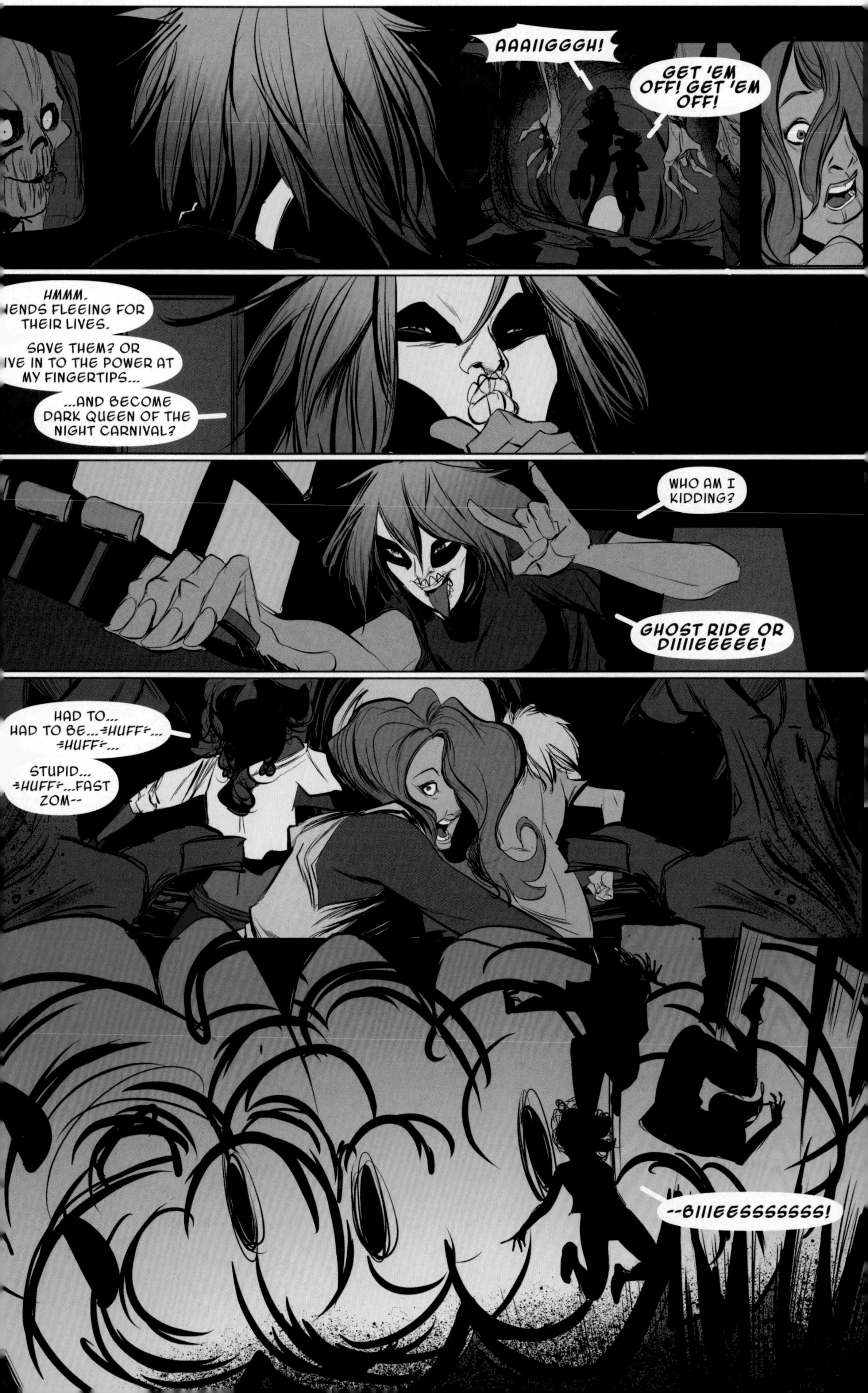
AAAIIGGGH!
GET 'EM OFF! GET 'EM OFF!
HMMM. IENDS FLEEING FOR THEIR LIVES.
SAVE THEM? OR IVE IN TO THE POWER AT MY FINGERTIPS...
...AND BECOME DARK QUEEN OF THE NIGHT CARNIVAL?
WHO AM I KIDDING?
GHOST RIDE OR DIIIIEEEEE!
HAD TO... HAD TO BE... =HUFF=... =HUFF=...
STUPID... =HUFF=...FAST ZOM--
--BIIIEESSSSSSS!

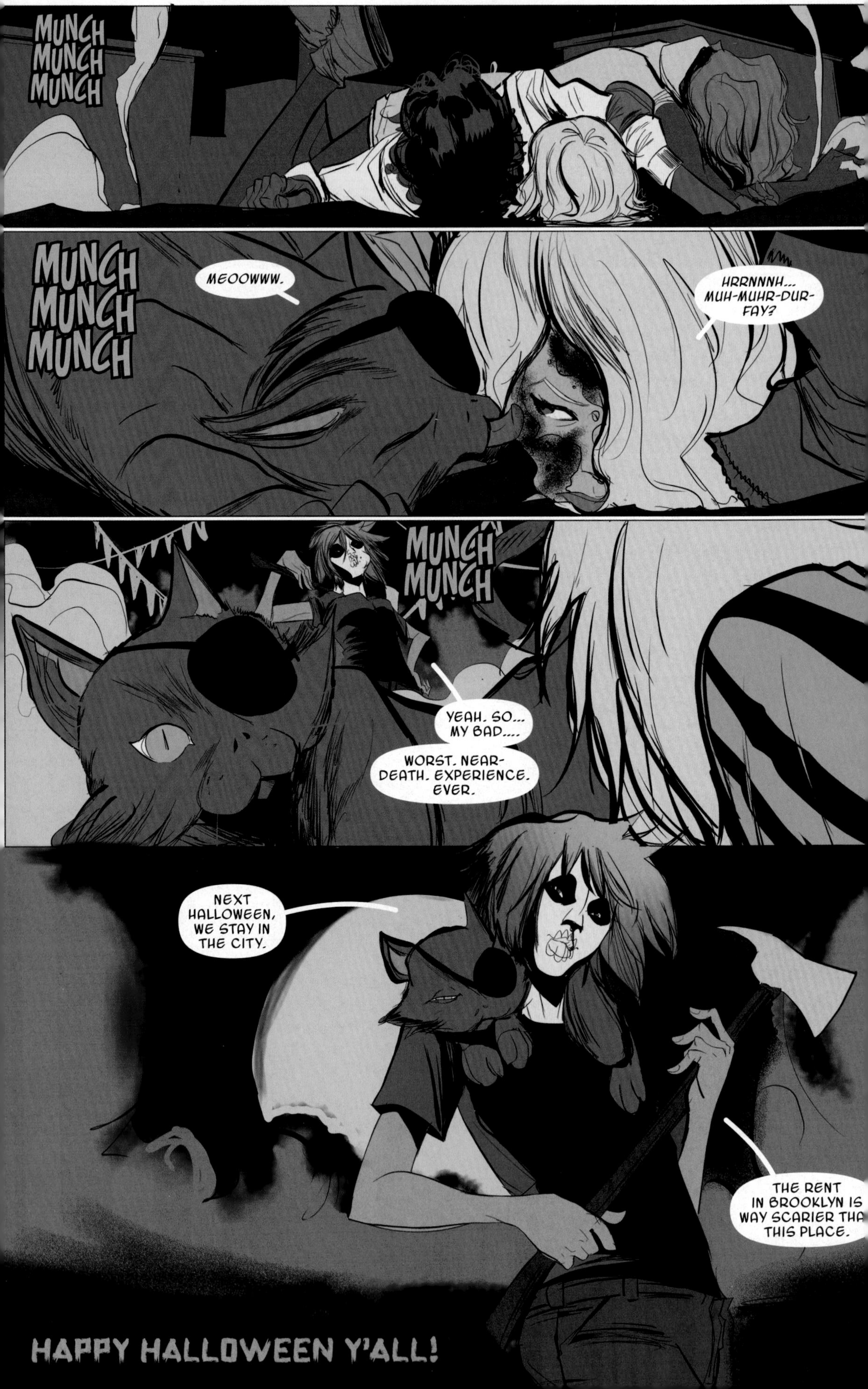
MUNCH
MUNCH
MUNCH
MUNCH
MUNCH
MUNCH
MEOOWWW.
HRRNNNH... MUH-MUHR-DUR-FAY?
MUNCH
MUNCH
YEAH. SO... MY BAD....
WORST. NEAR-DEATH. EXPERIENCE. EVER.
NEXT HALLOWEEN, WE STAY IN THE CITY.
THE RENT IN BROOKLYN IS WAY SCARIER THA THIS PLACE.
HAPPY HALLOWEEN Y'ALL!

#9 VARIANT BY J. SCOTT CAMPBELL & NEI RUFFINO

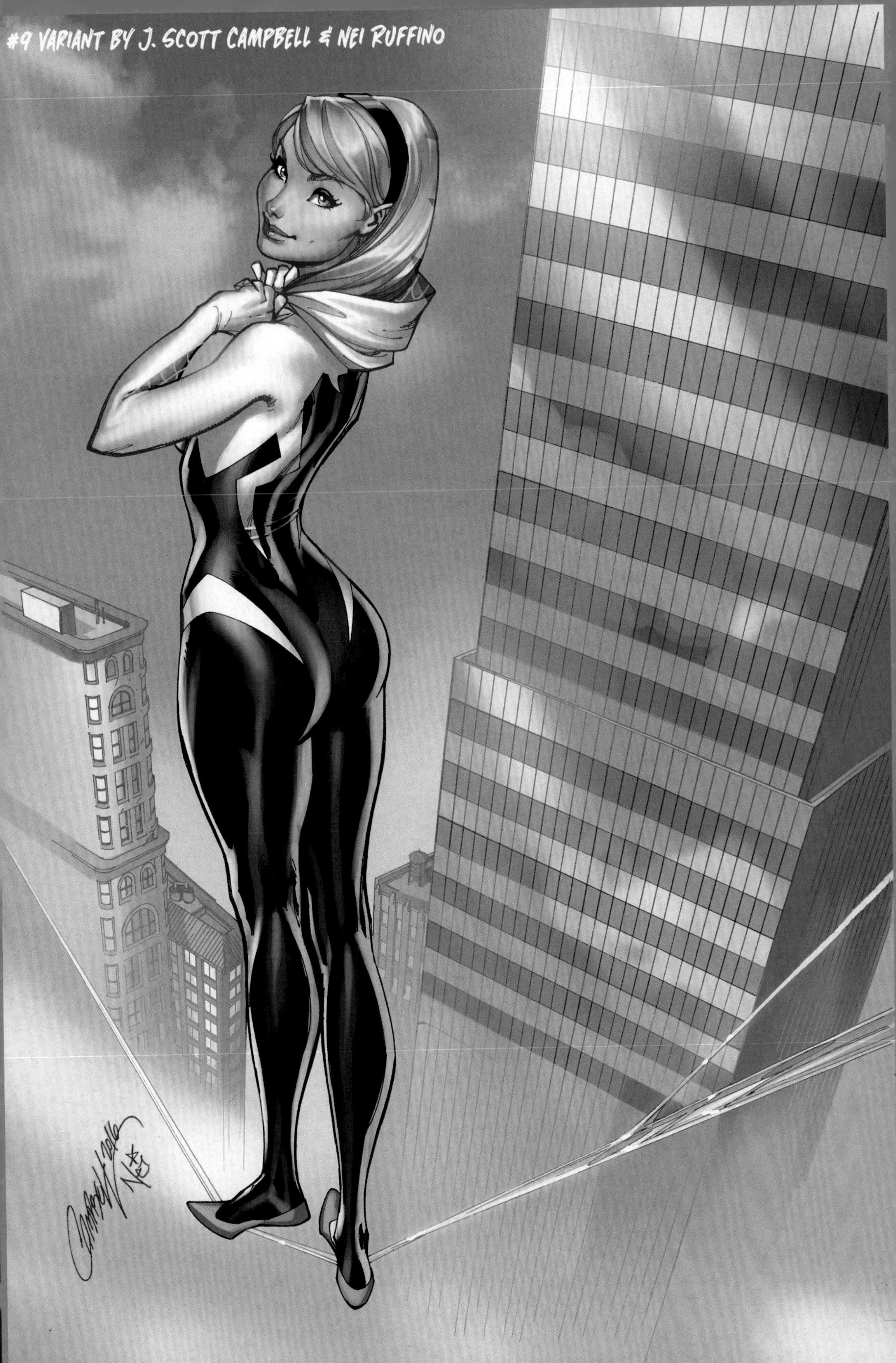